Active Learning for Fives

Debby Cryer

Thelma Harms

Adele Richardson Ray

Frank Porter Graham Child Development Center
University of North Carolina, Chapel Hill, North Carolina

Innovative Learning Publications

Addison-Wesley Publishing Company

Menlo Park, California ■ Reading, Massachusetts ■ New York

Don Mills, Ontario ■ Wokingham, England ■ Amsterdam ■ Bonn

Paris ■ Milan ■ Madrid ■ Sydney ■ Singapore ■ Tokyo ■ Seoul

Taipei ■ Mexico City ■ San Juan

This book is published by Innovative Learning Publications™, an imprint of the Alternative Publishing Group of Addison-Wesley Publishing Company.

Senior Editor: Lois Fowkes

Design Manager: Jeff Kelly

Production/Manufacturing Director: Janet Yearian

Production/Manufacturing Coordinator: Barbara Atmore

Cover and text design: Paula Shuhert

Illustrations: Cynthia Swann Brodie

Jane McCreary

Joel Snyder

Rachel Gage

ISBN 0-201-49401-9
 2 3 4 5 6 7 8 9 10-ML-99-98 97

Dedication

In the years that we have been involved in early childhood education, we have spent countless hours observing and talking with children and their teachers. In reality, every child who has shown us delight or interest in an activity has had a part in the creation of this book. And every teacher who has searched for and implemented activity ideas that we see children enjoying has had a part in the creation of this book.

The children whom we have known in closest relationships—our sons and daughters, nephews and nieces (and now grandchildren, too!), children of friends, and those we have taught in our own classrooms—have also had a great influence on our work. They have allowed us to watch, in a most personal way, the amazing details of human development. They have given us messages about developmental appropriateness that we could never have learned in any other way.

It is to all of these children and teachers, and to all who will use Active Learning activities in the future, that we dedicate this book.

Contents

Planning for Fives

Quality Programs for Fives

Most five-year-olds in group settings are in a kindergarten program. This means that many of them have made the leap from child care or preschool to an elementary school. Others may actually be having their first experience in a large group. Whatever their past experiences, Fives are a delightful mix of maturity and innocence. They are moving quickly toward wanting to spend time with friends instead of adults, but they are still closely tied to the important adults in their lives. They are at the edge of academic learning—often able to write their names and some letters, but not clearly; able to read some letters, but not perfectly; and able to count to 20 or higher, but not ready to begin adding or subtracting. A good kindergarten program will take Fives where they are developmentally and help them get ready for later learning without pressuring them to be first graders before their time.

Fives use many words when they speak and can understand many more. They speak in longer, more complicated sentences than younger children do. They can think ahead, plan a project, and then try to carry out the idea. Their self-help skills allow them to be quite independent. They can handle almost all of their own routine care—dressing, eating, bathing, and toileting—without much help. They are often responsible enough to walk to and from school by themselves in a safe neighborhood. A program for Fives should provide lots of activities so that children can improve all the skills that they are proud of doing by themselves and learn new skills, too.

Fives need a high-quality early-childhood program that enables them to develop both their minds and bodies in a safe and healthy place. But providing a program that meets the needs of five-year-olds is not always easy. There are often pressures from both parents and school staff to push children too fast, while in other cases, programs are not challenging enough. Sometimes it is difficult to find the right balance between play and academics or safety and independence for Fives. That is why kindergarten teachers have to remember where Fives are in their development and create a program that is just right for their age and abilities.

Even though Fives are able in many ways, they still have so much to learn. They need to practice getting along with others so that they will have the social skills required in the elementary grades. Just as important, they need to continue improving their thinking and talking skills. Most five-year-olds depend on the reassuring kindness of adults as they become adjusted to a faster, more demanding program. The key to working with Fives is to remember that they are still young children who enjoy learning through play, through hands-on activities, and through interactions with others. They learn more when given a wide range of experiences in which they can explore, think, and talk with others about what they are doing.

The Active Learning Series

The Active Learning Series is made up of activity books for infants, one-, two-, three-, four-, and five-year-olds. As part of the series, each of these books consists of a planning guide and four activity sections. There is also a companion book explaining how to adapt the activities for children with disabilities.

Active Learning for Fives has many ideas for children whose abilities are between 60 and 72 months of age. The book is divided into five sections, which are listed below.

Planning for Fives

This section has ideas for setting up your room and schedule to provide good care and education while avoiding problems. It includes ways of handling Fives that help them develop self-discipline. It shows how to plan activities so that things will run smoothly.

Activities for Listening and Talking

This section has ideas to help you make the best use of talking with and listening to Fives all through the day. It has play ideas using books, pictures, and puppets, as well as fun pre-reading and pre-writing activities for children. Activities are numbered 1 through 110.

Activities for Physical Development

This section has ideas to develop the large muscles in the legs, arms, and back. These muscles help children run, balance, and climb. It also has ideas to develop the small muscles in the hands and fingers that are so necessary when children begin to read and write. Activities are numbered 111 through 205.

Creative Activities

This section has art and carpentry, blocks, dramatic play, and music activities. These activities help to develop the senses, the imagination, and the skills children use to represent how they see and interpret their world. Activities are numbered 206 through 395.

Activities for Learning from the World Around Them

This section has activities that focus on science and nature and number, shape, and size (math). These activities help children enjoy and learn about the world around them while preparing them for the academics they will begin in first grade. Activities are numbered 396 through 506.

Sharing Ideas with Parents

Parents are interested in what you do with their children. It makes a parent feel good to know that you have been paying special attention to his or her child. You can share lots of information with parents, including the ideas in this book.

- Have a relaxed talk with each child's parents whenever possible. If you rarely see children's parents, send home short, friendly notes with the child. Tell parents about the activities their child likes and the progress the child is making in your class.

- Encourage parents to help you understand their child by talking about what the child enjoys doing at home, how he or she spends time outside of school, important changes the child has undergone, and the important people in the child's life.

- Have things on hand for parents to borrow and read. Cut out articles from magazines and put them in folders. Let parents know that you have materials they can borrow.

- Call state offices and agencies for free materials on early childhood topics. They may have materials on meals and snacks for kindergarteners, growth of children, getting ready for first grade, or ways parents can spot problems.

- Have a meeting for parents. Show a film or slides and talk about helpful ideas for raising children. Topics such as handling behavior problems, activities for Fives, or moving on to first grade will interest parents of Fives. Your local community college may be able to help with speakers, films, and other resources.

- Work closely with parents so that the child benefits from the feeling of trust and warmth you share with them.

- Keep a bulletin board for parents near the classroom entrance to post current information about school activities, notices about parenting education, and fun things to do with children.

Helping Fives Feel Special

Although five-year-olds usually seem so grown up and independent, you are still a very important person in their lives. Fives need to know that you really care about them. They know this from your kind tone of voice, your acceptance of them as individuals, and the interest you show in what they do. They feel good when you look into their eyes as you talk to them and really pay attention as they talk to you. Fives become hurt, fearful, or angry when you are strict or unfriendly, force them to do things they do not enjoy, or ignore their feelings. The way you relate to the children in your class is very important. It helps shape the way the children see themselves.

Children thrive in a program where you show that you value and like them. Throughout this book, you will find ideas to help children feel special and competent. Although there are no separate activities for social and emotional growth, emotional support is part of all the activities. Be sure to follow these ideas and you will be helping Fives develop the positive sense of self that will help them through future difficulties.

- Treat children as individuals rather than as a group. Arrange the room and most activities so that children are free to work and play in self-selected small groups. Then it is easier to relate to each child.

- Build a warm relationship by talking with Fives often. Listen to what they have to tell you.

- Make eye contact when you and the five-year-old talk together. It helps her feel important and special.

- Use the child's name when you talk with him. It makes what you say more personal. Limit talking to children as a large group and addressing them as "boys and girls."

- Listen to your Fives as they tell you about what interests them. Carry on extended conversations with them.

- Use a kind tone of voice and gentle touch. Help children when they ask or show frustration. It shows you care.

- Handle routines, such as meals and rest time, in a friendly, relaxed manner. It reduces the pressure of being in a large group.

- Show interest and delight with the things Fives can do. It helps them feel competent and valuable.

- Even when you have to correct your Fives or stop what they are doing, remember to treat them with respect so that they will continue to feel that you accept them for who they are.

Giving Fives Practice with Words

Success in school is heavily influenced by each child's language ability. During the kindergarten year you can help children expand their vocabularies in many ways. Fives need words for different things. They need words to *understand* what you and others are saying. They need words to *think* about things. They also need words to *talk* to others about their ideas. Your job is to help Fives get practice with words in all these different ways.

You are helping children understand words and ideas when you read stories, talk about what is happening, answer their questions, introduce new materials for them to explore and play with, and expand their world with new experiences. Fives need plenty of chances to talk with one another so that they can share ideas and practice communicating. Remember that a language-rich kindergarten has the constant sound of children talking.

You will find that it helps children to remember how to do something if you talk them through an action while you show them what to do. For example, if you are showing a child how to saw a piece of wood, you can help him notice what to do by saying, "See, I put the wood in the C-clamp so that it won't wiggle as I saw. I tighten the C-clamp so that the wood will not come loose. Now I run the blade across the wood to make a little groove on the place where I marked it. Now I am starting to saw." By talking, you have helped the child use words to think through all the steps.

Fives usually understand many more words than they use when they talk. Asking simple questions is a good way to give children practice using the words they understand but do not usually use. To encourage children to say more, try to ask questions that need more than a yes/no or one-word answer. You will find more information about encouraging children to discuss their ideas in the Conversations section of this book.

In most activities in this book, there are many examples of questions to use with Fives and topics to talk about with them. Try out some of these ideas and notice which ones help the children to talk most. Remember, the important thing is to make children feel free to talk. You can do that if you listen to them, discuss things with them, show that you enjoy what they tell you, and make your classroom a place for talking, not for silence.

Handling Problems

Although five-year-olds are competent and delightful in many ways, they can also test your patience. It helps if you can see everyday difficulties with Fives as part of the children's development and then ease children toward the behavior you want. For example, large-group times with 20 or more children are not always easy with Fives. They fight for space, complain that they can't see, and interrupt often. It helps if you remember that Fives do best in smaller groups and shorten big group times or divide the big group into two smaller groups until children can maintain their interest in a larger group. Fives may become rough or dangerous in their active play, so they need clear rules to follow as they challenge their large-muscle abilities. They sometimes fight with, exclude, or pick on other children, so lots of your teaching must be about feelings and getting along with others. Since you understand that Fives are still developing basic social skills and learning to control their feelings and actions, you can minimize difficulties by planning ahead. Problems that arise should be handled with understanding.

Like all young children, Fives are not very good at waiting with nothing to do. When they are in stressful situations, some children will fall apart. Fives can use words well and can (but do not always) remember much of what you say to them. Despite the rough edges, they are full of affection, excited about learning, and enjoy friends more than ever.

Patience and kindness are the way to work with Fives. If an adult gets angry, the children will respond with anger or fear. Children who are yelled at or severely punished learn to use these methods for solving problems. Punishment that shames or frightens a child hurts the entire adult-child relationship. Remember, Fives are copycats and are copying the way you treat them. That's how they learn. So you need to be sure that you model what you want them to copy.

The best way to handle Fives is to plan ahead so that there are fewer chances for things to go wrong. Plan ahead to have enough space and interesting activities so that children won't get irritable and aggressive. But planning ahead will not do away with all the problems.

Some Fives will still have difficulty working out problems by talking things through. They will need your help to learn to listen to another person's point of view, think about the feelings of others, and see how their actions affect others. Often, they need a lot of adult supervision to help make things go smoothly. You will get to know the signs before a child hits someone else, and that's the time to stop him if you can. If you stop things early by reminding the children about the words or actions they need to use, you can prevent a lot of fights.

The child who hurts needs lots of support to help him grow. When problems happen, step in and make it clear that you don't allow the troublesome behavior. Then help the child figure out what he did, how it made others feel, how he felt, and what he can do now or the next time so that things work out better. Also be sure to make it clear that you still respect him.

Here are some suggestions for handling the common problems of five-year-olds.

Problems Around Transition Times

Make transitions as short as possible, with little waiting. Arrange things so that children can move to the next activity in small informal groups rather than one large group. Have children move out to the playground or to wash up for lunch a few at a time while others are finishing up.

Be sure the next activity is ready before beginning a transition.

Avoid having children wait in a crowded space or in a large open space where they will want to tumble and wrestle. These are places where fights can start easily.

Help or supervise children a few at a time rather than all at the same time whenever you can. This makes it easier to prevent a rush when you're changing activities.

Keep children actively involved. Have them help by doing as much for themselves as possible. Allow children to play as long as possible and clean up when it is really time to go to lunch, outdoors, or special activities. Don't make them hurry to finish and then wait with nothing to do. If needed, use songs, fingerplays, and stories to prevent waiting with nothing to do.

Treat things with a light touch. Too much control is as bad as not enough. Make sure children know the big limits that are required for health and safety, but be more flexible with other issues.

Give children notice before a change in activity is coming: "You are having a good time building with blocks. You may play for a little while longer before it is clean-up time." Remind them again about two minutes before they have to finish up. Whenever possible, let Fives finish up what they are doing and then move on to the next activity in their own time.

Arrange things so that children are encouraged to work on long-term projects that they know they can return to. That means you will have to have a place to store projects safely so that children can continue working when they have time.

Have popular activities available over a long period of time so that children will be able to repeat the activity several times. This cuts down on competition and helps children improve their skills through practice.

Hurting and Fighting with Words

When Fives become angry, they can use words to hurt others because they are good talkers. It is just as important to deal with this way of fighting as it is to deal with physical fights. Constant bickering, name calling, and teasing can ruin the good feelings in a class and make everybody tense. Be careful never to use hurtful words or a mocking tone of voice yourself to any child. The way the teacher talks to the children sets the pattern for the children to follow.

It is necessary to make it clear that hurting with words is not acceptable, but this needs to be done in a calm, respectful way. If the teacher makes a big fuss when children hurt with words, this adds to the attention they are already getting from the children they are hurting.

Attention, whether it is approval or disapproval, can keep the negative behavior going. But you cannot ignore hurting with words because the children may interpret your lack of response as not caring or even approval. Instead discuss the problem calmly and help the children figure out better ways to deal with things the next time. Sometimes one or two children become the victims of most of the hurtful words. It helps to stop this if you can teach the children who are the victims to ignore the hurtful words and walk away.

Hurting and Fighting Through Actions

Some Fives can become very angry or upset. Their anger can be caused by a number of things, but often the child feels that things are unfair. That's why it is so important to help children talk things through so that different points of view can be discussed and a fair solution found.

If a child tends to fight physically, be aware of when problems start and why. Often problems happen during transitions and the fighter needs your help to keep occupied in a more constructive way. Always watch the children closely and stop things before they get out of hand. Help children to use the words they need to solve problems and to understand the feelings they and others have when problems happen.

Pick out a safe, cozy place for an angry child to quiet down and gain control. Suggest in a calm way that the child use this place if she needs to but avoid using the place as punishment. Make sure that you can see the child and that she is not a danger to herself or others. As soon as the child is calm, invite her to come out and join the group. Do not make a big fuss about it.

If anger is violent and happens often, talk to a child development specialist, a mental health consultant, or a social worker. Some problems are too hard for you to handle alone. If possible, get the specialist to come in and see the child in your group.

There may be something in your program or schedule that is triggering the child's problems.

Be sure to talk to the parents to find out how the child acts at home. Ask the parents for suggestions that work well with their child. Decide on one way that will work to handle problems at home and at school. Avoid problems by stopping an upsetting situation as soon as you can, before the child loses control.

Make sure you set a good example. *Never* hit a child who has hit someone else. Avoid yelling, being harsh, or using ridicule; children will copy what you do, not what you tell them to do.

Other Emotional Upsets

Many five-year-olds may be very sensitive and become frightened, insecure, or have their feelings hurt easily. Some children cry easily and seem much less resilient than others. Sometimes the temptation is to belittle the child's feelings and just expect him to deal with things. But it's important to remember that the feelings young children have are very real. A balance must be found between accepting feelings and expecting the child to cope more successfully. When the sensitive child falls apart, give some support and recognition to the feelings, discuss the problem, and help the child work out a solution. It is just as important to keep working with a sensitive child so that he learns to be more resilient as it is to work with an aggressive child so that he becomes more thoughtful and patient.

Problems with Sharing, Cooperating, and Taking Turns

Fives are usually great at sharing with their special friends, but problems can arise when children are asked to cooperate or share with a child who is not part of the small group of friends.

Have plenty of the materials needed for the most popular activities so that most of the time Fives are not pressured to share. Remember that sharing can be difficult, even for adults.

Whenever possible, let children know that you notice them sharing, cooperating, and taking turns.

Take every opportunity to be a good example of sharing and cooperating for the children to see.

Put up a waiting list for taking turns near each activity center and for popular activities so that children can take turns. Put the waiting list down low where the children can print their own names. (You can write names for those who need your help.) Teach children to check off their names when they finish their turn and go get the next child on the list. Always continue an activity until each interested child has had a turn. The waiting list works especially well when there are other interesting activities to do while the children are waiting.

Make sure there are enough interesting activities out at the same time so that children don't have to fight over the most popular ones. Continue special activities over several days so that every child gets at least one chance to do them.

"We don't want to play with you!"

As Fives learn to enjoy playing in small groups, they become more choosy about their friends. Sometimes children will be excluded from self-selected groups. In this case, it is important to view social development from a long-term perspective. As social skills develop, children will try out many relationships and interact with a variety of personalities. Unless things become nasty, it is best to allow relationships to grow naturally without too much manipulation by adults. You can be most helpful by maintaining a positive social environment in which all children are accepted by you with obvious delight.

Avoid forcing children to play with one another, but do try to promote new friendships. Provide lots of attention to children who are left out. Invite them to help you and to take part in small groups that you are working with. Help the left-out five-year-olds find other children who need friends. Set up groups so that children are near one another and involved in similar activities, but do not push friendships too hard. The children are the ones who are best able to choose their own friends. During group discussions, talk about feelings and getting to know new friends.

If you become especially frustrated with a small group of exclusive friends, remember that social groups for kindergartners are usually fleeting. Children are experimenting with different types of relationships and learning through each one. Maintain a pleasant social environment, model acceptance and appreciation of all personalities, and be amazed at how social groups change through the year.

Using Naughty Words

Often five-year-olds magically begin saying words that are considered unacceptable. Parents might contact you with complaints because their children never heard those words at home and therefore must have learned them at school. You can minimize this problem by setting limits, but children will continue to experiment with language, especially using words that upset adults.

Avoid emotional reactions to the "naughty" words a child might say. The quickest way to help a child stop saying a word is to ignore it. Never punish a child for using an unacceptable word. If you want to explain to the child that a word should not be repeated, do it gently, and then be very patient. The child will have to spend some time removing the word from her everyday vocabulary. Sometimes substituting a nonsense word for the unacceptable word helps.

Work cooperatively with parents. Let them know what you are doing to minimize the problem. Explain that children repeat what they hear, even if it is not acceptable in the home or classroom.

Rule Breakers and Tattletales

Rules are far more important to older five-year-olds than to younger children. They realize when rules are not followed and often want justice. On the other hand, they have trouble sticking to the rules when it means that things will not go the way they want, especially when playing card or board games. Teachers are caught up in this dilemma with constant complaints from some children (tattletales) and anger from others who are caught cheating at games (rule breakers). You must have lots of patience because children need time to move through this stage and do the learning that is required to resolve these typical problems by themselves.

You can help children talk through the rule-related problems and give support and reassurance. Often children feel hurt because they think things are not fair. You can help them understand their feelings and come to a reasonable solution. Children who feel that they must win and break rules to do so also need emotional support. You can help them learn that games can be fun whether you win or lose and that the important thing is to challenge yourself rather than others.

Tips on Handling Problems

- Have children help as you make a few clear rules. Write down the rules that they suggest. Ask them to explain why their rules are important. Then turn their many rules into a few big ones by having them help to sort all the rules they suggested into larger statements. Always stick to these rules.
- Help five-year-olds figure out a better way to act if they are doing something you or others don't like. Help them remember the rules and think about how their actions affect others.
- Encourage Fives to use words rather than actions such as hitting or shoving to solve problems. You may need to help them remember the words to use.
- When children hurt others' feelings, help them see how their words and actions make others feel. Then help them figure out better ways to solve problems.
- Talk with the children about the feelings people have and how words and actions can cause others to feel either happy or sad. Help them understand that feelings are fine, but hurting is not.
- Have plenty of the materials and equipment you expect children to share or use cooperatively, such as blocks and art materials, so that they will better be able to play together without fighting.

- Take Fives outdoors every day to play in a safe area. Leave enough indoor space for active play, too.
- Keep groups of children small by offering interesting activities in five or more activity centers at the same time. Make sure there is enough space for children to work because crowding causes fights.
- Give many chances to play with new toys and work with new activities by keeping them out for several days.
- Allow Fives to choose what they want to do. Keep big group activities short.
- Make sure lunch and rest are early enough so that Fives don't get too hungry or tired. If you are stuck with a fixed meal schedule, make sure the children can have a small, healthful snack when they are hungry.
- Keep Fives from having to wait with nothing to do. Have some books to look at, songs to sing, or fingerplays to present if they must wait. Try to avoid crowding children into one small area or having them line up to wait.
- Use imagination, humor, and a light touch to prevent emotional upsets. Step in early, before things get out of hand. Take children who are upset outside or to another room; a change of scene sometimes puts a new look on things.
- Keep an eye on the child who hits or hurts others so that you can catch that child when you see he is frustrated or angry and help him before he hurts someone. Make sure to pay attention to the many good things he does.
- Be calm.

Making Time for Activities in the Schedule

A regular schedule is important in creating a secure environment where Fives can do their best. They need to know what to expect and to be able to count on things. However, flexibility within the regular schedule lets you take advantage of all the interesting things that come up.

Since Fives have a longer attention span than younger children, it is important to plan long blocks of time when they can concentrate on one or two activities if they wish. The schedule and space should be planned so that the opportunity to work at length on a project is possible, even over a period of several days.

The schedule needs to be written and posted in an obvious place where parents and substitutes can refer to it. Your Fives will expect certain things to happen every day in the same order. If things go on as they should, children feel more relaxed, even if you are not with them.

The most important thing about a schedule is that it helps you think ahead. Then you can plan many activities for both morning and afternoon and get the things ready that you will need. If you have everything ready ahead of time you can quickly get the children started on a new activity. It is hard for Fives to wait with nothing to do.

As much as you can, let Fives choose their own activities and decide whether to play by themselves or in small groups. Try not to have all of them do things together in a large group. Expecting lots of young children to do things together is frustrating to you and to the children.

Make sure your schedule has both outdoor and indoor play times every day. Also make sure to schedule a balance of quiet play times and active play times. Plan a short time for group discussions, information sharing, and a story or music once or twice a day.

While you are actively supervising children, don't take time to clean up completely. Let the children help you with the initial cleanup. Then come back and finish when most of them have left for the day. When the children are with you, give them your full attention.

Always have a few extra ideas ready to use. It is better to have too many activities planned than too few. During bad weather it helps to have some new materials to put out and some active games to play.

Allow free-choice activities most of the day so that children can choose to return to an area and continue their work. Provide a safe place to store work in progress and protect unfinished work that children wish to return to, such as block buildings or carpentry.

Self-Directed and Teacher-Directed Activities

Fives want to do things by themselves. When Fives are free to choose and do their own activities, the activities are *self-directed*. Self-directed activities are possible when there are plenty of toys and materials on low shelves for children to use independently.

Activities should be changed regularly to add new interest and challenge. For many self-directed activities, you will have to show children how to use materials properly or how to play the game. Then they will be able to do the activity independently.

During the day, remind Fives to pick up and put back toys in the proper place as they finish using them. This keeps the materials ready and attractive looking for others to use. Also, cleanup is easier at the end of the day in an orderly room.

Some activities are dangerous or more complex. These activities are *teacher-directed;* they need to be done at times when you are free to supervise children more closely. Carpentry and cooking are examples of activities that should be teacher-directed. Once children have become competent at doing many teacher-directed activities, they may be added to the self-directed activities that children can choose freely. If you have enough self-directed materials out at all times, the children will have a lot to keep them busy. Then you can bring out the teacher-directed activities at scheduled times.

Activity Tips

Plan ahead to make things go smoothly.

- Set up five or more activity centers with plenty of everyday toys and materials for children to use in self-directed activities.

- Some activity centers to include are books, puppets, and picture games; blocks; dramatic play; puzzles and manipulatives; art; science; math; writing; and a quiet, cozy corner where one or two children can play alone.

- Plan new activities that can be added to ongoing activity centers and write them on a planning form.

- Choose activities to match children's skills. If an activity turns out to be too hard, try an easier one.

- Plan when and where you will do each activity.

- Include quiet and active, indoor and outdoor, small-group and individual activities.

- Frequently add new activities to old favorites.

- Always have extra activities ready in case you need them.

- Set special materials out ahead of time and make sure you have enough for everyone who wants to take part.

- Plan space and time for children to work on long-term projects. Have a safe space for children to store the things they are working on from day to day.

Activity Tips
Continued

Keep Fives interested and active.

- Allow five-year-olds to choose their activities for most of the day.

- Divide and organize big spaces into smaller play areas with low shelves and other furniture. Be sure adults can supervise the areas easily.

- Set up the areas to help Fives learn to do things for themselves. Have plenty of toys and materials on low, labeled shelves for Fives to use.

- Separate the quiet centers from the active centers.

- Provide both quiet and active activities outdoors. Bring lots of indoor activities outside in pleasant weather.

- Label shelves and other toy containers with clear pictures.

- Keep materials organized—put the same kind of toys in one area, put toys with small pieces in labeled dishpans or boxes, and so on.

- Help Fives remember how to take out, use, and put away the toys correctly.

- Set up an indoor active play area with some safe, large-muscle play things. This lets the Fives move around indoors, especially in bad weather.

- Be sure the outdoor and indoor large-muscle play areas are safe. Remember that Fives have not yet developed the same physical skills that older school-aged children have, so the play equipment should be the right size for them and have sufficient cushioning material underneath in case of falls.

Slowly help Fives learn to be part of a group.

- Begin with very short group times of fifteen to twenty minutes. Begin with two smaller groups instead of one big group if you can. Slowly increase the amount of time children are expected to spend in a large group as the year progresses.

- Encourage but don't force a child to be part of a group. Give the child the choice of a quiet alternative such as looking at a book while the rest of the group is together.

- If a group activity you planned isn't working, stop and try something else.

- Plan group times to be varied. Alternate listening times with times when children can participate actively.

Activity Tips

Continued

Make everything you do count twice.

■ Give children practice talking about what they and others are doing. Help them think things through by asking some questions.

■ Remember to speak often to each individual child. Look into the child's eyes as you talk and listen. This gives all children a turn to be special.

■ Use the same materials to do more than one activity.

■ After you have introduced materials for an activity, place them on a shelf in an activity center for children to use independently.

■ Try the same activity with all the Fives who are at about the same level.

■ Encourage children to do as much as they can by themselves: caring for their own personal needs, choosing the people they want to work with, getting out their own play materials, putting toys away.

Avoid safety problems.

■ Teach children about safety through special activities and, most importantly, through everyday conversations.

■ Create a safe environment. Store poisons or other dangerous items out of reach and be sure there is plenty of cushioning material under climbing equipment.

■ Have children pick things up and put them away as they go along so that no one trips and falls.

■ Have the Fives do activities that need to be closely watched, such as cooking, only while you are with them. Make sure that dangerous items, such as knives or hot plates, are out of reach when you can't watch carefully.

■ Have plenty of toys and materials out to avoid competition and fights. Provide more than one of the most popular toys and use a fair system for sharing. A sign-up sheet helps Fives take turns. Divide toys (Lego® bricks or watercolor markers) into several small containers so that there is a set for each child who needs one.

Gathering or Group Time

Fives can be gathered together in a larger group once or twice a day to sing, take part in short talks, or listen to a story. Keep them together only as long as everybody is really interested. Usually with young Fives, that means only 10 to 15 minutes. Older Fives might stay for 15 to 30 minutes if they are really involved in what is happening. If you have someone working with you, divide a big group into two smaller groups. The smaller the group, the easier it is to have a good gathering time and for children to take part in what you do.

For more ideas on group times, look at Ideas for Story Times at the end of the Listening and Talking section of this book.

Sample Schedule

Depending on your own situation, you can tailor the following schedule to fit your Fives' needs. Remember to be flexible and follow the children's interests. The main purpose of the schedule is for you to think ahead and plan so the day will go smoothly and things will get done.

Children arrive: Greeting time for each child and parents who drop off their children

Gathering time to discuss plans for the day
Planned play time with both self-directed and teacher-directed activities

Mid-morning: Cleanup
Toileting, handwashing*
Snack preparation and setup
Snack (if lunch is later than mid-day)

Late morning: Outdoor play time with both self-directed and teacher-directed activities
Gathering or group time: stories, music, talking about activities
Routines before lunch (handwashing and setup)

Mid-day Lunch

Early afternoon: Cleanup
Rest time with quiet self-directed activities
Routines (toileting, handwashing; cleanup)

Mid-afternoon: Snack (if lunch is earlier than mid-day)
Planned play time with both self-directed and teacher-directed activities
Outdoor play time

*Toileting should be self-directed throughout the day.

Late afternoon:	Routines to get ready to leave (gather artwork, get clothes ready)
	Reminders for next day
	Departure (help children with bus, talk with parents)
After most children are gone:	Clean up room
	Set up for next day

Making Spaces Safe and Healthy for Fives

If you do all you can to avoid health and safety problems, you will feel more relaxed and enjoy your work with the children more. Although Fives understand some safety rules, you will still need to prevent accidents by making safe spaces to use and by supervising carefully. You have to be very careful with Five-year-olds. In their active play they want to challenge themselves and do not always see dangers. They forget safety rules when their attention is on something else. Yet you can't always be close by, and you want to encourage Fives to do things by themselves.

Making the room and the outdoor area where children play safe takes a lot of thought. Think about what you can do to make it safe for your Fives at all times.

These questions will help you start thinking about the spaces used by Fives.

Where can I lock away medicines, cleaning materials, and other harmful things?

Where can I store things I don't want Fives to use by themselves?

Where can I put these things so that it's easy for me to get them out often for use when I can watch?

Is everything I have left out safe for Fives to use by themselves?

How can I make everything they will climb on safe?

Can I easily supervise what all the children are doing?

Tips on Health and Safety

- Never leave Fives unsupervised. They need to be within sight or hearing of a responsible adult.

- Be sure that *all* areas used at any time by the children are safe.

- Check to be sure that fire exits are not blocked and that the paths to the exits are clear. Practice fire drills with the children at least once a month.

- Make sure that Fives know what spaces they are allowed to use and that they follow the rules for not going beyond those spaces.

- Buy toys you can keep clean easily. Have children help wash toys in liquid dishwashing detergent and water when necessary.

- Make sure all the materials are safe for children (nontoxic paints, fabrics, and dyes).

- Use open, low shelves that are fixed so that they can't fall over. Do not store toys and blocks in a chest with a heavy lid that can fall down.

- Check indoor and outdoor toys for sharp edges, splinters, and other dangers that develop as toys get old.

- Be sure that children are safe outdoors. Use only safe, child-sized outdoor play equipment and be sure children are protected from traffic. A fence should be provided if the area is close to traffic or other dangers.

- Make sure that outdoor areas are free of tall grass, weeds, and harmful insects.

- Be sure that there is plenty of cushioning material under climbing equipment.

- Cover the sandbox to keep animals out.

- Teach children to flush toilets as soon as they are used. Check on toilets yourself. Disinfect once daily.

- Wash your hands with soap if you help children with toileting or nose wiping. Make sure that the children wash their hands after toileting, playing outside, and before eating. Handwashing cuts down on germs and illness.

Making the Most of Your Space

Fives need a lot of space in which to move around. There never seems to be enough usable space for play when you care for a group of young children. Planning how to best use space can help, even though it may not solve all the problems. Look around your room and ask yourself the following questions.

What can I store outside the room or in activity boxes?

How can I do indoor activities outdoors to make better use of all the space I have?

How can I organize the furniture to make clearly defined activity centers?

How can I divide my space into different areas but still supervise all the children?

What activities will work better outdoors than indoors?

Where can children do large-muscle play during bad weather?

How can I rotate activities so that they are not all out at the same time but there is plenty of variety?

Tips for Routine Care

- Use all the space you have. Use the same space and furnishings for both routines and play.

- If you have a rest time, set up children's mats in the different activity centers. This makes good use of space and gives children some privacy.

- Give each child a storage space for his coat, spare clothes, and art work.

- Teach children to help maintain routine care furnishings and space.

Tips for Play

- Set up six or more safe activity centers for play, some for quiet play and some for more active play. Remember to put some soft pillows with washable covers and cuddly toys in one quiet area. If possible, include an area for large-muscle play, too.

- Arrange the schedule so that children spend most of the day playing in activity centers, either indoors or outdoors.

- If there are two or more adults working with the group, plan to have some children doing activities outdoors with one teacher while other children are involved indoors with another.

- Use clear picture-word labels on shelves and materials so that children can clean up independently.

- Change the materials in the activity centers often.

- Have some very low tables in the activity centers for artwork, puzzles, and other fine-motor toys. Make sure chairs are child-sized and sturdy and that the children's feet rest on the floor when they sit down. (These chairs and tables can also be used for meals and snacks.)

- Set up a safe outdoor area that includes a fence if the area is not protected from traffic and other dangers. Have several outdoor activity times daily if you have a full-day schedule. Riding toys, balls, swings, a slide, a climber, and a sandbox with toys to use work well outdoors. Adding pretend play props, art and building materials, and water makes the outdoors even better.

Making Activity Centers

Activity centers are the heart of a good early-childhood program. They set the stage for most of the learning that your Fives will do every day. Schedules should be arranged so that children spend most of their indoor time working independently in activity centers. Once your space is set up in activity centers with basic materials and equipment, you can add all kinds of special activities to the centers.

An activity center is a place where the toys, materials, open storage, and play space have been set up for a special kind of play. For example, you might set up a Dramatic Play Center, a Book Center, a Block Center, an Art Center, a Science and Nature Center, and a Music Center. Some activity centers can be set up outdoors, too, such as a Sandbox Center and a Painting Center.

In each activity center make sure to have the following things:

- All the materials needed to do activities of a certain type, such as a variety of blocks and accessories for block play or a variety of art materials for creative artwork

- Open shelves with picture-word labels so that the children can get out the materials they need and put them back by themselves

- The right furnishings needed for the children to use the materials, such as soft pillows to sit on in the Book Center, a rug on the floor in the Block Center, an easel or art table in the Art Center

- Any special things needed to make the materials in the center easy and safe to use, such as a large towel under the water table, plastic aprons for the children to wear, a throw rug spread under the sand table, and a place to dry paintings

Activity Centers Fives Can Enjoy Every Day

It may not be possible to set up a separate center for each of the activities listed below, but that does not mean that you cannot present all of them. Some activities can be rotated in and out of the same center. This is easy to do if the materials are stored in boxes that are brought out only during the time an activity is being used. Centers that you set up should be suitable for noisy activities, for messy activities, for quiet activities, and so on. As you set up your room, you will have to decide which centers should be available all the time and which should be used for rotating activities.

Following is a list of the different types of activity centers Fives need access to on a regular basis.

- Dramatic Play Center with dishes, pots and pans, play sink, play stove, small table and chairs, dolls and doll beds, dress-up clothes, unbreakable mirror, play telephones, and other things commonly used in the home, plus a wide range of prop boxes with materials needed to extend pretend play into related areas such as store, office, school, and fantasy.

- Block Center with different kinds of unit blocks (wooden and plastic) and toy animals, trucks and cars, and airplanes to use with blocks

- Book Center with a soft, cozy place to read and a large supply of books, plus puppets and picture and story games

- Small-Muscle and Puzzle Center with many kinds of puzzles (some hard and some easy), small beads to string, small pegs with pegboards, and toys with pieces that go together and pull apart such as Lego® bricks

- Art Center with paints, paper, crayons, watercolor markers, safe scissors, tape, glue, paste, and play dough

- Sand and Water Center with a water table, sand table, containers of different sizes and shapes, strainers, shovels, and pails

- Large-Muscle Center with a small climber, crates or cubes for children to use for building obstacle courses, a low balance beam, large hollow blocks, and mats for supervised rolling and tumbling

- Science and Nature Center with often-changed examples of natural objects, such as stones, seeds, or flowers; living examples of the animal world, such as caterpillars or goldfish; magnets; magnifying glasses; and books and pictures

- Music Center with quiet rhythm instruments, a toy piano, a tape recorder with earphones, and tapes

- Math Center with many things to count, balance scales with things to weigh, number books and pictures, pencils and paper, and math activity boxes

- Writing Center with examples of letters to copy, paper and pencils, watercolor markers, and individual word tubs with clearly printed words children may want to write

- Listening Center with a tape recorder and earphones, books on tape, other tapes that interest children, and tapes children have made themselves

- Carpentry Center with sturdy workbench, real tools, soft wood pieces, sandpaper, nails, screws, wood glue, clamps, and goggles

- Computer Center with easy-to-use computer, computer games or software programs that are appropriate for young children (no violent games, games which encourage creativity and thinking rather than rote memorization), a timer to help remind child to limit the time spent in front of the computer and monitor, and a sign-up sheet

Tips for Setting Up Centers

- Before you make up your mind about where to put activity centers, look at your indoor and outdoor space. Decide which activity centers to set up indoors and which to set up outdoors. Centers may change with the seasons.

- Remember to keep pathways clear to enable children and adults to walk around and between activity centers.

- Set up quiet activities like books and art away from noisy activities like music and blocks.

- Keep toys and materials neat and organized so that the centers don't get cluttered. Store materials for some activities and rotate new materials into centers regularly.

- Keep toys with many pieces organized in labeled activity boxes so that it is easy to change what is out and keep sets of materials together.

- Make sure puzzles and other put-together toys have all their pieces before they are put away. Put-together toys with missing pieces are very frustrating to Fives and should not be used.

Stretching Space with Activity Boxes

You should have many more toys and materials for each activity center than you can keep out all the time. In order to keep these extra toys organized and ready to use, put them in activity boxes.

When you put everything you need for one kind of activity into a box or dishpan, you have made an activity box. This helps you keep many different things ready for children to play with without taking up much room. Activity boxes help you set up new activities quickly because you don't have to run around at the last minute to find the toys you need. You can store activity boxes in a closet or on a shelf. The activity boxes hold things that can be added to the materials you have in the activity centers every day. Label each box clearly so that you and the children know what's inside. A picture-word label on each box works well.

As you and the children put things back into an activity box, make sure that all the pieces are there and that they are clean. If you are careful to do that, you can count on the materials being in good shape the next time you need them. You will find many ideas for activity boxes in the activities sections of this book.

Outdoor Play

Be sure to set up an outdoor play space and use it every day as the weather permits. Check to see that the area is safe and free of any health hazards. Have weeds cut, be sure none of the plants is poisonous, and get rid of harmful bugs. Before you take the children out, check daily to see that there is no trash in the area.

A fence around the area makes it easier to keep the children safely inside. It will also keep dangers out. A rolling cart or wagon for carrying activity boxes with balls, wheel toys, sand toys, and other materials makes going outdoors easier. The children can help take things out. If you are doing a special activity or using large equipment, be sure to set up ahead of time. Once the outdoor area is set up, you need only get the children out and back inside again.

Outdoor space can also be organized into activity centers. Some of the centers you have outdoors will be fixed, but others can be moved in or out. When you make activity boxes, make some that can be used outdoors.

Some outdoor activity centers Fives enjoy include the following:

- Climbing Center with a safe climber and sturdy boxes and boards to use for building an obstacle course

- Sandbox Center with play dishes, shovels, and pails (be sure to cover the sand to keep animals out, and check to see that it's clean before letting the children play)

- Water Center with a sprinkler; a water play table; buckets and tubs for washing baby dolls and doll clothes, dishes, and pans

- Art Center where the easel or painting table can be brought out and where messy activities such as finger painting can be done

- Carpentry Center with a heavy woodworking table, boxes of wood, and carpentry tools

- Open Play Center where children can use wheel toys such as tricycles and wagons, play with balls of different sizes, or dance to music (be sure open play spaces are away from the quieter outdoor spaces and that the different types of active play do not interfere with one another)

Trips

Fives like to see new things, so field trips are important. But any field trip needs a lot of planning. Don't even think of taking a trip until every child feels secure about coming to the program. Ask parents and other helpers to come along on a trip so that you have enough adults to keep the children safe.

Walking trips are easier than bus or car trips. A car trip is a big job because each child must have his own seat belt or safety seat, and it often means coordinating the use of several cars. Anyway, most Fives like a short walk to a nearby place just as well as a longer trip. Even for a walking trip, you should have at least one adult for every five or six children. Be sure all children have partners that they hold hands with as they walk because there can always be one child who will wander off and get into danger. Adults should be at the front and back of the group and hold the hand of any child who needs more supervision. Walking trips should be short so that children don't get tired or bored. Before the trip, talk about things you might see, and then point them out on your walk.

Get written permission from parents for any trip that takes children away from your facility. Tell the parents where you will be going, when you will leave and return, and whether they need to do anything special for their children that day. Remind parents again the day before the trip.

You don't even have to take Fives away from your building to have some interesting trips. Try a trip to another part of your facility, such as the office or kitchen. A trip in your own playground can be fun if you take a small group out at a time when the other children are indoors. Do something different on a playground trip, such as catching insects or collecting leaves.

Fives are still very young children and do not need to be taken on big trips. Frequent walks in the neighborhood where children and adults share their discoveries work well with Fives. Short trips in your community, such as to the grocery store, post office, library, or the fire station help children learn a lot. A picnic or longer trip at the end of the year is a special treat and is best when all the families are involved.

Three Steps in Planning Activities for Fives

1. Plan and set up activity centers with basic toys and materials that most Fives will enjoy. Arrange the schedule so that children spend most of their day playing in these indoor and outdoor centers.

2. Find out what interests your Fives, and then plan special units about these topics. Add activities that go with these topics to the basic activity centers.

3. Find out what each child is interested in and the skills each is working on. Plan activities that are right for each child and show the child how to do them. These activities can be placed in the activity centers and done by any interested children.

Planning Activities Around Topics

Many teachers find that it helps planning when they pick a topic and look for activities related to it. In the first years of elementary school, teachers often plan units on subjects such as community helpers and the family. You can do this, too. However, you need to remember that five-year-olds have their own interests.

The most successful activities are those that build on the interests of the children in your group. Just about any topic is fine, as long as the children enjoy thinking and talking about it. It does not matter if they did the same topic when they were younger or that they will do it again when they are older. The topic is right for Fives as long as the children move beyond what they already know with curiosity and excitement.

Units can last only a few days or go on for several weeks. For example, you may notice that children are digging up stones on the playground and making collections of them. To build on this interest, you may want your Fives to learn about the stones they find and other kinds, too, by doing a unit on rocks and gems.

As part of the unit, you could put picture books about rocks and gems into the book corner and put pictures of rocks up where the children can see them. You could talk about rocks with the children to see what they can tell you and then give them more information. You and the children could find pictures of their rocks in the books to discover their names. You might put different kinds of rocks in the water table so that children can see their colors when they are wet, have the children sort rocks by color or textures, or use tiny pebbles to make mosaics or sand castings. You might add a special walk to discover new rocks in your neighborhood.

Once you pick a topic, you can find related activities in the sections of this book, including stories, songs, and fingerplays. Following are some topics that you could build a unit around. You can add your own ideas, too.

Myself:	■ What I like, what I used to like
	■ My toys
	■ My clothes

Who lives at my house:
- ■ Parents
- ■ Grandparents
- ■ Brothers and sisters
- ■ Other adults and children

Mothers and babies:
- ■ Animal babies
- ■ Human babies
- ■ When I was a baby
- ■ Baby brothers and sisters and friends

The weather:
- ■ Cold/warm, rainy/sunny
- ■ Clouds
- ■ Clothes for different kinds of weather
- ■ Play in different kinds of weather
- ■ Seasons
- ■ Kinds of storms

Animals:
- ■ Pets
- ■ Birds
- ■ Zoo animals
- ■ Farm animals
- ■ Animal families
- ■ What animals eat
- ■ Where animals live

Nature:
- ■ Water: rivers, ponds, ocean
- ■ Rocks
- ■ Plants and flowers
- ■ Sun, moon, and stars
- ■ Fire and heat
- ■ Ice and cold

Going places:
- ■ On the ground: walking, running; cars, trucks, buses, bicycles, trains
- ■ Riding different animals
- ■ In the air: airplanes, helicopters, hot air balloons
- ■ In the water: swimming, boats, submarines

Health and safety:
- ■ Healthful eating
- ■ Brushing teeth, washing hands, bathing
- ■ Fire safety
- ■ Traffic safety

Our neighborhood:	■ Stores: grocery, pet, book, department; shopping center
	■ Restaurants
	■ Library
	■ Fire station
Helping to save the earth:	■ Saving energy: water, electricity
	■ Recycling waste
Moving on to first grade:	■ Where will we be going?
	■ Riding a school bus
	■ Eating in a school cafeteria
	■ First grade visit
	■ New friends
	■ New activities

Sample Unit

As an example of how you might choose related activities on a topic for a month, let's think through how a unit on "Fire and Heat" might work. This example is for a long unit with many topics. Some of your units may be much shorter and last only a few days or a week.

M O N T H L Y   U N I T   T O P I C

FIRE AND HEAT

Fire and heat help us in many ways.

Week

1

Have children think of and discuss all the hot things they know about.

What are some sources of heat and fire, such as gas stoves, electricity, wood, matches?

How is heat or fire used at home? How is it used at school?

How can you tell if something is hot without touching it?

Discuss how heat and fire can be dangerous. Encourage children to tell about personal experiences.

Materials and Activities

Present pictures and books that show uses of fire and heat: people cooking, drying clothes, sitting in front of a fireplace, and so on.

Take a field trip around the building to find where fire and heat are used.

Put together a child-created book about the ways we use fire and heat.

Provide props in the Dramatic Play Center that encourage thinking about fire and heat, such as a pretend fireplace, stove, space heater and clothes dryer.

Talk about safety rules use to prevent getting burned by heat or fire.

Emphasize not using matches or lighters and using caution around hot items.

There is a lot to learn about fire and heat.

How does it look?

What can be used to measure heat?

Discuss rules for handling fire and heat safely. Rules can be posted on a large chart.

Present an art project with fire colors, such as red, yellow, blue, and orange.

Display pictures of the sun and sunny places.

Present science experiments about hot and cold, such as using thermometer to measure temperature or feeling substances that differ in temperature, such as metal, marble, wood, paper, and soft toys.

Demonstrate science activities such as looking at a lighted candle to see what the flame looks like and experimenting with different ways to extinguish the flame. (Careful supervision by an adult is needed.)

Fire fighters help keep us safe.

Discuss how fire fighters help the community.

How do firefighters find out about fires?

Explain use of emergency (911) numbers: how and when to use them.

What do firefighters do when an alarm is sounded?

What are fire hydrants?

How do firefighters reach tall buildings?

How do firefighters help people get out of burning buildings?

How can fires be prevented?

Use a fire safety checklist from the fire department.

Materials and Activities

Display books and pictures about fire-fighters in the Book Center.

Add fire engines and rescue trucks to the Block Center.

Take a field trip to the fire station.

Put together a child-created book about firefighters.

Act out the sequence that a firefighter would follow when an alarm sounds: waking up, getting dressed, sliding down the fire pole, driving the fire engine, holding the hose, climbing ladders, using an ax, carrying someone to safety, and so on.

Provide firefighter props, such as short hoses, hats, and so on in the Dramatic Play Center.

Walk around the neighborhood to locate fire hydrants.

Present a science experiment to show how water can extinguish a flame.

Create a play pretend fire engine by using chairs in rows.

Provide riding toys in the outdoor area that can be used to play firefighter with other props.

Check school for fire hazards.

Send home newsletter on fire safety for parents to talk about with their children.

We can protect ourselves from fire.

Discuss fire warning devices we use: smoke alarms, fire alarms.

Why it is dangerous to use these when there is no fire?

Discuss what to do in case of fire: fire drills at school and emergency evacuation plans for home, stop-drop-roll procedure, use of fire extinguishers.

Materials and Activities

Explore the building and home to spot fire-warning devices.

Set off an alarm so that children will know the sound.

Show children how a fire extinguisher works.

Practice fire drills.

Add a fire drill bell to the Dramatic Play Center.

Practice stop-drop-and-roll procedure.

Ask your librarian for fire safety songs and rhymes to use at group time.

Send a newsletter to parents so that they can discuss fire evacuation procedures with their child at home.

Add a photo album to the Book Center about a visit to a fire station and children doing various fire awareness activities.

Provide small fire engines and people toys for the sand table.

Have children dictate and illustrate stories about fire fighting.

The sun is a heat source that can burn, too.

Discuss how the sun is a source of heat.

What is the difference between sun and shade?

How do clouds block the sun?

Discuss sun safety: checking playground equipment to be sure it is not too hot, wearing sunscreen on sunny days, wearing protective clothing, sunglasses.

Materials and Activities

Present pictures and books about the sun.

Do a science experiment to see how things left in the sun are warmer than things left in the shade.

Take a playground field trip to find things in the sun and things in the shade. Note that the location of sunny spots changes throughout the day.

Play a game in which children find and stand in a sunny spot or a shady spot.

Try on different sunglasses to see how vision differs with each.

Add sunglasses, sun hats, and clean, empty sunscreen bottles to dress-ups in the Dramatic Play Center.

Weekly and Daily Planning

Unit activities are fun and can add special excitement to a classroom, but it is important to remember that units are not the only things to plan. A wide range of activities in the various activity centers are necessary in a good early-childhood program. When you plan for the week, remember that you will need to provide many self-directed and teacher-directed activities for the children every day in addition to the unit activities. The unit can help you bring many different ideas and facts to the children's attention. The repetition in a unit also helps five-year-olds learn some basic ideas and build vocabulary. But you will need to plan other activities for children to do both indoors and outdoors.

When you get down to practical planning for children, you need to think of what you will do day by day. Making a daily plan can help you think of activities that you can add to the children's play in the activity centers or to group activities. The daily plan can help you think of new toys or materials to bring out that day and ways to change activity centers by using some different activity boxes. In your daily plan, try to include activities from all four sections of this book.

There is a sample form for a weekly plan on pages 44 and 45. You could put your completed plan up on the wall as a reminder. Also use the plan as a guide when you get your materials ready for the next day.

Planning for Individual Children

Every five-year-old is an individual with his own pattern of what he can and cannot do. No two children of the same age will be able to do exactly the same things. By using the "Fives Can" lists on pages 50 and 51, you can find some of the things each one of your children can do. Using the "Fives Can" lists, take a few minutes to watch each one of your Fives and write down what he or she can do.

The "Fives Can" lists are not meant to be used in screening for problems. They cannot tell you how fast or slow a child is in his development. These lists can only help you notice more of what the children can do. Without the help of a list, you usually see only the big advances a child makes. A list can help you become a better observer so that you notice the little advances a child is working on every day.

When you know some of the things each child in your group can do, then you will know which activities best suit the children. For each of the activities, a reference to the "Fives Can" list tells what skill is practiced. If you think a child can do that skill or is trying to learn to do it, then try the activity with her.

When you plan, try to think of several children who would enjoy the activity you choose. Jot down their names on the written planning form so that you will remember to encourage them to try the activity. During a slow time of day, try that special activity with the children. You might try it when many children are already actively involved in activities or when another adult has taken some of the children outdoors. The important thing is to plan some activities that are right for each child in your group every day.

Most of the activity ideas in this book can be introduced to children, and then the toys and materials needed for the activity can be placed in an activity center. The children will be able to do the activity over and over again until they are no longer interested. You will find that children will show their friends how to use the materials, too.

Writing an Activity Plan

It is easy to write up an activity plan using the activities and planning form in this book. Put the number and name of the activity you want to use on the planning form. Some activities can be presented to a small group of children who meet the "Fives Can" requirements listed for the activity. Jot down the names of the children near the activity to remind you.

On pages 44 and 45, there is a weekly planning form. Post your weekly plan where you can see it. Having the children's names on the written plan helps you to make sure that you are keeping each child in mind. If another teacher has to take over for you, things will go more smoothly with a written plan.

Your written plan should list the *new* activities you want to try. You will also want to repeat familiar activities that Fives enjoy. It is better to plan too much than too little. Always have some extra things ready in case you need them. This way the children will be happy and learn new things all day, during routines and at play times. When you have written your activity plan, look it over and ask yourself the following questions:

Have I used routines to encourage learning and independence in children as much as possible?

Have I planned for both morning and afternoon activity times?

Are there outdoor play activities daily, weather permitting?

Are a wide range of self-directed activities and toys available all through the day?

Have I planned a variety of activities that will enrich children's knowledge?

Remember, in carrying out your written plan to prepare for activities by getting the materials together and going over the instructions, think of questions to ask the children and topics to discuss for different activities.

On the next four pages you will find a sample Activity Plan Form. The first one is filled in to show you how to use it. Copy the blank form if you wish, and change it to fit your needs. If you are already using a written planning form and you are happy with it, by all means stay with it. Remember, this is only a sample to help you come up with the written planning form for Fives that suits you best.

Activity Plan

Write the names of the activities you plan for the different activity areas in your classroom. If there are specific children who will benefit especially from an activity you plan, write their names next to the activity and encourage them to take part.

Activity Areas	Monday	Tuesday	Wednesday	Thursday	Friday
Large-Group Time	Talk about emotions— name feelings	Talk about things that make me happy/sad	Talk about things that make me calm/angry	Talk about things that make me frightened	Talk about things that make me excited

Activity Centers	Monday	Tuesday	Wednesday	Thursday	Friday
Books 7, 47, 48, 53	Add books on feelings to book corner	Read and Ask Sarah	Acting Out Poetry Emma Clint Jimmy Kenisha	Copycat Writing William Robert Elizabeth Susan	Matching Coupons Dave Amanda Vanessa
Art 223, 222, 226, 229, 233	Paper-Plate Masks	Yarn-and-Ribbon Pictures	Great Big Pictures	Using Tape Sidney Rasheed	Paper Box Sculpture
Blocks 290, 293, 295	Building a Big House (leave it up!)	Building a Big House	Big Boxes as Outdoor Blocks	Big Boxes as Outdoor Blocks	Build Around Me Emma Clint
Music 357, 360, 367, 362, 371	Dance Your Own Way (talk about emotions)	The Popcorn Dance	Relaxing to Music (talk about calm)	Fast/Slow singing (talk about calm, excited)	Many Drums Jimmy Kenisha
Dramatic Play 321, 326, 313	Afraid of the Dark (talk about emotions)	Playing Doctor and Nurse (talk about emotions)	Playing Doctors and Nurses	Feelings Pantomime	Feelings Pantomime

Activity Centers	Monday	Tuesday	Wednesday	Thursday	Friday
Large-Muscle 125, 127, 128, 136	Quiet-Moving Game Sidney Rasheed Sarah	Beginning Golf	Beginning Golf	Beanbag Toss Emma William	Jumping on Stepping Stones
Small-Muscle 170, 173, 192	Tying Knots with Help William	Bead Patterns	Bead Patterns	Tying Knots with Help William	Pickup Sticks William Robert
Science/Nature 433, 432	What Will Ants Eat? Jimmy Clint Amanda	What Will Ants Eat? Elizabeth Jonathan Vanessa	What Will Ants Eat? Emma Megan Sarah	What Will Ants Eat?	Pressed Flowers
Math 474, 495, 500, 503	Fraction Words Sarah Jonathan	Delivering Mail to Houses	Delivering Mail to Houses	Estimating How Many	Taking Surveys—Who Wore What Color? Emma Clint
Other	Children make pictures that show emotions	Children make pictures that show emotions		Cooking—make cheese pretzels (Emma's mom will help)	Cooking—make cheese pretzels (Rasheed's mom will help)
Other	Add books about emotions to Book Corner	Stories about what ants eat	Music teacher at 10:30		

Activity Plan

Write the names of the activities you plan for the different activity areas in your classroom. If there are specific children who will benefit especially from an activity you plan, write their names next to the activity and encourage them to take part.

Activity Areas	Monday	Tuesday	Wednesday	Thursday	Friday
Large-Group Time					

Activity Centers	Monday	Tuesday	Wednesday	Thursday	Friday
Books					
Art					
Blocks					
Music					
Dramatic Play					

Activity Centers	Monday	Tuesday	Wednesday	Thursday	Friday
Large-Muscle					
Small-Muscle					
Science/Nature					
Math					
Other					
Other					

Finding the Right Activities

The activities for Fives have been broken into two age groups. Each group is shown by a picture.

stands for what a child 60 to 66 months can do.

stands for what a child 66 to 72 months can do.

Every activity has one of these two pictures to make it easy to pick out the right activities for the children you are teaching. You can use these activities for a five-year-old who is developing typically, more slowly, or faster than usual for his age. Just choose an activity based on what each child *can do.* Each activity in this book gives an idea of what the five-year-old should be able to do in order to take part in the activity. Remember, what the child can do is more important than the child's age in choosing the right activity.

If you have used *Active Learning for Threes* or *Active Learning for Fours,* you may notice that some activities from those books are similar to activities for Fives. Some are the same activities. Remember that when the same open-ended materials are given to a group of children, it is the children themselves, not the adult, who make something developmentally different out of the activity. Each time an activity is done, it is experienced with new understandings.

The first activities in each section are easier than those that come later. For example, in the first Books, Pictures, Pre-Reading, and Pre-Writing activities, children dictate their words and you write down what they say. The later activities in this section are used to encourage children to write a few words on their own.

On pages 50 and 51 you will find a list of many things Fives can do in each of the age groups. Take time to look at these pages. It may surprise you to see what you can or can't expect from Fives.

When You Start to Use the Activities

- Look at the "Fives Can" lists. Watch and think about each child. What can each one do?

- Pick out the best "Fives Can" picture for each of your children. This will help you plan for each one of them.

- Decide which children seem to be on a similar level in large- and small-muscle skills, in listening and talking, and in play interests. Plan some activities for those small groups.

- Look at all four activity sections and ask yourself the following questions:

  Which activities do I have the materials for?

  Which activities do I think each child will be able to enjoy?

  Which activities do I have time to do?

  Which activities would I like to start with?

  Can I relate any of these activities to a topic and add it to a simple unit?

- Encourage children to try the activities. Show children how to do an activity if necessary. Whenever possible, add the activity to a center for any interested children to use by themselves.

- Go back over the plan at the end of the week, and ask yourself these questions about how things went:

  Which activities went best?

  Do I need to make any changes in the interest centers?

  Do I need to make any changes in the daily schedule?

  Do I need to make any new activity boxes?

Writing Your Own Activities

A number of the activities you will find in this book may be familiar to you. That's because many of the activities have always been used by parents and teachers to encourage children to grow and learn. There will also be some activities you've never used before because no one can think of every activity or even remember all the activities that have been done in the past. That's why activity books keep you on your toes with lots of new ideas. There may be some activities that you have enjoyed doing with Fives that are not in this book. As you remember them, write them down in the blank activity boxes at the end of each section. This will make it easier to remember and use the activities as you write your activity plans.

When you work with five-year-olds, you will find that you have to think up some of your own activities to meet their needs and make the best use of the resources you have on hand. Here's how to write your own activities.

- First, think about what one child can do. Use the "Fives Can" lists to help focus on a skill the child would like to practice.

- Next, think about what you need to do to help the child practice the skill. Ask yourself the following questions:

  Will the activity be teacher- or self-directed?

  What toys, equipment, or other materials will I need?

  What will I have to get ready ahead of time?

  Exactly what must I do to make the activity happen?

  What kinds of things can I say to help with the child's learning?

  Where will the activity work well?

  How long will the activity take?

  How many children can take part in the activity?

- Write your activity in a blank space on the planning form. Try it out to see how it works. Make changes if you need to.

Activity Checklists

At the beginning of each activity section in this book, you will find a checklist. The checklist is to help you see how well the setting you create for children meets their needs for learning in that area. It's a good idea to try out these checklists to see the strengths and weaknesses of your early childhood setting for each type of activity in the book. Then you can see where improvements are needed and use the checklists as a guide for making changes.

You can do all the checklists at one time if you wish, or pick one or two to work on at first, and then do the others when you are ready. As you carefully read each statement on the checklists, look around your early childhood setting and think about the things you do with the children.

Carefully follow these directions as you do the checklists.

1. On each checklist you will find that the statements are followed by check boxes under two age ranges, one for younger Fives and one for older Fives. Note the ages of the children in your setting and rate the statements for those ages.

2. If you find clear evidence that a statement is *true* for an age group, put a check in the box.

3. If you find clear evidence that a statement is *not true*, put an X in the box.

   Make notes next to a statement if you are not sure about whether it should get a check or an X.

If people who do not work in your classroom want to use the checklists, they will need to spend enough time observing children in your room to really find out what they need to know. It takes about two hours in a morning to get most of the information needed to complete all the checklists. If the other observers do not see or hear everything needed to complete the checklists, then they will have to set aside time to ask you some questions about your preschool setting. However, they should be sure to observe first.

Observers may see things differently from the way you do. If there is a chance to talk about the differences, both of you will probably end up with some good new ideas.

"Fives Can" Lists

The following pages give you more information on what Fives can do. It is important to remember that these lists are only general guidelines and cannot be used to find out whether a child is or is not developing typically. These lists are not a screening test. If you are worried about a child in your care, you should advise the parents to find a professional who can do some special tests. The parents could talk to their family doctor for suggestions. Or you might help by asking the early childhood professionals who come to your classroom, such as the child care consultant, social worker, or school counselor, about special services.

The "Fives Can" lists are meant to help you become more aware of some of the things most five-year-olds can do. The lists are actually made up of many of the "Fives Can" indicators from the activities. Without a list to follow, it is hard to be aware of the new little steps each child takes. But these little steps are what we need to encourage in order to help children grow. We want to help each child practice these small advances as he plays with toys, listens to stories, answers our questions, and takes part in all the play activities. Then the big advances will come more easily in their own time.

Fives Can List

60 MONTHS

From 60 to 66 months, some things Fives can do:

- get along well in small groups
- try to catch a small ball with two hands
- have an idea for artwork before beginning to create
- like to play house and baby
- eat well with a fork, cut with a knife
- print name, but not too clearly
- hear the beginning sounds of words, like "d" in dog
- ask for adult help only when needed
- know colors and color names well
- answer the telephone and call correct person to telephone
- begin to tell one letter from another
- enjoy animal stories or fairy tales
- know shapes and do shapes puzzles well
- say numbers from 1 to 20
- understand place words (*on top of, over, under*)
- build complex block buildings
- draw person with head, body, legs, arms, and other parts
- enjoy exploring the neighborhood
- choose friends
- handle toileting by self, usually dry through the night
- listen well to a story read to a large group of children
- cooperate quite well with friends
- make up rhyming words
- comfort friends who are upset
- sort things in different ways, usually by color
- understand size—which things are biggest, tallest, and so on.
- brush or comb hair quite well
- begin to understand clocks and time
- use classroom tools appropriately

66 MONTHS
- skip well

Fives Can List

66 MONTHS

From 66 to 72 months, some things Fives can do:

- use time words (*morning, night*) to tell when things happen
- hop in a straight line for about six feet
- have best friends, but change friends often
- confuse some similar words, such as *ask* and *tell*
- begin to understand money and how it is used
- begin to jump rope
- prefer to use either left or right hand
- tell a story from a picture book very well
- begin to know what a ruler and thermometer are used for
- know when something is cut in half, thirds, or quarters
- bathe self, but still need help to be sure all parts are washed
- cut well with scissors
- protect younger children and pets
- name feelings that others are having
- tell left shoes from right shoes
- make only a few mistakes when speaking
- write some numbers and tell their names
- play easy table games (checkers, lotto) with a friend and often follow rules
- draw most easy shapes
- count things quite well
- name most uppercase but not most lowercase letters
- dress and undress well alone
- say numbers above 20
- read a few words
- usually tell one letter from another
- use long sentences, tying thoughts together
- write some, but not all, letters of the alphabet
- catch a small ball with two hands quite well
- do very easy adding using 1, 2, 3, 4 (1 + 1, 2 + 3)

72 MONTHS
- share secrets with friends that are not shared with adults

Activities for
Listening and Talking

Index

of Activities for Listening and Talking

Here's Why

Talking with others is important for five-year-olds as a way of telling what they think and how they feel. Fives have also learned to depend on talking for most of the socializing with friends that they enjoy so much. Fives use words to solve problems and remember. The sentences Fives use are generally long, with strings of words and ideas put together. They ask many questions and answer them, too. But Fives still have lots to learn before they can talk as adults do. Although the speech of your kindergartners should be easy to understand toward the end of their year with you, their vocabularies and grammar will still be developing.

You can help children continue to make gains in their communication skills by asking questions, listening with interest, and adding to what they say. You can also be sure that your classroom is set up for talking rather than being quiet, with plenty of free-play activities children can choose from during most of the day. You can help them accumulate a larger vocabulary by introducing them to a wide range of experiences and ideas.

In the Books/Pictures/Pre-Reading/Pre-Writing section you will find ideas for using pictures and picture and word combinations to help your Fives practice some new thinking skills, such as naming, matching, guessing, and comparing. You will also find activities in which children get the warm, personal experiences with books that make learning to read more fun later on. Many activities will help children learn that what they say can be written down and read back to them.

The Conversation and Group Talk activities give you ideas for helping Fives use talking to get along with others, share feelings and ideas, work on self-help skills, follow directions, and show what they know and remember. Some of the activities in this section are just meant to be fun as you and your Fives play with words together. Communication should be a big part of everything you do with children. The activities in this book can get you started helping Fives improve their skills with words.

Throughout the day, informal conversations should take place as part of the children's activities. It is also important to bring a more formal group of Fives together to talk about something of interest so that they can learn how to take turns as they listen and talk.

Materials and Notes

Books/Pictures/Pre-Reading/Pre-Writing

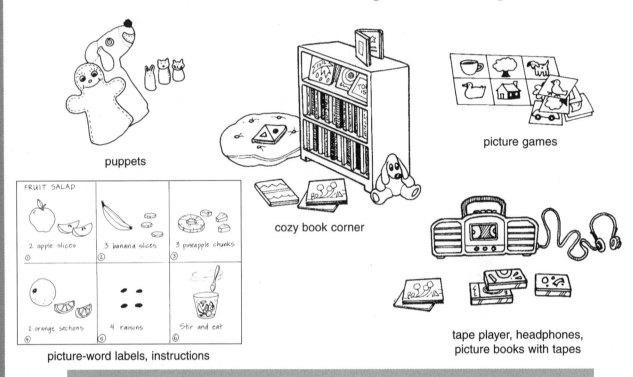

puppets

cozy book corner

picture games

FRUIT SALAD

2 apple slices ①

3 banana slices ②

3 pineapple chunks ③

2 orange sections ④

4 raisins ⑤

Stir and eat ⑥

picture-word labels, instructions

tape player, headphones, picture books with tapes

- Remember that listening and talking about many new experiences is the best way for Fives to get ready to read and to write when they are ready.

- Give interested children lots of chances to try writing or reading when they choose. But spend most of your time encouraging Fives to do fun, interesting activities that enable them to learn many words and talk a lot.

- Do most book activities with small groups of children. Read often to a few Fives in the Book Center. Have large-group story times that do not last too long. Be sure children are uncrowded and comfortable when they listen to stories.

- Use lots of books and pictures in all areas of the room to show information about topics you are discussing with the children.

- Many of the activity ideas for younger and older Fives can be used with either age group because they are open-ended and can be challenging to children with a wide range of abilities.

- Give children many chances to tell stories (about pictures, activities, and so on) and to watch you write down exactly what they say. Read their words back to them.

Activity Checklist

Books/Pictures/Pre-Reading/Pre-Writing

Book, picture, pre-reading, and pre-writing activities for Fives include the use of picture books, picture games, and pictures in the room that add information about things you talk about with the children. Fives enjoy being read to and love looking at books on their own. They are likely to notice the letters and words printed in books, and some children may be ready to read some words. They enjoy playing easy picture games with a few friends. They are interested in retelling or pretending to read familiar stories, as well as making up their own. Many Fives understand that what they say can be written down and read. Some Fives will be interested in trying to write some letters and words, and this should be encouraged, but not hurried.

Check for each age group

	60–66 months	66–72 months
1. Many pictures that show things that are interesting to the children and that the children talk about with adults are placed where children can see and touch them.	❑	❑
2. A cozy Book Center with a variety of books that are sturdy and in good condition is available to the children most of the day.	❑	❑
3. Pictures and picture books show people of different races, ages, cultures, and abilities in positive, nonsexist ways.	❑	❑
4. New pictures and books are added often.	❑	❑
5. Adult reads with children several times every day, mostly in small groups, but also during larger group times where children are not crowded together.	❑	❑
6. Children use simple picture games, puppets, and flannelboards with teacher help when needed.	❑	❑
7. Children see many printed words, such as names on cubbies or picture/word labels on toy shelves.	❑	❑
8. Picture/word recipes and printed instructions to guide activities are used often, such as picture/word instructions for feeding classroom pets or printed instructions for using a new art material. Adult reads these instructions to children and refers to them during the activities.	❑	❑

Activity Checklist

9. Children often have what they say (stories about pictures, activities, and so on) written down for them by an adult. The child sits so that he can see the letters being printed right-side up. The adult reads back what the child said. ❐   ❐

10. A Writing Center, where children can pretend to write, copy letters and words, and write some words on their own is available for children to use if they choose. ❐   ❐

11. Interested children are encouraged to read and write some letters, their names, and other simple words. Children who are not interested are not pushed to take part in these activities. ❐   ❐

12. Adult helps children learn to associate alphabet letters with their sounds in discussions that come up naturally, not through rote memorization methods. ❐   ❐

1

Fives can

- look at books on their own
- clean up play areas quite well

Using the Book Center

Set up a Book Center for your Fives to use. (Book Center Ideas on page 87.) Talk with the children about how to use books carefully and how to clean up the center when finished.

Add books that come from the library, books the children have made, and photo albums of the children in your group. Have a special little place where children can safely put books they bring from home. Talk with the children about taking special care of books others wish to share.

 indoors   5–20 minutes   1–4 Fives

2

Fives can

- print name, but not too clearly
- begin to tell one letter from another

The Writing Center

Set up a Writing Center for Fives to use if they wish. Put a small table with two or three chairs and a small shelf in a quiet part of the room. On the shelf put neatly organized pencils, colorful watercolor markers, and white paper (some with lines and some without). Have an example of the alphabet for children to look at if they want to.

Explain to the children that this is a place where they can write (or pretend to write). Tell them that you will write words for them to see or to copy if they wish.

Ramika, do you want to write house? *Watch while I write it. H-O-U-S-E. Now you can copy it onto the picture you drew.*

 indoors   2–10 minutes   1–3 Fives

3

Fives can

- show interest in print materials

The Reading Classroom

Make your classroom a reading classroom. Add children's magazines and more children's books to the Book Center. Put the daily newspaper, magazines, catalogs, menus, and coupons in the Dramatic Play Center so children can pretend with these. Post the menu for meals and snacks where children can see and point it out as you read about what they will be eating each day. Read a variety of stories, poetry, jokes, and riddles. Put children's stories on a bulletin board at child height and read them to your Fives at least once a week.

Help children learn to read by watching others read for work and for play. Set an example for your Fives by reading in the classroom. Talk with parents about the importance of home reading too.

 indoors   3–10 minutes   1–10 Fives

4

Fives can

- show interest in printed words

Using Printed Words to Guide Fives

When setting up activities for your Fives to do, add signs with printed words to guide them. For example, put up a sign next to a sink-or-float game in the Science and Nature Center that says "Which things sink? Which things float?" Or for a new art activity using a new type of paper, you might put up a sign that says, "What can you make with this paper?" Point out the printed words and read them to the children.

When talking about the activities children have done, refer to the signs again and ask children how the questions can be answered.

Do you remember what these words say, Demitrius?
That's right. They say, "What things stick to the magnet?"
What did you find out?

 in or out   1–3 minutes   1–8 Fives

Activities for Listening and Talking

5

Fives can

- print name but not too clearly
- recognize a few names of friends

The Name Box

Neatly print each child's name on a sturdy card that is 8" wide and 4" tall. Have each child watch as you print his or her name. Start with the first name and add the last name when the child is ready. Talk about the letters as you write them and the sound the first letter makes. See if the child knows what the letters are. Put these cards into a box in the Writing Center.

When children want to write their names, have them find their card in the box. Then they can copy what the card says.

Look at all the names in the box with a small group of children. See if they can tell which names belong to the different children in the group.

 indoors   2–20 minutes   1–4 Fives

6

Fives can

- begin to tell one letter from another
- hear some beginning sounds of words

Books of Different Reading Levels

Place two types of picture books in the Book Center. First, have plenty of picture books with many words for children to look at and that you can read to them. But also add picture books with just one or two words per page that are closely tied to the pictures children look at. Encourage children to use both types of books, based on their own interests. Point out some of the words in the simple books as you read with your Fives. See if interested children begin to recognize some of the words.

There are all kinds of dogs on this page, Jimmy. Here's a Scottie, and here's an Airedale. That's right. That word is dogs. *Dogs* starts with a d, *just like* daddy. *That's right! Your friend Debby's name starts with a* d *too!*

 indoors   4–20 minutes   1–5 Fives

7

Fives can

- talk about stories they know
- answer simple questions

Read and Ask

Read a short picture book to a small group of Fives. (See Story Times Ideas, page 87.) As you finish reading a page, see if the children can answer some questions about what is happening. Be sure the children can see the pictures. Then use questions that ask what, when, why, and how things are happening in the story.

Why was the little bird unhappy? What did he decide to do? Why did he think all the different animals were his mother? How did little bird finally find his mother? What do you think the little bird's mother was doing while her baby was searching for her?

 in or out 5–15 minutes 1–10 Fives

8

Fives can

- enjoy listening to stories
- begin to recognize the first letter in their names

Alphabet Books

Read your Fives some alphabet books. Point out the letters of the alphabet as you read. Try to find rhyming stories, silly stories, and stories with new words.

Talk with your Fives about other words that start with the same letter of the alphabet.

Baby, banana, bacon.
Can you think of another word that starts with b?
That's right, Alonzo. Brother *and* boy *start with* b.

 in or out 3–10 minutes 1–20 Fives

9

Fives can

- print name, but not too clearly

- learn that what they say can be written and read

The Class Book

Have your Fives help you make a <u>book</u> that shows each child in the class. Have a page for each <u>child</u> where they can write their names. Give help as needed. Then talk with the children so that you can write what they tell you about what they like to do, where they live, and other things they want on their page. Add <u>photos</u> of each child or <u>pictures</u> they draw. Read this book to small groups of children. As they get to know it well, let them tell you about their friends.

Whose page is this? It says she likes to ride a bike.
That's right, it's Patricia. This is Marika's page.
Do you remember what Marika likes to do?

Put the book in the Book Center so that the children can look at it by themselves.

 indoors   5–15 minutes   2–6 Fives

10

Fives can

- talk about pictures

- learn that what they say can be written and read

Poster Making

Have your Fives help you make picture posters to go with the ideas you talk about. For example, if you are talking about animals they would like to have as pets, make posters that show the different animals. Let your Fives cut out lots of the <u>pictures</u> you need from <u>magazines</u>. Then your Fives can <u>glue</u> them onto a large sheet of sturdy <u>paper</u>.

Talk with the children about the pictures as they work. Write down some of the things they say on the poster, too. Read their words back to them. Encourage children to write their own words, too, if they wish. Have the children help hang up the posters when they are done. Look at and talk about them often. Take the posters down after a week or two, but save them to look at again.

 indoors   15–30 minutes   1–8 Fives

Activities for Listening and Talking

11

Fives can

- talk about things they know
- guess easy riddles

Picture Card Riddle Game

Use a set of picture cards that has many different pictures. Show your Fives three pictures of things they know about. Encourage the children to talk a little about the three pictures. Then give clues about one of the pictures and see if anyone can guess which picture you are talking about.

This creature has eyes, a nose, and a mouth.
Hmmm. Some of you think it's the fish, some the dog, and some think it's the rabbit. Here's another clue. It has long ears. All of you know it is not the fish!

Give your Fives chances to take turns giving the clues and guessing. Show four or five pictures to make the game more challenging. Put the game on the shelf in the Book Center so that children can play it with friends.

 in or out   5–15 minutes   1–10 Fives

12

Fives can

- figure out familiar sequences
- tell what comes next

Sequence Card Story

Buy or make a set of easy, five-step sequence cards. (You will find some examples to copy on page 95.) Point to each picture and encourage your Fives to talk about what is happening. Then see if they can figure out the order the cards should be in, from what happens first to what happens last. Help the child put the cards in order from left to right. Ask questions that help the child figure things out.

The woman is going into the store. Which picture comes next?
Does she check out, put groceries into the shopping cart, or put groceries into the car?

Put the cards in the Book Center for the children to use with friends. Many Fives will have good reasons for putting the cards in a different order.

 in or out   5–15 minutes   1–3 Fives

13

Fives can

- recognize some familiar things by touch
- show interest in printed words

Feelie Box Picture Game

Put a plastic margarine tub into a large, stretchy sock to make a feelie box. Have some familiar things that will fit into the box, such as a ball, a marble, or an eraser. Make picture cards that show these things. Add words for the things on the cards, too.

Put one of the things into the feelie box while the child looks away. Then show the child three cards, one of which is a picture of the thing in the box. Read the words on the cards to the child. Let the child reach into the box and feel. See if he can choose the picture of the thing he feels.

Encourage children to play this game with friends. Add challenge by showing more pictures or by using things that are similar, such as a crayon and a pencil.

 in or out   3–10 minutes   1–3 Fives

14

Fives can

- make up stories or tell familiar stories
- cooperate with friends

Story with Puppets

Show your Fives how to use hand puppets to tell a story. Then encourage a few children to work together to create a puppet story. They can make up their own story or tell a familiar one. See if children can work on the story alone, but be ready to jump in to help them work out problems. Remind children that stories have a beginning, middle, and end. Some children may want to work on their puppet stories over several days. Encourage children to perform their puppet stories for a voluntary audience.

Which puppet is supposed to talk first, Rosa?
And then what will happen?

Fives can make stick puppets, too. (See Directions for Making Stick Puppets on page 92.)

 in or out   10–40 minutes   1–4 Fives

15

Fives can

- make up a silly story
- learn that what they say can be written and read

Making Silly Story Books

Have children help as you make a new silly book for the Book Center. You can start the story and then have the children continue it. Write down what the children say.

We're going to make up a silly story.
Tell me about the silly character.
Alfred says, "There is a silly dog with green fur."

Ask the children to draw pictures for the story. Cover pages with clear contact paper. Tie the pages together with yarn or string. Write the book's title on the front. Make lots of silly books with your Fives. Read them the stories they helped to write.

 indoors   5–30 minutes   # 1–6 Fives

16

Fives can

- begin to hear beginning sounds of words

Alphabet Posters

Collect pictures (from magazines, catalogs, advertisements) that show things that begin with clear letter sounds. Ask parents to help collect pictures, too. Work with your Fives to sort the pictures by their beginning sounds. Use large pieces of paper and glue to make a separate poster for all the pictures that begin with each sound. Allow children to arrange the pictures and glue them in place. Label the pictures on the posters, spelling out the letters and helping children notice the sounds.

Hang the posters where children can easily see and reach them. Talk often about the different pictures on each poster.

 indoors   10–20 minutes   # 1–6 Fives

Activities for Listening and Talking

17

Fives can

- talk about self and others in pictures
- learn that what they say can be written and read

Kids' Photo Album

Take photos of the children and other familiar people often. Take pictures on special occasions, such as birthdays, but be sure to have many pictures of your Fives doing everyday things, too. Include pictures from home. Put the photos into a sturdy photo album with plastic pages.

Have children talk about the pictures. Write down some of the things they say and put their words next to the photos. Put the album in the Book Center for the children to use. Talk with the children about the pictures and read their words to them.

Do you remember where this photo was taken, Marlys? That's right. We visited the pumpkin patch in the fall. Why did we visit the pumpkin patch?

 indoors   2–20 minutes   1–6 Fives

18

Fives can

- talk about familiar things
- answer many questions

"Things We Talk About" Picture Box

Make picture cards with words on them to go with the things you are talking about with your Fives. (See Ideas on Pictures for Fives on page 90.) Put them into a special box that you keep in the Book Center. Look at and talk about the pictures with the children.

That is quite a big dinosaur, isn't it, Tracy? What do you think this part of his body was for?

Ask questions to help children talk about each thing, but keep things relaxed. Do not pressure children to answer if they are not interested. Leave the pictures in the Book Center for children to share with their friends.

 indoors   3–15 minutes   1–5 Fives

Activities for Listening and Talking

19

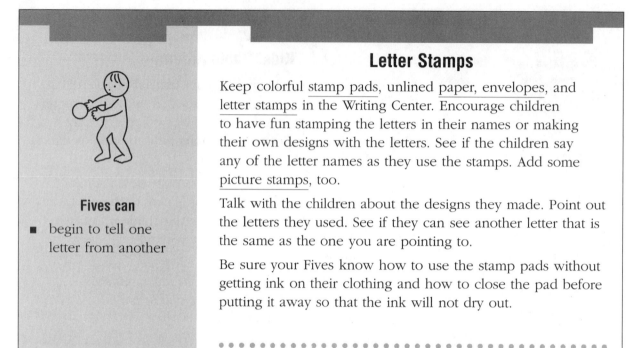

Fives can

- begin to tell one letter from another

Letter Stamps

Keep colorful stamp pads, unlined paper, envelopes, and letter stamps in the Writing Center. Encourage children to have fun stamping the letters in their names or making their own designs with the letters. See if the children say any of the letter names as they use the stamps. Add some picture stamps, too.

Talk with the children about the designs they made. Point out the letters they used. See if they can see another letter that is the same as the one you are pointing to.

Be sure your Fives know how to use the stamp pads without getting ink on their clothing and how to close the pad before putting it away so that the ink will not dry out.

in or out   1–5 minutes   # 1–4 Fives

20

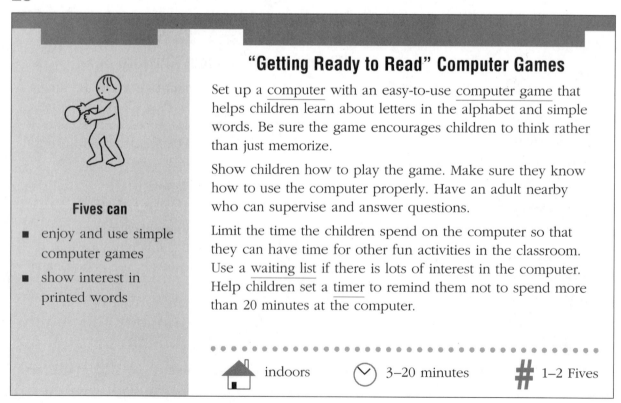

Fives can

- enjoy and use simple computer games
- show interest in printed words

"Getting Ready to Read" Computer Games

Set up a computer with an easy-to-use computer game that helps children learn about letters in the alphabet and simple words. Be sure the game encourages children to think rather than just memorize.

Show children how to play the game. Make sure they know how to use the computer properly. Have an adult nearby who can supervise and answer questions.

Limit the time the children spend on the computer so that they can have time for other fun activities in the classroom. Use a waiting list if there is lots of interest in the computer. Help children set a timer to remind them not to spend more than 20 minutes at the computer.

indoors   3–20 minutes   # 1–2 Fives

21

Fives can

- tell about things they have done
- learn that what they say can be written and read

Sunshine Notes

When you and a child are happy about something she has done, write a short Sunshine Note for the child to take home and share. (Sample Sunshine Notes for you to copy are on page 96.) Have the child tell you what to write.

What do you want to say in this Sunshine Note, Hiromasa? You tell me and I'll write.
OK. "I helped Maria tie her shoe."
Do you want to say anything else?

Be sure to include all the children in your classroom. Read the notes you've written back to the children and encourage families to read them aloud, too. Keep plenty of blank notes handy.

 in or out   2–5 minutes   # 1–2 Fives

22

Fives can

- sort familiar things by category

Sorting Board Fun

Make some picture sorting games for your Fives to use with a sorting board. (See How to Make Sorting Boards on page 439.) Have sets of pictures, such as toys, animals, clothes, foods or dinosaurs, that the children can sort. Put out a sorting board with four sets of the cards. Show the child how to sort the cards by what they are.

Can you put all the trucks into the row where they belong, Kyle? What's this picture? Right. It's a tyrannosaur. Does it go here with the dinosaurs, with the trucks, with the flowers, or with the toys?

Children can sort cards into boxes rather than sorting boards if you wish. Make the game more challenging by adding more sets of cards.

 indoors   5–15 minutes   # 1–3 Fives

Activities for Listening and Talking

23

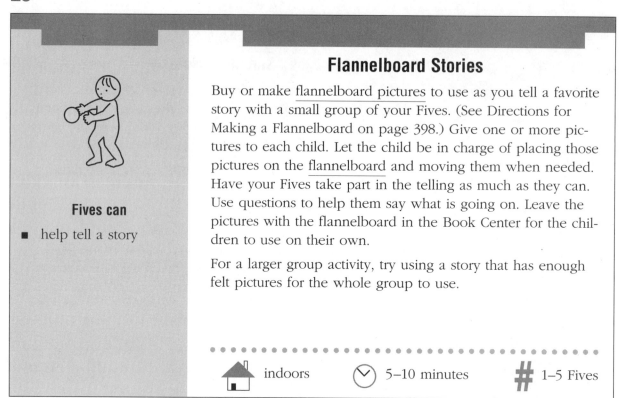

Fives can

- help tell a story

Flannelboard Stories

Buy or make flannelboard pictures to use as you tell a favorite story with a small group of your Fives. (See Directions for Making a Flannelboard on page 398.) Give one or more pictures to each child. Let the child be in charge of placing those pictures on the flannelboard and moving them when needed. Have your Fives take part in the telling as much as they can. Use questions to help them say what is going on. Leave the pictures with the flannelboard in the Book Center for the children to use on their own.

For a larger group activity, try using a story that has enough felt pictures for the whole group to use.

indoors   5–10 minutes   # 1–5 Fives

24

Fives can

- enjoy stories
- follow simple directions

Books with Records or Tapes

Play a record or tape that goes with a picture book. Show the children how to listen to the story and turn the pages when they hear the signal that tells when to turn the page. Teach the children how to operate the record or tape player and let them take over once they know how to do it. Encourage children to take turns holding the books and turning the pages.

Provide headphones so that Fives can listen without disturbing others.

Try making your own tapes of favorite books. Read slowly, ring a bell as you turn the page, and wait ten seconds before starting the next page. Ask some fathers, mothers, or other special friends of the children to read and record stories.

indoors   5–20 minutes   # 1–5 Fives

25

Fives can

- enjoy being read to
- make up simple rhymes

Poems

Read to your Fives from a book of poems. Fives especially enjoy rhyming and hearing new words. Find poems with different rhythms, some that show different feelings, some that represent different cultures, some that tell stories, and some that are just fun. Include poems the children have written. Read slowly and show that you enjoy the poems. Talk about things the Fives might imagine as you read.

Here's a poem about clouds. Close your eyes while I read. Pretend you see clouds up in the sky. Tell me what you see.

 in or out   3–12 minutes   1–20 Fives

26

Fives can

- help tell a familiar story
- take turns telling a story

What Will Happen?

Begin to tell a familiar story to your Fives. Do this without a book so that the children listen without looking at pictures. Once you are into the story, encourage children to tell what happens next. Be ready to hear lots of different ideas besides the ones you expect.

Ernestine was riding on Jonah the goat.
Just then she lost her grip.
What happened next?

Try to make up a story with your Fives. See if they can help you make up what happens as the story grows. This can get pretty silly, so be ready to laugh. Write down the stories you and the children make up so that they can be read over and over.

 in or out   3–10 minutes   1–5 Fives

Activities for Listening and Talking

27

Fives can

- help tell a story
- name pictures

Rebus Picture Stories

Read a <u>story</u> that combines words and rebus pictures. Rebus pictures are small pictures that are used in place of a written word that is repeated over and over in a story. For example, a picture of a bear might replace the word *bear* in the text of the story. (A sample Rebus Picture Story can be found on page 97.) Or you can ask at your public library for books with rebus stories, such as *Ready . . . Set . . . Read* by Joanna Cole and Stephanie Calmenson, published by Doubleday Books, 1990.

Begin reading the story with one or two children. Have them follow your finger as you point to each word you read. When your finger comes to a picture, see if they can fill in the word.

 in or out   5–10 minutes   4–6 Fives

28

Fives can

- talk about pictures
- show interest in printed words

Special Picture Place

Set up a "Special Picture Place" on a wall, the back of a bookcase, or a bulletin board. Put up <u>pictures</u> of the things your Fives are interested in or things you and the children are talking about at the time. As topics change, be sure to change the pictures. Point out the pictures in your talks. Ask questions to help the children talk about them.

What happened to this house, Emeka? It caught on fire. Let's look at our special picture place. Can you find someone who can help put out a fire? The fireman? Can you find someone else who can help?

Add words to the pictures and talk with the children about what the words say.

 indoors   2–4 minutes   1–20 Fives

Activities for Listening and Talking

29

Fives can

- print name, but not too clearly

- learn that what they say can be written and read

Individual Word Tubs

Collect clean margarine tubs so that you have one for each child. Write each child's name on his or her tub. Let children know that these tubs are for keeping their special words in. When children ask how to spell or write a word, print it neatly on a paper strip for the child to copy in his own way. Then the child can store that word in his own word tub. Word tubs can be kept in individual cubbies or in the Writing Center.

You want to know how to write love, *Adele?*
What are you writing? "I love you, Mommy"?
That's a sweet thing to write for your mom.
Watch while I write. L-O-V-E. Keep this word in your word tub.
Then you can write it all by yourself whenever you want!

 indoors   5–15 minutes   1–2 Fives

30

Fives can

- enjoy stories

- apply what they know in many different activities

Story-Book-Based Units

Choose a picture book that you can build a unit around. Then plan and do activities in many of the centers of your room that relate to the content of the book.

For example, read "The Gingerbread Man" to the children. Then add cookie sheets, gingerbread men cookie cutters, and even a gingerbread man mask to the Dramatic Play Center. Put out brown play dough and paints to see if children make their own gingerbread forms, and place flannelboard cutouts for children to use to tell the story in the Book Center. You can also set up a cooking activity so that children can make their own gingerbread men to eat. Play a group game like tag in which children pretend to be the gingerbread man while someone tries to catch them.

 in or out   20–60 minutes   1–20 Fives

31

Fives can

- write some letters
- read some words
- hear beginning sounds of words

Letter of the Week

Help children learn about the sounds associated with letters of the alphabet by highlighting one letter each week. Serve foods for snack that start with the letter. Have a special letter place where you display things that begin with the letter being talked about. Notice if any children's names begin with the letter of the week. Talk with the children about the letter and the sound it makes at the beginning of words.

What things are on the letter table, Trina?
Right. There is a pencil and a paper clip.
Do you hear the sound in pencil *and* paper clip?
They both begin with p—/p/.
What else do you see?

 indoors   3–8 minutes   # 1–6 Fives

32

Fives can

- tell a story quite well

Tape Record Fives' Stories

Use a tape cassette recorder to record one child or a small group of children as they tell a familiar story. Play back the story for them to listen to. Label the tape and store it where children can play it to listen to on their own. Encourage children to make a book with pictures that can be used with the tape. Help them write a few words in their homemade book if they wish.

You and Jeffrey recorded the story about the three pigs, last week, Maurice. Myra says she would like to listen to that tape today. Can you help her find the book that you made to go with the tape?

 indoors   5–15 minutes   # 1–4 Fives

33

Fives can

■ read a few words

■ listen quite well in a large group

News of the Day

Write down on <u>chart paper</u> the activities that will happen in your classroom each day and read them to the children during morning group time. Point to the words as you read so that children can follow along. Give clues to see if they can guess any of the things that the news tells them.

Today our news says, "In the Art Center we will..." What do you think we will be doing? We talked about it yesterday. That's right, Carina! It says, "In the Art Center we will be making our own watercolor paints." See the words watercolor paints?

Look at and read the news from past days to see if children can think back and remember the things they did.

 indoors   4–7 minutes   1–20 Fives

34

Fives can

■ tell some words that rhyme

■ play sorting/matching games

Matching Rhyming Words

Talk with your Fives about words that rhyme and give some examples. Make a set of <u>picture cards</u> that includes pictures of things that rhyme. Be sure to write the names of the pictures on the cards. Look at all the pictures with the children. Have them tell what all the things are. Read the labels for them. Then see if the children can match the rhyming cards together. Some rhyming words you might draw onto picture cards are

■ *pig* and *wig*
■ *hat, cat,* and *bat*
■ *cake, rake,* and *snake*
■ *dragon* and *wagon*
■ *mop* and *top*

■ *tree* and *bee*
■ *wall* and *ball*
■ *bear* and *pear*
■ *bed* and *sled*
■ *spoon* and *moon*

 in or out   5–20 minutes   1–4 Fives

35

Fives can

- tell a simple story
- know that what they say can be written and read
- read and write a few words

Creating Picture/Word Stories

Put out large sheets of paper for children to draw on. They can fold the paper in half and make the picture on the top half, while the other half is folded underneath. When a child is finished drawing, ask if he wants to write a story to go with the picture.

He can unfold the paper and then write the story under the picture. If the child is not interested in doing his own writing, you can write down exactly what he tells you. Use another piece of paper if you run out of space and the child wants to continue. When the child is done, you and he can read the story. Display children's stories on a bulletin board at child height for others to see. You can make a book of all the stories and read them often.

 indoors 5–20 minutes 1–2 Fives

36

Fives can

- recognize many letters of the alphabet
- recognize familiar printed words

Letters of the Alphabet

Buy or make alphabet letters in metal, felt, plastic, wood, sandpaper, or cardboard. Put baskets of letters in the Book Center and the Writing Center. Encourage your Fives to have fun sorting them in many ways and finding the letters of their names or letters of words that are in their own word tubs. Help them use the letters to spell out words they want to see.

Hang a steel cookie sheet (not aluminum) on the side or back of a shelf. Put a basket or box of magnetic letters on the shelf. Then children can stick the letters onto the metal sheet to spell out words or to sort the letters into different groups.

 indoors 1–5 minutes 1–3 Fives

37

Fives can

- follow directions in a simple game
- recognize first and last names when written

Skip to Your Name Game

Write children's names in colored chalk on the sidewalk outdoors, or if they want to, have them write their own. Move away from the names and have children stand next to you. Then give a direction that tells children to go to their name in a special way. Ask them to hop to their names, skip to their names, or stand on their names and follow your directions for what to do next. If children want more challenge, use last names rather than first names for children to find.

Walk backward to your names.
Maria, turn around three times, touch your toes,
and touch your nose.
Jasmond, put your arms in the air, jump three times, and
touch your shoes.

 in or out   4–15 minutes   1–12 Fives

38

Fives can

- recognize familiar printed words

Word Field Trip

Take a field trip with your Fives to look for words. Point out the words on stores, street signs, trucks, gas stations, and fast-food restaurants. Note any words your Fives recognize by themselves. When you return from the field trip, ask your Fives if they remember some of the words they saw.

What words did you see, Dovi?
You saw MILK on the truck and EMERGENCY at the hospital.
What do you think emergency *means?*
Yes. It shows the ambulance where to go when someone needs
help fast.

 outdoors   10–20 minutes   4 Fives per adult

39

Fives can

- know that what they say can be written and read

- read and write some words

Stories About Classroom Activities

Sit in the Writing Center with a five-year-old who wants to write a story about activities she has done. Ask the child what she would like to say and write down her words exactly as she says them. Be sure the child is sitting right next to you so that she can see you print the letters, or have the child write as much as she can by herself. Read back what she said or wrote, or she can read to you if she wishes. See if she would like to add a picture to the story. Read what children have said to other children if they are interested.

Here's Margaretta's story about what she did this morning. "I played with David in the little house. Then I made an airplane in carpentry. Then I drew a picture of my family." I saw you in carpentry, too, Mamie. What did you do?

 indoors   5–10 minutes   1–4 Fives

40

Fives can

- learn that what they say can be written and read

- share feelings of a friend

Letters to Sick Friends

When a child is not present due to illness, talk with your Fives about how people send get-well letters to people who are sick. Show them some examples of get-well cards. Then help your Fives write get-well letters to their sick friend. Talk with them about what the letter should say. Write their words on a large sheet of paper. Read back the letter to them.

Here's what we wrote in our letter so far. "Dear Ann. We are sorry you have the chickenpox. We miss you. We saved you a piece of Nico's birthday cake." Do you think we should add anything else?

Let the children see you address an envelope. Then they can put a stamp on it and, if possible, help you mail it.

 indoors   5–10 minutes   1–20 Fives

41

Fives can

- show interest in printed letters
- type letters and some words on a typewriter

Typing

Set up a table, typewriter, and paper for your Fives to use. Carefully explain how to use the typewriter without hitting all the keys at once. Then let the children type letters freely as they are interested.

Look at what the child has typed. If she is interested, ask her to point out and name some of the letters she used. See if she can type the letters in her name.

Heather, you typed a Z here. I see another Z. Can you see it? Oh, you typed some words, too. I see "I love you" right here!

 indoors 1–15 minutes 1 child per typewriter

42

Fives can

- hear beginning sounds of words
- tell some letter sounds from others

Which Pictures Start with a Different Sound?

Buy or make a collection of picture cards that show pictures of things that start with the same sound and letter. For example, have cards that show things that start with a *w*, such as wagon, witch, and window, cards that show things that start with *d*, such as dog, doll and duck, and so on. Show children two pictures that start with the same sound and one that is different. Have them name each picture and then try to figure out which one does not start with the same sound.

That's right, Susie. Pumpkin *and* pitcher *sound the same. They start with a* p. Wagon *starts with a* w.

You can also give children sets of pictures that start with several different letters and see if they can sort them by beginning sounds.

 in or out 5–20 minutes 1–4 Fives

43

Fives can

- write many letters of the alphabet
- read a few words
- hear beginning sounds of words

Invented Spelling

Encourage interested children to write as much as they can on their own, using their own "invented spelling." This means that children spell things by listening to the sounds they hear as they say words and then write the letters they hear. For example, a child who was inventing spelling for the word *dinosaur* might write something like *dinosaw* or a child writing the word *snake* might write *snak*. (You will find more information about Fives' Use of Invented Spelling on page 100.)

Give children lots of experiences in making the connection between the letters and the sounds associated with them in everyday conversations and activities. Then encourage invented spelling as children begin to write.

 in or out 3–20 minutes 1–4 Fives

44

Fives can

- know that what they say can be written and read
- talk about things they remember

Writing Outdoor Stories

Bring paper, pencils and watercolor markers outdoors on a nice day when you plan to spend lots of time outdoors with your Fives. When a child has run off lots of energy and wants something new to do, see if he would like to tell you a story about what he likes to do outdoors. Write down what he says and read his words back to him.

Here's what you wrote about playing outdoors, Kenny. "Brian and I were monsters. We chased all the kids and put them in a cave. Then they escaped." Do you want to add anything else to your story?

See if children want to add pictures to their stories. Show them a good place to draw outdoors.

 outdoors 5–20 minutes 1 Five at a time

45

Fives can

- pretend to write a letter
- learn about sending mail

Sending Letters

Put out envelopes, pencils, colorful watercolor markers, and paper so children can write letters to other children, teachers, or parents. Encourage children who are interested to write themselves, by scribbling, or printing letters or words. Encourage children to add pictures to their letters if they wish.

Have each child fold the paper and put it into an envelope. You can help children write the names they want on the envelope or they can copy the names from index cards.

If possible, address and stamp the letters so children can mail them to their own homes. Take a walk to the mailbox to mail the letters. Ask the children if their letters reached them at home.

 indoors   5–8 minutes   # 1–6 Fives

46

Fives can

- follow a simple sequence
- enjoy cooking and eating

Using Picture/Word Recipes to Cook

When cooking with children, have a recipe that uses pictures with words that show them what to do. For example, have each child make a fruit kabob for snack time by using the picture recipe on page 101. Before cooking, show the recipe cards and talk about what the pictures/words say to do. After cooking, look at the recipe cards again and see what the children can tell you about how to make fruit kabob.

This picture shows what to put on your skewer, Vinetta.
Can you tell what it is?
Yes, and this word says "orange."

(Look for many other picture/word recipes for children in *Cook and Learn,* by Beverly Veitch and Thelma Harms, published by Addison-Wesley Publishing Company.)

 indoors   5–10 minutes   1–6 Fives

47

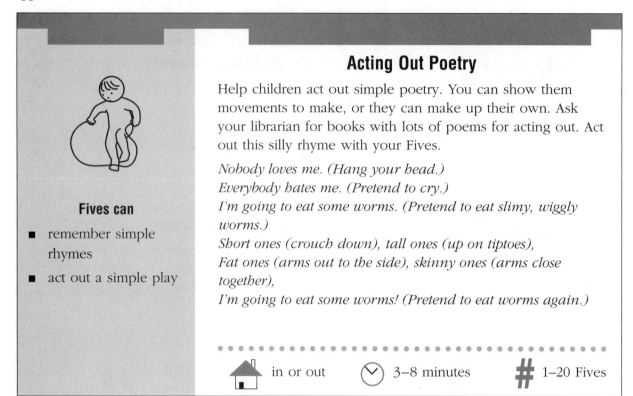

Fives can

- remember simple rhymes
- act out a simple play

Acting Out Poetry

Help children act out simple poetry. You can show them movements to make, or they can make up their own. Ask your librarian for books with lots of poems for acting out. Act out this silly rhyme with your Fives.

Nobody loves me. (Hang your head.)
Everybody hates me. (Pretend to cry.)
I'm going to eat some worms. (Pretend to eat slimy, wiggly worms.)
Short ones (crouch down), tall ones (up on tiptoes),
Fat ones (arms out to the side), skinny ones (arms close together),
I'm going to eat some worms! (Pretend to eat worms again.)

in or out   3–8 minutes   # 1–20 Fives

48

Fives can

- copy simple words

Copycat Writing

Write simple words on index cards. Put them into a basket in the Writing Center for children to copy if they wish. Put a picture of each word on the back of an index card and cover it with clear contact paper. Include simple words children might enjoy copying such as *cat,* and *dog,* or more difficult popular words, such as *tyrannosaurus rex* or *rainbow.*

Don't worry about how children form their letters or whether they write them in order.

Leave blank index cards in the writing area so that you can write down other words the children want to copy.

indoors   3–15 minutes   # 1–5 Fives

49

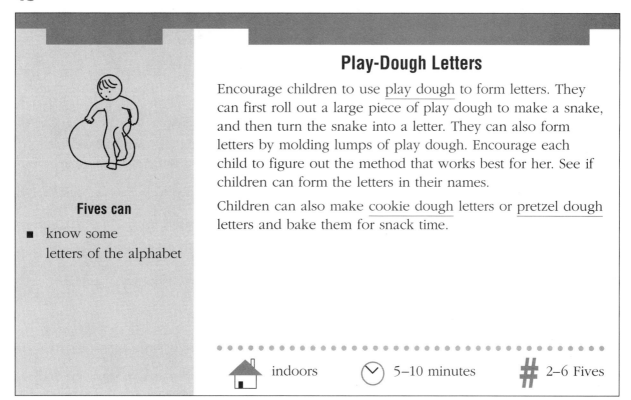

Fives can

- know some letters of the alphabet

Play-Dough Letters

Encourage children to use play dough to form letters. They can first roll out a large piece of play dough to make a snake, and then turn the snake into a letter. They can also form letters by molding lumps of play dough. Encourage each child to figure out the method that works best for her. See if children can form the letters in their names.

Children can also make cookie dough letters or pretzel dough letters and bake them for snack time.

indoors   5–10 minutes   # 2–6 Fives

50

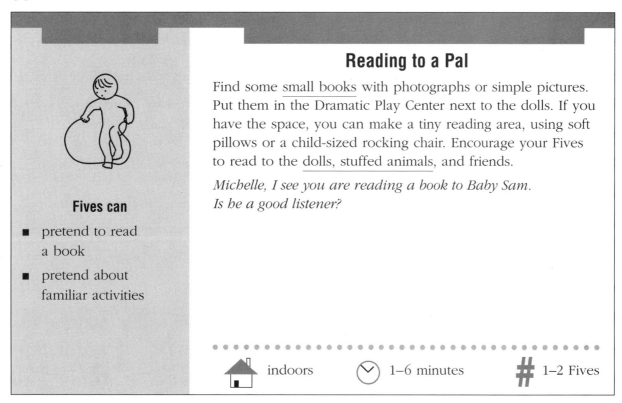

Fives can

- pretend to read a book
- pretend about familiar activities

Reading to a Pal

Find some small books with photographs or simple pictures. Put them in the Dramatic Play Center next to the dolls. If you have the space, you can make a tiny reading area, using soft pillows or a child-sized rocking chair. Encourage your Fives to read to the dolls, stuffed animals, and friends.

Michelle, I see you are reading a book to Baby Sam. Is he a good listener?

indoors   1–6 minutes   # 1–2 Fives

51

Fives can

■ recognize their printed first and last names

Names Hunt

Write the first and last names of each child in your group on a sturdy index card. Hide these cards in easy-to-find places, either indoors or outdoors. Have the children go on a Name Hunt. Let them search until they find their own name cards. Give help to children who are having difficulty finding their names.

Keep looking, Jimmy. You are close. You found Jimmy Smith. Are you Jimmy Smith? No, you are Jimmy Tate. T-A-T-E. Can you find it? Yes, there it is. Jimmy Tate!

 in or out 4–8 minutes 1–20 Fives

52

Fives can

■ try to read books by talking about pictures and/or remembering the story

Children "Read" to You

Sit with a very small group of Fives. Ask one of the children to choose a favorite picture book to use as he tells you the story. Listen with interest as he goes through the book and tells the story in his own way. See if he pretends to read or makes up a new story to go with the pictures. Whatever he does, show delight with the way the story is told.

Encourage children to read to each other in this way often.

 in or out 4–10 minutes 1–4 Fives

53

Fives can

■ play a simple table game

■ find pictures that match

Matching Coupons

Collect coupons for foods your Fives enjoy. Be sure to get at least two of each brand so that the children can find pairs that match. Put 20 coupons in a labeled shoe box. Play a matching game with several of your Fives. Give each child three coupons and take three for yourself. Put the rest in a pile in the middle of the table. Tell your Fives that you are trying to find two of a kind.

I've got a Cheerios coupon.
I need to find another one.
Then I'll have two of a kind.

Show your Fives how to draw from the pile on the table to find new coupons to match.

 indoors   5–10 minutes   # 1–5 Fives

54

Fives can

■ play a simple table game

■ find pictures that match

What Letter Sound Does It Begin With?

Make a collection of small things that begin with the different consonant sounds. You can often buy sets from school supply companies, but they will be more interesting when you and the children add special things you have found. For example, you might find these small things for the letter *d:* a small toy dog, a dime, a toy dish, a dinosaur, and so on. Ask parents to help you collect things for the letter sounds. Store each set in its own container that is labeled with the letter. Encourage your Fives to look at the letter on each container and name the things inside to hear how each word starts with the same sound. Mix up the things in two sets and see if children can sort them into the correct containers. When children are very good at sorting two sets, add another for more challenge.

 indoors   5–10 minutes   # 1–5 Fives

55

Fives can

- talk about the things they do
- read or write some words

Keeping Children's Journals

Make books with blank pages for each of your Fives. Explain that each day they can tell about the important things they are doing, either at home or at school, and you will help them write those things down in their journals. Keep the journals in the Writing Center. Encourage each child to make a journal entry every day. You can write what they dictate, or the child can write if he or she wishes. Read back what was written. Go through the pages of past days, rereading with the child about what he entered.

Children can decorate their journal covers and illustrate their daily entries, too.

 indoors   5–10 minutes   1–5 Fives

- Keep the Book Center small, so that only about four children use it at a time. Make it comfortable and well-lighted. Have a small bookshelf with plenty of children's books. Add pillows, carpet, and a small chair or two near a little table.

- Change many of the books in the Book Center often, but always keep children's favorites. Add books with pictures and information about topics you are discussing with your Fives.

- Place some of the books so that children can see the front covers.

- Be sure the books show people of many cultures, races, ages, and abilities in a positive way.

- Add some other Book Center materials. Put out soft puppets in a container, a flannelboard with shapes or pictures, and some sets of picture cards. Have a clear place in the center where children can use these things.

- Keep the Book Center organized and neat. Replace books that are not in good shape. Talk with the children about careful use of books and other materials.

- Plan at least one special time in your schedule for stories with your Fives. If the time works well, have a story or other talking activity at the same time every day. Stories work well at the table after snack is cleared away or before lunch preparation begins. A story as children wake up from nap or rest is also good.

- Be patient. Begin with a ten-minute story time. As children learn to listen with interest, have a longer story time. Stop as soon as interest is gone.

- Use a fingerplay, riddle, song, or puppet to catch children's attention. Then read a book. Also use pictures, books the children have written themselves, and flannelboard stories at this time.

Place

- Plan a regular place for your story time. Choose a large enough space so that no one will be crowded. A rug helps let children know where they should be.

- Choose an out-of-the-way place where you won't be disturbed.

- Find a place where children will pay attention; for example, away from toys on open shelves.

- Give each child her own special space to sit. You can put chairs with names on them in a circle or names on labels around a table if you wish. You can also try putting names on a masking-tape circle that you have put down on a rug. Or try giving each child his own carpet square or pillow to sit on.

- Make sure every child can see and hear.

- Keep the story place the same every day unless it does not work well. Changing children's places, making story times shorter, or having stories with fewer children might help.

Group Size

- Many Fives will be able to listen and participate in a large group of about 20 children while others will be less attentive. Encourage children to take part with the group, but don't force them. Some children may prefer sitting quietly and listening away from the group.

- If there are two adults, have two groups if one big group does not work well. Or have one person read while the other sits with the children and helps them listen.

- Read to children alone or in a very small group during the day whenever you can. Be especially sure you read to the children who cannot listen to stories in a larger group.

Reading

- Choose the book you will read ahead of time.

- Use books with big, clear, colorful pictures. If there are too many words, tell the story in your own words instead of reading it.

- Hold the book up facing the children so that all of them can see the pictures.

- Point out things on the pages that interest the children. Help them talk about what they see.

- Give the children a chance to help tell the story with you. For example, if the story is a familiar one, see if they can say what is coming next. If the story is a new one, have them guess what will happen.

- Show interest with your face and voice. Change your voice to match the story.

- Use a quiet voice when you want children to listen. Children pay more attention to a quiet voice than to a loud one.

- Look into each child's eyes often as you read or talk.

- Pick books that go with the ideas you are talking about at the time. For example, if it's fall and children bring in pretty leaves from outside, read a book about fall leaves.

- Read books the children have chosen from the library or bookmobile. Try to read all the books they have chosen before they have to be returned. If you can't read each book in a group, try to read to the child individually or with a friend.

- Put books you read in the Book Center for children to look at by themselves. Remind children to handle books carefully.

- Read a variety of written materials, including poems, stories, magazines, comic strips, and letters.

- Read favorite books often.

Other Ideas

- Use puppets, a flannelboard, pictures, or real objects as you tell a story.

- Add to your book collection by using your public library. Ask if a bookmobile will visit you and your Fives.

- Help children act out a very short, simple story that they know well.

Pictures

Choosing Pictures

■ Choose clear photographs or colorful pictures that show things Fives know about—families, food, clothes, animals.

■ Choose clear pictures of new things you will be talking about and teaching your Fives—holidays, community helpers, things that are different, people doing things.

■ Make picture collections of different subjects—toys, different kinds of buildings, letters and numbers, animals, birds.

■ Choose big and small pictures.

■ Choose pictures that show one thing at a time and pictures that show many things.

■ Choose pictures that show people of all ages and races doing many positive things, alone or together.

■ Include many nonsexist pictures that show men and women doing a variety of jobs.

Adding Words to the Pictures

■ Label the pictures with simple words.

■ Print clearly and be sure words are spelled correctly. If you wish, use computer-printed words, but be sure that the print is large and easy to read.

■ Ask the children to help you think of the words to go on the cards. Write down the words they say.

■ Point out the words that are on the picture cards, but do not expect children to read or write all of the words yet.

Storing Pictures

■ Make picture cards with the pictures you want children to use a lot. Glue the pictures onto sturdy cardboard. Cover with clear contact paper. Keep card sets together.

■ Put picture cards into separate, labeled boxes or use a picture file box.

■ Add topics based on the interests of your Fives.

Finding Pictures

■ Use the following sources to find pictures: school supply

catalogs; department store catalogs; colorful newspaper ads; junk mail; photographs, post cards; old calendars, magazines, picture books, newspapers, coloring books

- Have parents and friends provide pictures. Tell parents why you need pictures so that they can use some of your ideas at home.

- Send for free photos from organizations and groups such as the Dairy Association or dental groups.

- Ask managers if you can have posters used as ads in stores, car showrooms, and supermarkets when they are no longer needed.

Displaying Pictures

- Hang pictures where Fives can see, reach, and touch them. Hang them on furniture, on walls or doors, or on bulletin boards.

- Use tape or clear contact paper to hang pictures. If you use bulletin boards, use thumbtacks or staples that are out of Fives' reach.

- Change pictures often.

- Put pictures into large, page-sized, soft vinyl photograph holders. You can usually get them in stores where cameras are sold. Hang these around the room where children can see and touch them. Put some in the Book Center.

- Use three-ring binders with clear vinyl pages to make a book of pictures. Change the pictures in the pages often.

- Put sturdy picture cards you have made into a box or on a tray. Put these on a shelf in the Book Corner.

Making your own Picture Books

1. Glue pictures onto sturdy cardboard.
2. Add your own words or the children's if you wish.
3. Cover pages with clear contact paper.
4. Punch two or three holes on the left side or top of each page.
5. Tie pages together with strong string or narrow ribbon. Do not tie too tightly. Leave pages a bit loose so that they can be easily turned.

Directions for Making Stick Puppets

1. Find or draw a picture of what you want to use as the puppet. Try faces, animals, or anything else you or a child wants to make talk.

2. Cut out the picture, glue it to a larger piece of cardboard, and cover it with clear contact paper, or simply draw the picture onto the cardboard.

3. Make a holder for the picture. Try these ideas:

   Glue smaller pictures to ice cream sticks. Make them more secure with tape.

   Use 1" brass brads or paper fasteners to hold the picture onto an empty paper towel or toilet paper roll. Poke two brads through the picture and into the roll. Then open the brads so they stay in place.

   Glue pictures to tongue depressors. Make them more secure with tape.

   Cut out a cardboard holder as part of the cardboard you use to mount the picture. Make it sturdier by attaching a stick or some extra cardboard where it might bend.

Activities for Listening and Talking

Sequence Cards

What They Are

- Sequence cards are picture cards that show the steps in a story. They show what happens at the beginning, middle, and end of the story.

- Often there is more than one right answer when using the cards with young children. But it is likely that Fives will be able to order sequence cards correctly. Use the cards to help children talk about what they see and think.

How to Use Them

- Use sequence cards that show familiar activities. Begin with cards that show four or five clear, familiar steps in what is happening.

- Some Fives may not put the cards in the same order you do. They might order the cards in their own creative ways. Listen to how they tell the story and enjoy it together.

- You can put the cards in order and tell the children how you see the story. Use the words *first, second, third, fourth,* and *last* as you talk.

How to Make Them

1. Find or draw pictures of the steps in the story you want to show.

2. Cut out the pictures.

3. Glue them to sturdy cardboard squares.

4. Cover them with clear contact paper.

5. Store the cards in a box or container. Keep each set separate with a rubber band or in its own little sandwich bag.

Topics for Cards

Getting up in the morning

- Child sleeping in bed
- Child getting dressed
- Child all dressed and walking away from bed
- Child eating breakfast cereal
- Child putting bowl in sink

Cooking and eating

- Putting food in pot
- Stirring food on stove
- Serving food onto plate
- Eating food
- Putting plate in sink

Getting dressed

- Child with shirt, socks, and underclothes on, holding pants
- Child putting on pants
- Child putting on shoes
- Child tying shoes
- Child dressed

Taking a bath or getting washed and dressed

- Child with clothes on, parent running water in bathtub
- Child in bath
- Child drying off with towel
- Child putting clothes on
- Child combing hair

Sweeping the floor

- Dirty floor
- Person with broom, floor partly swept
- Person with dustpan, sweeping trash
- Person emptying dustpan into trash can
- Person putting broom away, floor clean

Grocery shopping

- Person entering grocery store
- Person with empty shopping cart
- Person with full cart
- Person paying at register
- Person with bags of groceries

- Cut these out. Color them if you wish.
- Glue the cards to cardboard squares.
- Cover them with clear contact paper.
- Have children put them in the order they see.
- Talk about the pictures.

Sunshine Note

Sunshine Note

Sample Rebus
Picture Story

Once upon a time, there were three little  .

The  decided that they wanted to build their

own 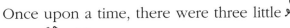 .

The first decided to build his out of .

It did not take long to build his , and he quickly

moved in.

The second decided to build his house of  .

He worked more than the first to build his ,

but he soon moved in.

The third decided to build his house of .

It took a long time and lots of work to build his , and

he moved in.

A came up to the first little pig's  and he

said, "Little little  , let me come in."

The frightened little  locked the and said,

"Not by the hair on my chinny chin chin!"

The 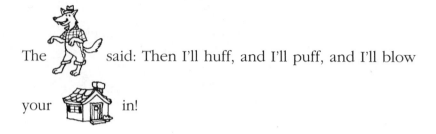 said: Then I'll huff, and I'll puff, and I'll blow

your in!

So he huffed and he puffed and he blew the in.

The little  ran to the house of the second .

They locked the .

The came up to the second little pig's and

he said: "Little , little , let me come in."

The little said, "Not by the hair on our chinny

chin chins!" The said, "Then I'll huff, and I'll

puff, and I'll blow your in!

So he huffed and he puffed and he huffed and he puffed

and he blew the in.

98

Activities for Listening and Talking

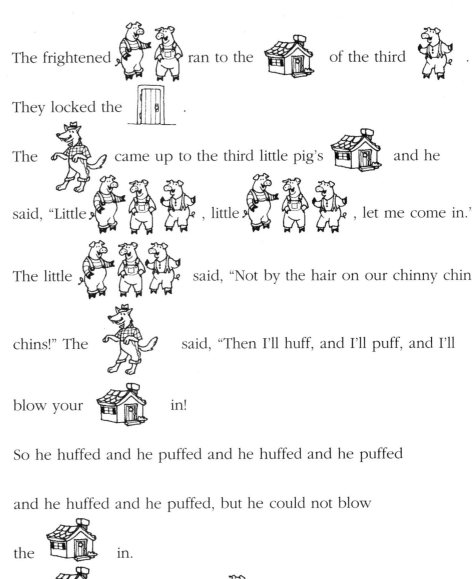

The frightened ran to the of the third .

They locked the .

The came up to the third little pig's and he

said, "Little , little , let me come in."

The little said, "Not by the hair on our chinny chin

chins!" The said, "Then I'll huff, and I'll puff, and I'll

blow your in!

So he huffed and he puffed and he huffed and he puffed

and he huffed and he puffed, but he could not blow

the in.

The of the third little was too strong for the

, so he went away to find supper somewhere else.

The three little were very happy!

Fives' Use of Invented Spelling

Invented spelling is a predictable stage of children's writing development. Through invented spelling, children begin to sound out words and write them as they sound. Of course they will not be able to do this if adults do not help them make a connection between the words they say or see and the sounds associated with the letters in those words. The first words they write may have just one letter, usually the first sound they hear in a word. As they sound out more words, they begin to write more letters, using the consonants they hear. Next, vowel sounds are added. At this stage, children begin to use capital letters at the beginning of sentences and periods at the end. Spelling gradually becomes more complete and is phonetic. You can help children move to correct spelling when you rewrite what they have written correctly, above their own writing. But it is important to show acceptance and delight with the way children spell out the words by sounding them out.

To promote the use of invented spelling in your classroom:

- Provide examples of print throughout the classroom.

- Put out pencils, pens, markers, paintbrushes, and lined and unlined paper.

- Call children's attention to the sounds they hear in spoken words. Talk about the letters associated with the sounds.

- Let children see you write notes, lists, and so on.

- Write with children so that they can see how letters are written, and talk about letter sounds as you write them.

- Encourage children to keep journals by writing what they have to say as they watch.

- Encourage children who are interested to write for themselves. Ask children to read to you what they have written.

- Accept and enjoy the children's invented spelling.

See also the following references.

Hayes, L.F. (1990). From scribbling to writing: Smoothing the way. *Young Children.* 45(3): 62–68.

Roskos, K.A., and S.B. Neuman. (January 1994). Of Scribbles, Schemas, and Storybooks: Using Literacy Albums to Document Young Children's Literacy Growth. *Young Children,* 49(2): 78–85.

Schickedanz, J.A. (1986). *More than the ABC's: The Early Stages of Reading and Writing.* Washington, DC: National Association for the Education of Young Children.

Picture Word Recipe
for Fruit Kabobs

① skewer
② banana
③ strawberry
④ orange

Directions for the teacher:

1. Copy the recipe cards shown above onto sturdy posterboard. Protect them with clear contact paper or laminate them if you wish.

2. Slice bananas and strawberries, and separate oranges into slices. Children can help with this. Put each fruit into a separate bowl.

3. Cut the points off wooden skewers.

4. Set up the cards on a long table, with the first card on the left and the last card on the right.

5. Put the skewers in front of the first card, the bananas in front of the next, and so on, so that each real fruit is in front of the card it matches.

6. Show children how to follow the recipe from left to right to make a fruit kabob.

7. Make the first kabob with your Fives. Put on a slice of banana, a slice of orange, a strawberry, and a slice of orange. Point to the recipe as you work.

8. Eat the kabobs for snack and make more if the children want to.

Materials and Notes

Conversation and Group Talk

things children bring in

Jimmy

things children make

group discussion

talker's turn

- Fives enjoy talking, both to you and to each other. Try to keep the happy, busy sound of talking going on most of the day.

- Show children how much you enjoy their talk. Look at children as you listen to things they tell you. Ask many questions to encourage them to say more. (See page 132 for hints about different kinds of questions.)

- Include parents in the talks you have with your Fives. Ask them about things the child does at home. Ask questions to help the child add to what they say.

- Keep discussion groups small so that everyone can have several turns to talk and share ideas. If you have larger discussion groups, make the time shorter.

- Gently help your Fives understand that a conversation means that people listen when someone talks. People take turns listening and talking to each other.

Activity Checklist

Conversation and Group Talk

Conversation and Group Talk activities with Fives make use of the informal talking times that happen throughout the day, as well as the planned group time many programs include. By five years of age, most children can talk quite well and use many words in sentences. They enjoy talking to adults and other children who will listen to them. They ask plenty of questions and answer many of the questions you ask. With your help, Fives can use words to solve problems and avoid fights. Most conversations don't have to be planned. They will happen when children find out that what they do is important to you and that listening and talking are ways of sharing ideas and feelings.

Check for each age group

	60–66 months	66–72 months
1. Children are free to talk to adults and each other during most of the day. There are very few times when no talking is allowed.	❑	❑
2. There is much talking with every child about things that interest the child, including classroom routines, play experiences, and home experiences.	❑	❑
3. Adult speaks clearly and uses a pleasant tone of voice.	❑	❑
4. Adult shows interest when children begin conversations or ask questions.	❑	❑
5. Adult asks different types of questions to encourage children to talk and listen to children's answers.	❑	❑
6. Adult makes eye contact when talking with children.	❑	❑
7. Adult adds more information to what children say.	❑	❑
8. Adult encourages children to talk and listen to each other in small groups, so that each one can have a turn.	❑	❑
9. Adult encourages children to use talking to solve problems with each other and supplies words as needed.	❑	❑
10. Adult plays word games, such as opposites or rhyming games, and provides other playful language experiences.	❑	❑

56

Fives can

- tell about things they have done
- use many words
- take part in group discussions for ten to fifteen minutes

Early Morning Talks

Show children how happy you are to see them each morning. Plan time to greet each one individually. Make time to do this even when you are busy or when everyone seems rushed.

Include parents in the little talks. See if they will help their children remember some nice things they did the night before or what they plan to do over a weekend. Make sure you, the parents, and the children all take turns talking and listening to each other at this time.

How exciting that you have a kitten, Petra.
What color is it? Have you chosen a name yet?
What does your brother think about the kitten?

 in or out   1–5 minutes   **#** 1–2 Fives

57

Fives can

- remember what happened
- talk about things that will happen

Goodbye Talk

As children get ready to go home, talk with each child. Look at and talk about things children are taking home and about what they have done that day. Ask about what the children will do when they get home. Say something about the plans for the next day.

What are you going to do at home, Kristin? Play with your puppy?
I'll see you tomorrow, Paul. Do you remember what we will do tomorrow?

 in or out   1–3 minutes   **#** 1 Five at a time

58

Fives can

- use many words
- talk in sentences
- take part in group discussions for ten to fifteen minutes

New Information for Fives

Think of a special idea you want your Fives to know more about. (A list of some special ideas for units that you might like to work on with your Fives is in the Planning Section, page 34.) Choose an idea that you and the children will find fun and interesting. An example might be "things with wheels." Then write down many ways to talk about the idea. Use real things, books, pictures, field trips, and anything else you can think of to help the children learn about the idea. Ask easy questions to help Fives talk and think about what they know.

What things with wheels do people use for work?
That's right, Juan. They use cars, trucks, and trains. What about play? Yes, Patrick. People use roller skates and bicycles.

 in or out   3–10 minutes   5–10 Fives

59

Fives can

- ask many questions
- answer some questions

They Ask, You Answer

Try to listen to and answer the many questions your Fives ask. Show them how pleased you are with the asking they do. If you don't know an answer, don't worry. Just say that you don't know but will try to find an answer for the child as soon as you can.

Keep the talking going by asking the child a question and then listening to the answer.
I don't know where coyotes live, Kevin.
We can look them up in a book and find out.
Where were you when you saw the coyote?
What did it sound like?

Hints for asking different types of questions are on page 132.

 in or out   1–5 minutes   1–4 Fives

60

Fives can

- tell about what they are doing or planning to do

Pretend Play Talk

When children are playing in the Dramatic Play Center, ask questions so that they will tell about what they are doing. Choose the right time to ask questions so that you don't spoil the play. Add your own ideas to the children's answers to help the play go better.

You're getting all dressed up, Aretha. What are you planning to do in that fancy dress?

Ask about children's play in other centers, too.

 in or out   1–3 minutes   1–3 Fives

61

Fives can

- remember new things

Who Are Your Parents? Where Do You Live?

Help all your Fives learn their parents' first and last names and addresses. Have parents help with this. Teach the children this information and help them repeat it often. Try to get each child to say it slowly and clearly. Then print the names and address on a piece of paper for the child to keep.

What's your daddy's name, Emma?
Jim? That's his first name. Do you know the rest?
That's right. And where do you live?

Help children learn their telephone numbers, too.

 in or out   1–3 minutes   1 Five at a time

62

Fives can

- play easy circle games
- remember people's names
- take part in group discussions for ten to fifteen minutes

Name Riddle Game

Always help your Fives learn to use people's names. Tell everyone the names of new children and adults, including visitors. Help children use names to get people's attention. Also make sure to use each child's name in your many conversations throughout the day.

Sara, you don't need to pull Tamara when you want her to listen. Say her name. Then she will look at you.
The new teacher's name is Miss Jane, and she wants to learn all our names.

Play this game with your Fives. Have children sit in a circle. Begin describing one of the children. Have the others name the child after you have given enough clues. Play again. Make sure everyone is described.

 in or out 5–15 minutes 1–20 Fives

63

Fives can

- remember names of children and teachers

Who's Here and Who's Absent?

When the children know the names of their classmates and teachers, you can ask them who is missing from the circle at group time. If you know the reason for a child's or teacher's absence, tell the group about it.

Who isn't here today? Who is absent?
Yes, Bobby, Cathy, and Tyler are not here.
They're on vacation.

If someone is sick for a long time, the children can make a get-well card at the art table for them later. Be sure to welcome children and staff back when they return.

 indoors 2–4 minutes 1–20 Fives

64

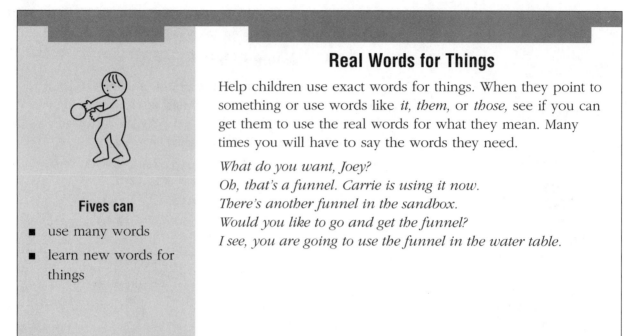

Real Words for Things

Help children use exact words for things. When they point to something or use words like *it, them,* or *those,* see if you can get them to use the real words for what they mean. Many times you will have to say the words they need.

What do you want, Joey?
Oh, that's a funnel. Carrie is using it now.
There's another funnel in the sandbox.
Would you like to go and get the funnel?
I see, you are going to use the funnel in the water table.

Fives can

■ use many words

■ learn new words for things

⌂ in or out   🕐 1–2 minutes   # 1–8 Fives

65

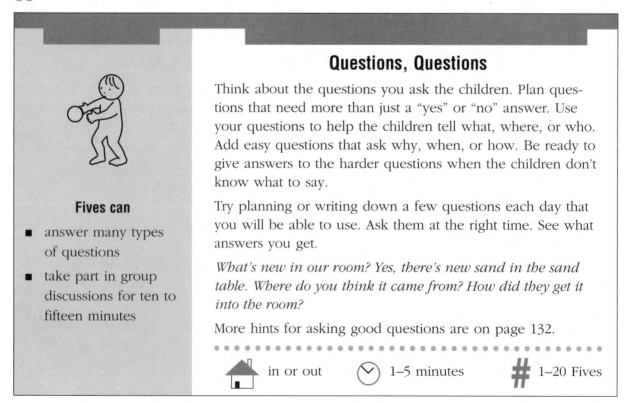

Questions, Questions

Think about the questions you ask the children. Plan questions that need more than just a "yes" or "no" answer. Use your questions to help the children tell what, where, or who. Add easy questions that ask why, when, or how. Be ready to give answers to the harder questions when the children don't know what to say.

Try planning or writing down a few questions each day that you will be able to use. Ask them at the right time. See what answers you get.

What's new in our room? Yes, there's new sand in the sand table. Where do you think it came from? How did they get it into the room?

More hints for asking good questions are on page 132.

Fives can

■ answer many types of questions

■ take part in group discussions for ten to fifteen minutes

⌂ in or out   🕐 1–5 minutes   # 1–20 Fives

66

Fives can

- say what they are doing
- describe a familiar sequence

Sequences We Follow Talk

Help children talk about the steps they take as they do familiar things, such as washing hands.

You need to wash the paint off your hands, Betty.
Let's see, what do you do first?
Yes. You turn on the water. Then what?

See if children are able to explain sequences to their friends.

Brandon, could you please tell Maude how to clean the paint brushes? She has never done it. Tell her first. Then use the words while you show her what to do.

 in or out 2–5 minutes 1–4 Fives

67

Fives can

- help with cleanup
- remember and talk about routines

Clean-Up Talk

Help children learn about cleanup by talking about each thing they need to do. Ask questions to help the Fives think through their work.

Now what goes in this dishpan? That's right, the little people.
You saw the label, didn't you?
Do you know where these little cars go, Sidney?
Yes. Please find the rest and put them in the box.
Now what do we need to put away? The blocks. How can we tell where they go?

Pretty soon you may find your Fives are able to remind their friends about how to clean up by talking about the process.

 in or out 5–15 minutes 1–20 Fives

68

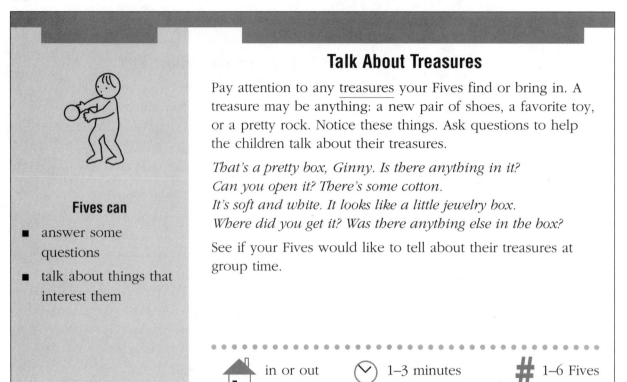

Fives can

- answer some questions
- talk about things that interest them

Talk About Treasures

Pay attention to any <u>treasures</u> your Fives find or bring in. A treasure may be anything: a new pair of shoes, a favorite toy, or a pretty rock. Notice these things. Ask questions to help the children talk about their treasures.

That's a pretty box, Ginny. Is there anything in it?
Can you open it? There's some cotton.
It's soft and white. It looks like a little jewelry box.
Where did you get it? Was there anything else in the box?

See if your Fives would like to tell about their treasures at group time.

🏠 in or out   🕐 1–3 minutes   # 1–6 Fives

69

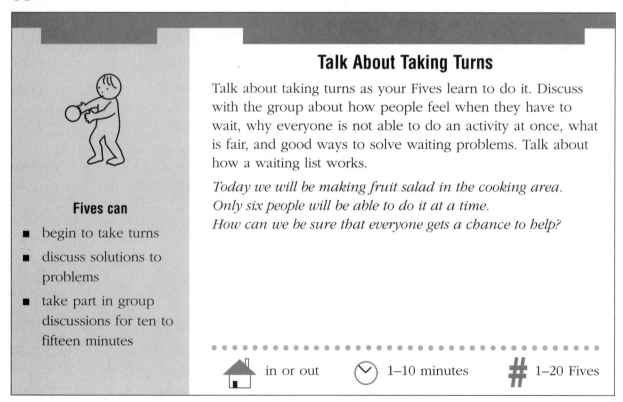

Fives can

- begin to take turns
- discuss solutions to problems
- take part in group discussions for ten to fifteen minutes

Talk About Taking Turns

Talk about taking turns as your Fives learn to do it. Discuss with the group about how people feel when they have to wait, why everyone is not able to do an activity at once, what is fair, and good ways to solve waiting problems. Talk about how a waiting list works.

Today we will be making fruit salad in the cooking area.
Only six people will be able to do it at a time.
How can we be sure that everyone gets a chance to help?

🏠 in or out   🕐 1–10 minutes   # 1–20 Fives

70

Fives can

- understand many common dangers
- discuss solutions to problems

Why Be Careful? Discussions

Remind your Fives to be careful about things that may be dangerous. Do this when it relates to what is happening. Help the children talk about why care must be taken.

Sammy brought balloons for his birthday today.
Balloons are fun, but we have to be careful with them.
Do you remember our rule about balloons?
That's right, Andy. Don't put balloons in your mouth.
Why don't you put balloons in your mouth?

Being careful is a good topic for group discussions. You could talk about care in climbing, building, crossing the street, cutting with scissors, and so on. Give the children lots of chances to talk about their ways to be careful.

 in or out   2–5 minutes   1–20 Fives

71

Fives can

- talk in sentences
- use many words

Special Talking Time

Plan to have a special talking time with each child every day. Make this a warm time when you listen to and talk with just one child. Fit these times in whenever you can. Keep a checklist, if you need to, to be sure you talk to everyone. This will help each child feel special.

You've been working so hard, Keith.
Tell me about your work in the sandbox.

Sarah, what nice new boots.
Are they like your mom's?
Tell me how you got those boots.

 in or out   1–4 minutes   1 Five at a time

72

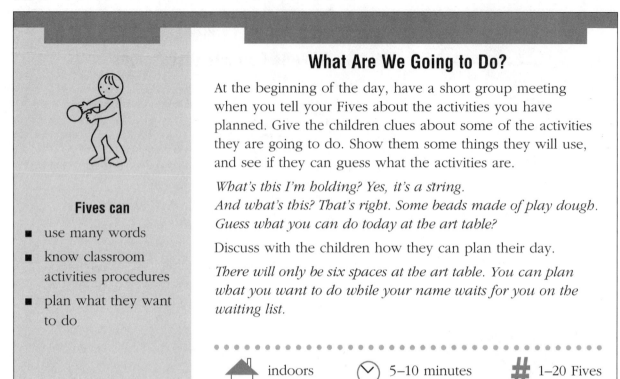

Fives can

- use many words
- know classroom activities procedures
- plan what they want to do

What Are We Going to Do?

At the beginning of the day, have a short group meeting when you tell your Fives about the activities you have planned. Give the children clues about some of the activities they are going to do. Show them some things they will use, and see if they can guess what the activities are.

What's this I'm holding? Yes, it's a string.
And what's this? That's right. Some beads made of play dough.
Guess what you can do today at the art table?

Discuss with the children how they can plan their day.

There will only be six spaces at the art table. You can plan what you want to do while your name waits for you on the waiting list.

🏠 indoors   🕐 5–10 minutes   # 1–20 Fives

73

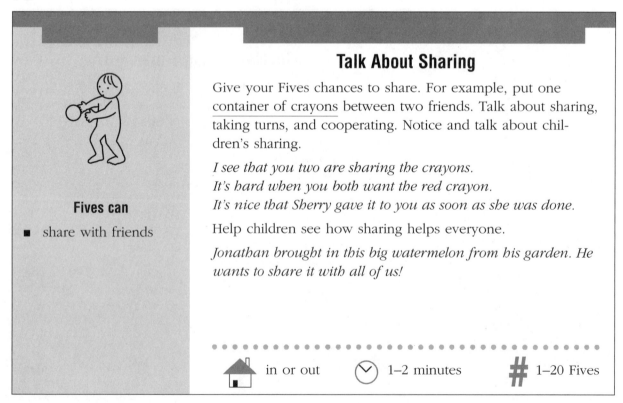

Fives can

- share with friends

Talk About Sharing

Give your Fives chances to share. For example, put one container of crayons between two friends. Talk about sharing, taking turns, and cooperating. Notice and talk about children's sharing.

I see that you two are sharing the crayons.
It's hard when you both want the red crayon.
It's nice that Sherry gave it to you as soon as she was done.

Help children see how sharing helps everyone.

Jonathan brought in this big watermelon from his garden. He wants to share it with all of us!

🏠 in or out   🕐 1–2 minutes   # 1–20 Fives

74

Fives can

- talk in sentences
- enjoy playing with friends
- take part in group discussions for ten to fifteen minutes

Talk—Don't Hit

Help Fives learn words to solve problems they have with others. Tell them to use words to say what they do not like. You will often have to help them find the words they need and make them feel safe as they work things out.

What's the matter, Andrew?
Benjamin is taking the blocks you are using?
Tell him you need them. Tell him to get his own.
Show him the blocks he can use on the shelf.

Be sure that when children do "use their words" you are right there to be sure the words can work to solve the problem. The children may need you to help them listen and solve the problem. Solving problems also works well as a group talking time activity.

 in or out   2–5 minutes   1–6 Fives

75

Fives can

- tell about things they make

What Did You Create?

Ask questions to help your Fives tell you about the things they create. Help them talk about their artwork, carpentry, block building, and more. See if they can remember what they used and how they completed the process.

What did you make with the play dough, Danny?
A dog and a dog house? How did you make them?
Would you like to bake your sculptures so that you can keep them?

 in or out   1–2 minutes   1–6 Fives

76

Fives can

- talk about things they have done
- take part in group discussions for ten to fifteen minutes

Remember Play Time

Ask questions to help the children tell about things they did at play time. Make notes if you need to about who did what so that you can ask the right questions.

I saw you making a tall block building, Terry.
What kind of building was it? Who was working with you?

Help children remember and talk about other things that happened during the day, such as what snack they ate or what story you read. The remember game can also be played by asking the children to tell what others were doing:

Who was playing firefighters outside today?
Who worked on the dinosaur model?

 in or out   1–10 minutes   1–20 Fives

77

Fives can

- play simple guessing games
- give clues

Places We Know

Tell your Fives all about a very familiar place, but don't name it. See if they can guess what the place is. Try this with a supermarket, library, park or playground, zoo, shopping center, or farm.

Guess what place I'm talking about.
When you go in, you see all kinds of foods.
There are fruits, vegetables, foods in cans, frozen foods, milk, and bread.
You put things into your cart to buy.
Do you know what place it is?

Let the Fives give clues about a place and have the other children guess.

 in or out   2–7 minutes   1–15 Fives

78

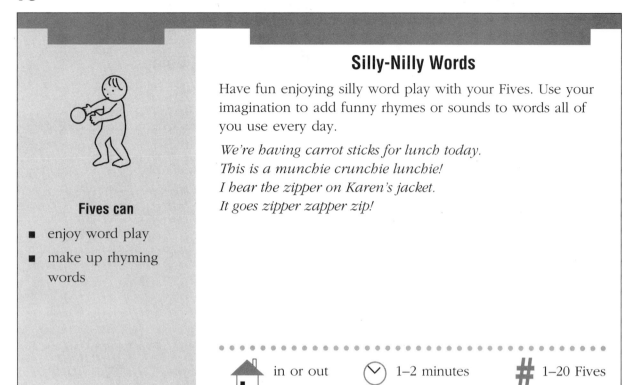

Fives can

- enjoy word play
- make up rhyming words

Silly-Nilly Words

Have fun enjoying silly word play with your Fives. Use your imagination to add funny rhymes or sounds to words all of you use every day.

We're having carrot sticks for lunch today.
This is a munchie crunchie lunchie!
I hear the zipper on Karen's jacket.
It goes zipper zapper zip!

in or out   1–2 minutes   # 1–20 Fives

79

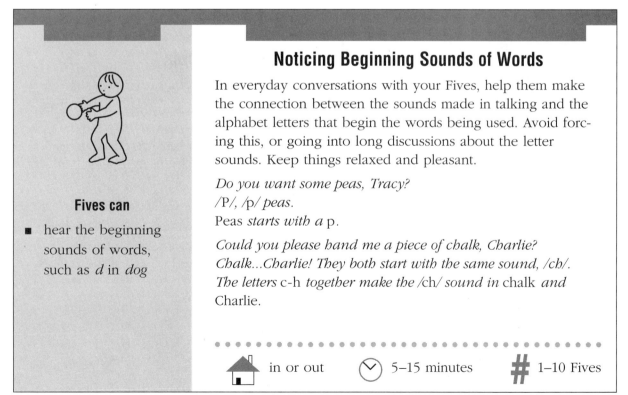

Fives can

- hear the beginning sounds of words, such as *d* in *dog*

Noticing Beginning Sounds of Words

In everyday conversations with your Fives, help them make the connection between the sounds made in talking and the alphabet letters that begin the words being used. Avoid forcing this, or going into long discussions about the letter sounds. Keep things relaxed and pleasant.

Do you want some peas, Tracy?
/P/, /p/ peas.
Peas *starts with a* p.

Could you please hand me a piece of chalk, Charlie?
Chalk...Charlie! They both start with the same sound, /ch/.
The letters c-h *together make the /ch/ sound in* chalk *and* Charlie.

in or out   5–15 minutes   # 1–10 Fives

80

Fives can

- name actions
- take part in group discussions for ten to fifteen minutes

Guess What I'm Doing

Act out some very familiar, easy-to-guess things your Fives do often. Act out getting dressed, drinking, eating, going to sleep, or taking a bath. Do the actions without words. See if the children can say what you're doing.

If they have trouble guessing, then add words to your actions.

First I get two pieces of bread. Then I get the jar of peanut butter. And then I get the jar of jam and a knife. Can you guess what I am doing?

After you act out one or two things, give children a chance to be the actors.

 in or out   3–7 minutes   1–20 Fives

81

Fives can

- repeat rhymes

Rhyming Words

Point out and repeat words the children say or hear that rhyme. Be excited about these words and show that rhymes can be fun.

Listen, Paul. You made a rhyme! You said, "My coat is new, it's blue." The words new *and* blue *rhyme. That was a little poem you made up!*

Don't expect Fives to do rhyming on purpose at first, although they will begin to notice rhyming words. This will come later and be easier if they have enjoyed rhymes with you. It helps to read simple poems and point out the rhymes, too.

 in or out   1–2 minutes   1–20 Fives

82

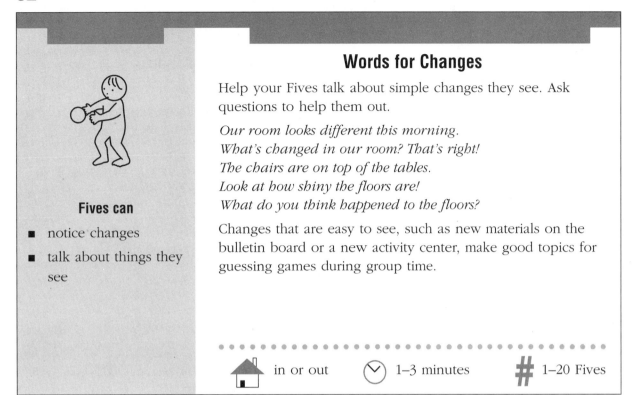

Fives can

■ notice changes

■ talk about things they see

Words for Changes

Help your Fives talk about simple changes they see. Ask questions to help them out.

Our room looks different this morning.
What's changed in our room? That's right!
The chairs are on top of the tables.
Look at how shiny the floors are!
What do you think happened to the floors?

Changes that are easy to see, such as new materials on the bulletin board or a new activity center, make good topics for guessing games during group time.

in or out   1–3 minutes   # 1–20 Fives

83

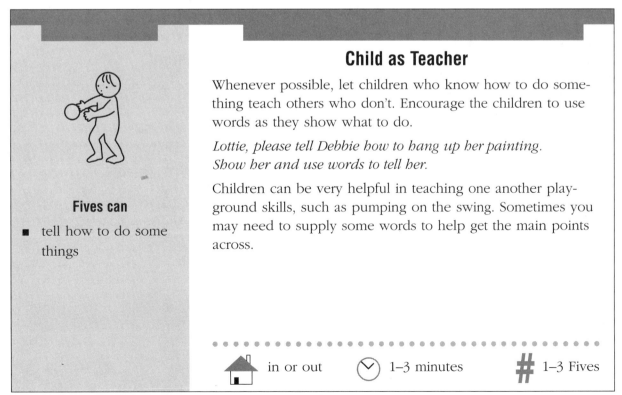

Fives can

■ tell how to do some things

Child as Teacher

Whenever possible, let children who know how to do something teach others who don't. Encourage the children to use words as they show what to do.

Lottie, please tell Debbie how to hang up her painting.
Show her and use words to tell her.

Children can be very helpful in teaching one another playground skills, such as pumping on the swing. Sometimes you may need to supply some words to help get the main points across.

in or out   1–3 minutes   # 1–3 Fives

84

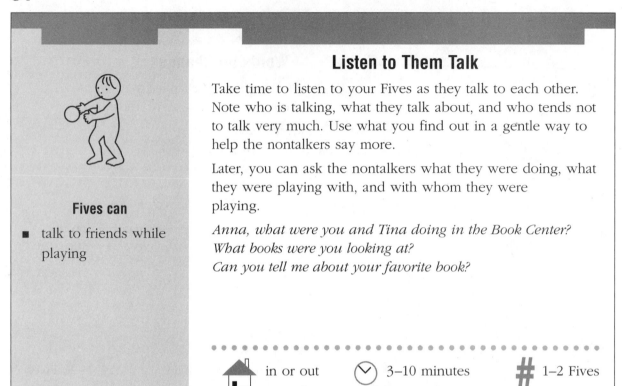

Fives can

- talk to friends while playing

Listen to Them Talk

Take time to listen to your Fives as they talk to each other. Note who is talking, what they talk about, and who tends not to talk very much. Use what you find out in a gentle way to help the nontalkers say more.

Later, you can ask the nontalkers what they were doing, what they were playing with, and with whom they were playing.

Anna, what were you and Tina doing in the Book Center?
What books were you looking at?
Can you tell me about your favorite book?

🏠 in or out   🕐 3–10 minutes   # 1–2 Fives

85

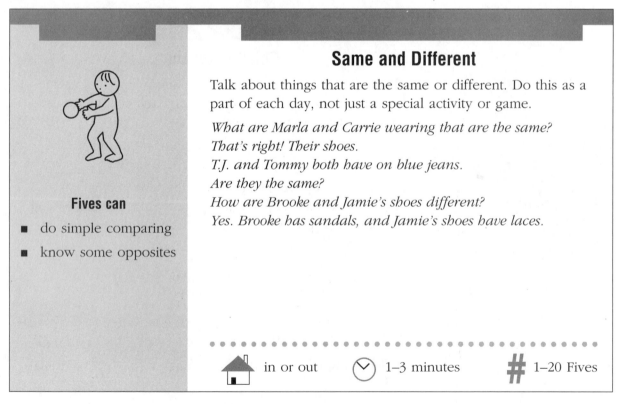

Fives can

- do simple comparing
- know some opposites

Same and Different

Talk about things that are the same or different. Do this as a part of each day, not just a special activity or game.

What are Marla and Carrie wearing that are the same?
That's right! Their shoes.
T.J. and Tommy both have on blue jeans.
Are they the same?
How are Brooke and Jamie's shoes different?
Yes. Brooke has sandals, and Jamie's shoes have laces.

🏠 in or out   🕐 1–3 minutes   # 1–20 Fives

86

Fives can

■ tell about things they see

Talk-About Table

Set aside a little table where you and your Fives can put new things to talk about every day. You can put out something that goes with a unit you and the children are working on. For example, if you're doing a unit on fruits, put a new fruit on the table to taste and talk about each day.

The children can add whatever interests them to the table. Make sure that things on the Talk-About Table are safe to touch and hold.

As your Fives stop by the table, talk about the name of each thing, what you do with it, and how it looks or feels. Be sure the children know that the things on the table need to stay on the table. Change the things every day.

 in or out   3–5 minutes   1–6 Fives

87

Fives can

■ follow three-step directions

■ understand place words such as *over, under, near*

Hunt and Find

Hide a familiar thing somewhere in the room. Tell the children what you have hidden. Give them three-step directions to follow until they find the thing.

I have hidden a little brown teddy bear.
Do what I say and you will find it.
Go to the block shelf.
Look on the bottom shelf behind the triangle blocks.

When children get good at this game, see if they can hide something and give directions for someone else to find it.

 in or out   2–5 minutes   1–6 Fives

88

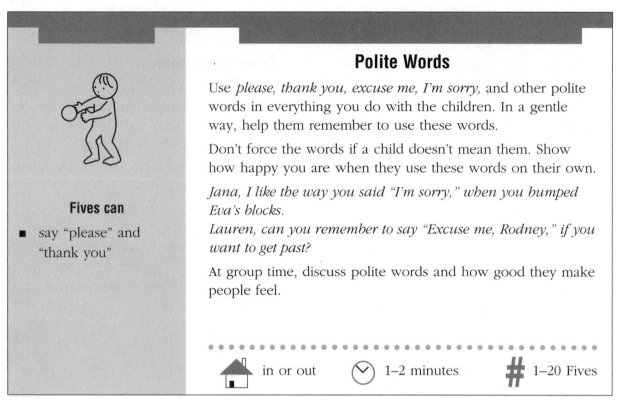

Fives can

■ say "please" and "thank you"

Polite Words

Use *please, thank you, excuse me, I'm sorry,* and other polite words in everything you do with the children. In a gentle way, help them remember to use these words.

Don't force the words if a child doesn't mean them. Show how happy you are when they use these words on their own.

Jana, I like the way you said "I'm sorry," when you bumped Eva's blocks.
Lauren, can you remember to say "Excuse me, Rodney," if you want to get past?

At group time, discuss polite words and how good they make people feel.

in or out   1–2 minutes   # 1–20 Fives

89

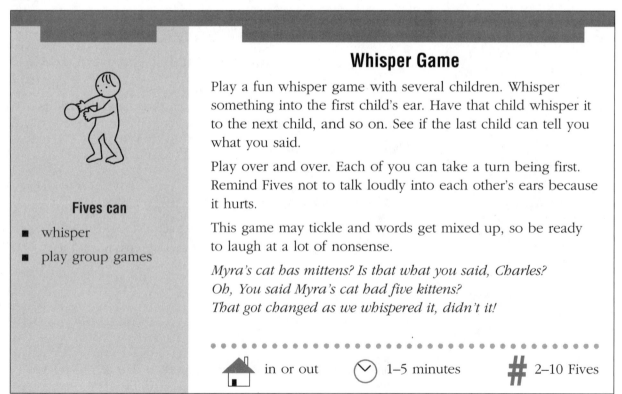

Fives can

■ whisper

■ play group games

Whisper Game

Play a fun whisper game with several children. Whisper something into the first child's ear. Have that child whisper it to the next child, and so on. See if the last child can tell you what you said.

Play over and over. Each of you can take a turn being first. Remind Fives not to talk loudly into each other's ears because it hurts.

This game may tickle and words get mixed up, so be ready to laugh at a lot of nonsense.

Myra's cat has mittens? Is that what you said, Charles?
Oh, You said Myra's cat had five kittens?
That got changed as we whispered it, didn't it!

in or out   1–5 minutes   # 2–10 Fives

90

Fives can

- plan activities
- choose what they want to play

Planning the Day

A short group talk time in the early part of the day can help Fives learn to plan. This is a good time to introduce the special activities of the day and to get each child to choose where he or she wants to start to work. A system for making activity choices, such as a waiting list for each special activity, is helpful so that children can plan ahead even if they can't be among the first to take part in the activity.

Jerry wants to start in blocks. Susan is going to paint. What will you do first, Debby? Yes. You can start in the playhouse and put your name on the list for carpentry.

 in or out   5–10 minutes   # 1–20 Fives

91

Fives can

- take part in a short group time
- tell about something they did

Gathering-Time Talk

Gather your Fives together for a short talking and sharing time. You may do this as part of a story time. Have the children talk about what they did at play time, something they made or brought in, or things that go with what they are working on. Have one child at a time speak to the group. Ask questions to help the children along with their talk. Encourage the other children to ask questions, too.

To call attention to the talker, have the talker hold something special, like a pretend microphone or a speaker's badge, which is passed from talker to talker. Help the others look at and listen to the one who is speaking. Be sure each child gets a turn to talk at least once a week, but have only a few talk on one day.

 indoors   3–7 minutes   # 5–20 Fives

92

Fives can

- guess simple words

Guess the Word

Play a guessing game with your Fives. Give them easy clues until they guess the familiar thing you are talking about.

Guess what animal I'm thinking about.
It has four legs and a round ball for a tail.
No, it's not a dog. Listen to all the clues.
It has long ears. It lives in a hutch. It goes hop, hop, hop.

Encourage your Fives to give clues and have others guess the answers. Be ready for some pretty silly clues and hard-to-discover answers.

 in or out   2–7 minutes   1–20 Fives

93

Fives can

- ask permission to use things
- know about sharing

The Sharing Table

At group time, ask your Fives to bring some things they want to share. Explain that you will put their toys on a sharing table. When someone wants to play with their toys, the person will ask their permission. Set up a table near the entry door with a marking pen, some slips of paper and tape. As children bring in their sharing toys, print each child's name and the toy on a slip of paper and tape it near the toy on the table. You may also want to label the toy.

This is Blake's car, Rachel. You can ask him if it's OK to play with it. Remember to bring it back to the table when you're through.
Yes, Craig. You need to make a waiting list for your toy.
Lots of kids want to play with it.

 indoors   2–10 minutes   1–20 Fives

94

Fives can

- understand rhymes
- enjoy guessing games and riddles

Rhyming Riddles

When the Fives can recognize rhyming words, you can play this game with them at group time.

I'm thinking of an animal whose name rhymes with hair. *Yes, bear.*
I'm thinking of an animal that rhymes with log. *Yes, dog.*
I'm thinking of something that people ride in that rhymes with jar. *Yes, car.*

See if the children can make up rhyming riddles, too.

 in or out   2–5 minutes   1–20 Fives

95

Fives can

- follow directions
- understand *close/closer* and *far/farther away*

Giving Hints

Pick one child to be the hunter. The hunter has to hide her eyes so that she can't see where one of the children hides a toy. Help everyone in the group pay close attention to where the toy is hidden. Tell the hunter what she is hunting for and the side of the room where it is hidden. As the hunter tries to find the toy, have the children tell her if she is getting closer or farther away.

Is Ellen close now? Let's help by telling her.
Closer, closer. Very close! Very close!
Ellen, you're a good hunter.
You found the red block Nathan hid.
How did you know where to look?

 indoors   2–6 minutes   1–20 Fives

96

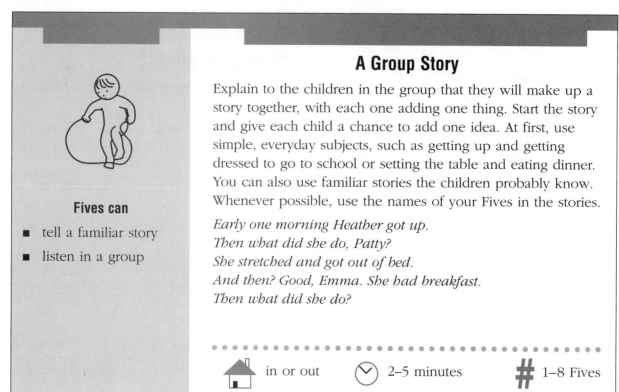

Fives can

- tell a familiar story
- listen in a group

A Group Story

Explain to the children in the group that they will make up a story together, with each one adding one thing. Start the story and give each child a chance to add one idea. At first, use simple, everyday subjects, such as getting up and getting dressed to go to school or setting the table and eating dinner. You can also use familiar stories the children probably know. Whenever possible, use the names of your Fives in the stories.

Early one morning Heather got up.
Then what did she do, Patty?
She stretched and got out of bed.
And then? Good, Emma. She had breakfast.
Then what did she do?

 in or out   2–5 minutes   # 1–8 Fives

97

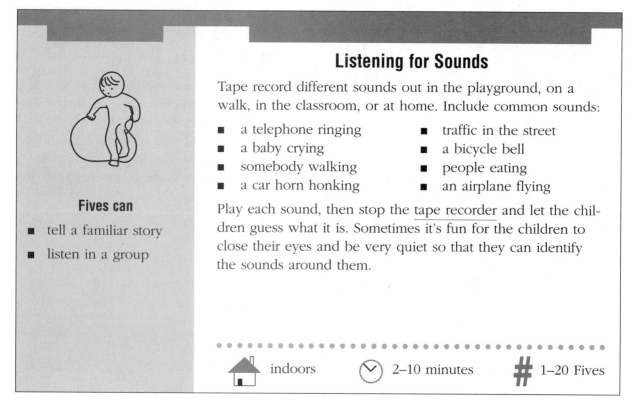

Fives can

- tell a familiar story
- listen in a group

Listening for Sounds

Tape record different sounds out in the playground, on a walk, in the classroom, or at home. Include common sounds:

- a telephone ringing
- a baby crying
- somebody walking
- a car horn honking
- traffic in the street
- a bicycle bell
- people eating
- an airplane flying

Play each sound, then stop the tape recorder and let the children guess what it is. Sometimes it's fun for the children to close their eyes and be very quiet so that they can identify the sounds around them.

indoors   2–10 minutes   # 1–20 Fives

98

Fives can

- remember rules
- behave well in public

Preparing for Field Trip Talks

Before a field trip, gather the children in small groups to discuss where you are going and rules for how to behave. If parents are coming along, tell the children who they are. Talk about how you will get where you are going and whether children will have partners to walk with or go in a small group with one adult.

Remind your Fives that they need to stay close to the leader, a teacher, or a parent. They must also remember the safety rules for riding in a car and for crossing the street.

And, of course, spend time talking about what you will see and do on the trip. If possible, bring in pictures of what you might see so that the children can start to think about and notice things that will help them get the most out of the trip.

 indoors   5–10 minutes   1–20 Fives

99

Fives can

- tell about what they did

Remembering a Trip

Take a camera along on trips you take with your Fives. Take pictures of anything of interest that you and the children see. Include the children, their parents, and the teachers in your photos.

After you return, talk about what you remember about the trip. Let the children draw pictures, tell stories, ask questions, talk about the photos, and write about the trip. Encourage children to remember as many details about their trip as they can.

Put the pictures, drawings, and stories on a bulletin board where the children can see and talk about them.

 indoors   5–30 minutes   1–20 Fives

100

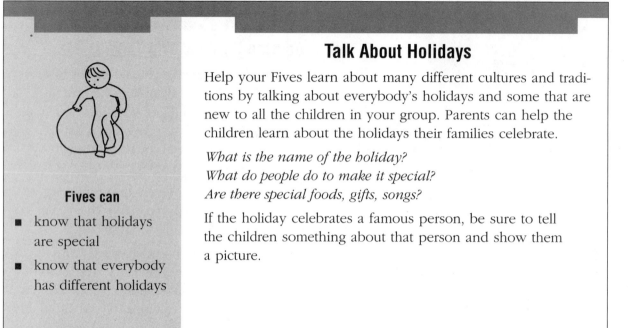

Talk About Holidays

Help your Fives learn about many different cultures and traditions by talking about everybody's holidays and some that are new to all the children in your group. Parents can help the children learn about the holidays their families celebrate.

What is the name of the holiday?
What do people do to make it special?
Are there special foods, gifts, songs?

If the holiday celebrates a famous person, be sure to tell the children something about that person and show them a picture.

Fives can

- know that holidays are special
- know that everybody has different holidays

indoors   2–10 minutes   # 1–20 Fives

101

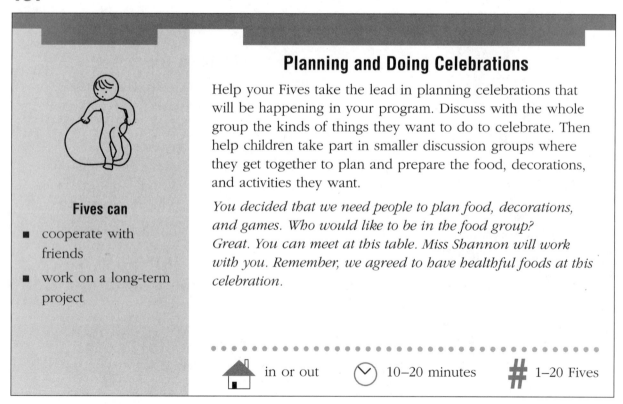

Planning and Doing Celebrations

Help your Fives take the lead in planning celebrations that will be happening in your program. Discuss with the whole group the kinds of things they want to do to celebrate. Then help children take part in smaller discussion groups where they get together to plan and prepare the food, decorations, and activities they want.

You decided that we need people to plan food, decorations, and games. Who would like to be in the food group?
Great. You can meet at this table. Miss Shannon will work with you. Remember, we agreed to have healthful foods at this celebration.

Fives can

- cooperate with friends
- work on a long-term project

in or out   10–20 minutes   # 1–20 Fives

102

Fives can

- tell about what they did
- take part in small discussion groups

What Did We Do Today?

Give your Fives a chance to talk with other children about their work and show them the work they do daily. After the children have worked in the different activity centers, bring them together in a group of no more than ten children to talk about what they did. They can show their drawings, paintings, and other work and talk about their block buildings, pretend play, and games.

Use this group talking time as a chance to point out some new ideas and ask questions to help children think. Encourage the children to communicate with and listen to others.

 indoors   5–15 minutes   1–10 Fives

103

Fives can

- tell about things they know
- take part in short discussions

Work Our Dads and Moms Do

Start a conversation about the work the Fives' dads and moms do. See if they can take turns telling what they know about their parents' work.

Peg's mom is a doctor. Have you been to see her at work, Peg? Tell us about what she does.

You can invite some of the parents to tell about their work, too. Remind them to bring along things they use at work or pictures of themselves at work to show the children if possible. Encourage your Fives to ask lots of questions.

 in or out   5–15 minutes   1–20 Fives

104

Fives can

- talk in sentences
- tell about things they know
- take part in group discussions for ten to twenty minutes

Talk About Details

Sit with a group of Fives and have them all concentrate on looking at the same thing. Then encourage them to say as much about that one thing as they can. Ask questions to help them talk about the details.

Let's look at Henry, our guinea pig.
Really look hard and tell me about what you see.
Right, Tessa. He is white and brown.
Yes, Jason. The insides of his ears are pink.
What is his fur like?

Keep talking until the children have told you as much as they can about something. Try looking at something else next time. You can write what the children say on a chart and read their words back to them if you wish.

 in or out   5–15 minutes   1–20 Fives

105

Fives can

- tell about things they know
- remember details about trips
- talk about imaginary ideas

Vacation Talk

When the children come back from a vacation, have them tell others about what they did. Ask the parents to send in anything that will help the children understand more about the vacation experiences your Fives describe, such as shells collected at the beach or pictures taken on the trip.

Later, have the group let their imaginations take off as they describe pretend vacations they would like to take. Encourage the children to add to what others say, giving as many imaginary details as possible.

What do you think you would eat if you took a vacation in a spaceship to a star, Antoine? What clothes would you take?

 in or out   2–10 minutes   1–20 Fives

106

Fives can

- tell what they like and dislike
- suggest solutions
- take part in group discussions

What Do We Like? What Would We Change?

Have group discussions in which children talk about the things they are experiencing in the classroom. Encourage them to talk about what they like best, what they like least, and what they would change if they could. Keep things open, allowing children to say what they really think. Allow time to think about possible solutions to problems.

Emma says she hates lunchtime because it is so noisy in the cafeteria.
You hate it, too, Josh?
It is true that there is hardly any time to eat.
What do the rest of you think?
How could we improve lunchtime?

 in or out   5–15 minutes   1–20 Fives

107

Fives can

- begin to understand clocks and time
- understand time words

What the Clock Says to Do

Using a clock whose hands can be moved, talk about what the clock tells us to do at different times. Discuss what we do:

- in the morning before school starts
- when school starts
- at noon
- when school ends
- when we go to sleep

Use time words such as *morning, noon, afternoon,* and *evening* as you move the hands on the clock to show the times. Throughout the day, call children's attention to the time as the schedule progresses.

 indoors   5–10 minutes   1–20 Fives

108

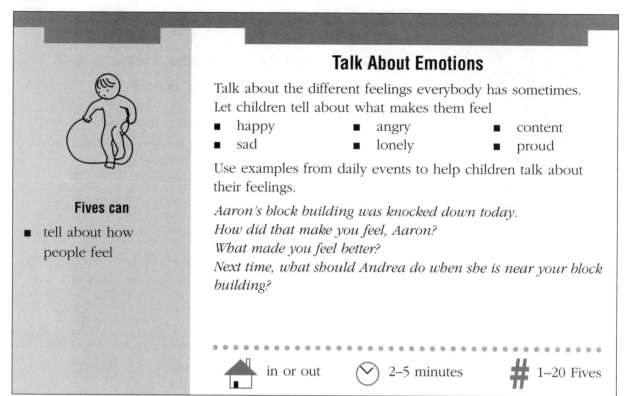

Fives can

- tell about how people feel

Talk About Emotions

Talk about the different feelings everybody has sometimes. Let children tell about what makes them feel

- happy
- sad
- angry
- lonely
- content
- proud

Use examples from daily events to help children talk about their feelings.

Aaron's block building was knocked down today.
How did that make you feel, Aaron?
What made you feel better?
Next time, what should Andrea do when she is near your block building?

in or out   2–5 minutes   # 1–20 Fives

109

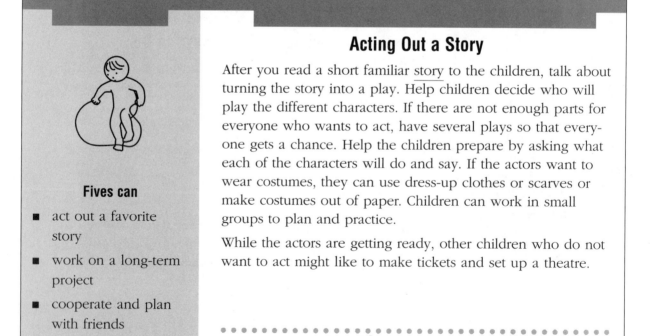

Fives can

- act out a favorite story
- work on a long-term project
- cooperate and plan with friends

Acting Out a Story

After you read a short familiar story to the children, talk about turning the story into a play. Help children decide who will play the different characters. If there are not enough parts for everyone who wants to act, have several plays so that everyone gets a chance. Help the children prepare by asking what each of the characters will do and say. If the actors want to wear costumes, they can use dress-up clothes or scarves or make costumes out of paper. Children can work in small groups to plan and practice.

While the actors are getting ready, other children who do not want to act might like to make tickets and set up a theatre.

in or out   5–30 minutes   # 2–20 Fives

Fives can

- cooperate with friends
- work on a long-term project

Planning Their Own Special Activities

Have a group time where children plan a special activity on their own. Encourage them to brainstorm to choose an activity and then help them work through planning and carrying it out. Children may need help choosing an activity to begin with, so you might suggest some ideas, such as a circus or a talent show. Let the whole group decide the kinds of things they want to do and then have them divide into smaller groups to work on their parts. Keep things simple—do not turn this into an adult extravaganza!

Myron, you, Dennis, Abraham, and Sheila want to be the clowns. You can talk about what you will do in this corner. I'll help you in a minute. Who wanted to plan the horse show? Great. You can work at this table with Alison's mom.

 indoors   5–15 minutes   1–20 Fives

Group Talk

■ Keep the group small (under ten) so that each child can have a chance to ask and answer questions and make comments several times during the meeting.

■ Sit in a circle so that the children can see one another. Sitting on a rug is not so disruptive as wiggling in chairs.

■ Decide on a signal to give when someone wants a turn to talk. Putting up the index finger is a good quiet signal.

■ When the children are learning that only one person speaks at a time while the others listen, have the speaker hold something to show that it is his turn to speak. A yarn ball, a toy microphone, or something else that is easy to pass around will do.

■ Keep the group time short because it is hard for young children to sit still and listen for a long time. When children are allowed to get bored or restless in group time, they learn to dislike large groups.

■ Talk about things the Fives are interested in—what they did, what they want to do, and what happened to them.

■ Bring in things to look at and touch to make the topics more lively.

■ Remember that a group can't learn; only individual children can learn. Make eye contact and talk to each child in the group.

Hints About Asking Questions

■ Use different types of questions to help children think about their activities in many different ways.

■ Always be sure that your questions sound friendly and that they do not cause stress and pressure.

■ Count to ten as you calmly listen for an answer. Remember that it takes time for children to think of an answer.

■ If a child can't find an answer to your question, then answer the question for him and share the information that way.

■ In order to help young children think, you'll need to practice asking different types of questions.

An *open-ended question* has no right answer. It is a good type of question to start with because it gives the child a chance to show the adult how he organizes his ideas and expresses himself in words. An example of an open-ended question is "Can you tell me all about your painting?"

Open-ended questions can be used in many situations. When you are reading a story, you can stop and let children tell about one of the pictures by asking, "Can you tell me all about what is happening here?"

An open-ended question may get very different answers, depending on the child's level of understanding. One child may be able to pull together all the details and tell you what the whole picture means. Another child may just be able to name the different parts of the picture. The adult can help this child by asking questions that focus his attention on the details. After the child has told about the details, the general question can be asked again: "Now can you tell me what's happening here?" The child can then give the main idea of the picture.

"How" questions give the child a chance to describe a process or tell about a sequence. "How did you make your pancake when we did cooking today?" "How did you build this tall building?" This is very different from asking a child, "What did you build?" "What" questions usually get short answers. A "how" question helps the child remember and organize a lot of information about the process.

"How" questions can also help children recognize relationships, such as same and different, more and less, big and little. "How are these blocks different from one another?" "How are they the same?"

"Why" questions ask children to try to find reasons for the things they see happening. "Why do you think the ice cream became hard in the freezer?" "Why did it melt outside on the table?"

"What if" questions help children think about what might happen next, to predict. "What might happen if you spill water and children walk on the wet floor?"

- In order to build skills in asking questions, it helps to plan the questions you want to ask. Story time is a good time to plan for asking a few questions. You might ask an open-ended question about one of the exciting pictures that has a lot going on in it. You might ask a "how" or a "why" question when they are right for the story. The children can also be asked to predict what will happen next before you turn the page and continue reading.

- Planning can help you learn to ask a variety of questions. With practice, questions will become a comfortable way to encourage your Fives to talk more.

Active Learning
for Fives

Activities for
Physical Development

Index

of Activities for Physical Development

Here's Why

Fives enjoy physical activity. While they are indoors, they usually want to move about as they work on activities. Sometimes it is hard for them to sit quietly during group time; they tend to fidget and move about. They always rush outdoors and race around after being indoors for any amount of time. We know that Fives need plenty of time for physical play in order to build strong bodies, yet many kindergarten programs emphasize quiet activity and limit active times. It is important to maintain a healthful balance of quiet and active play for a group of Fives.

While they are using their muscles, Fives can learn more than physical skills. They learn about how things move and balance in space. They are open to learning the words they need to think and talk about what they are doing. As children become more competent, physical play is a way to help them learn to cooperate in simple games and sports. The ideas in this section give children many safe and enjoyable large-muscle activities.

Five-year-olds also need lots of practice in using their fingers and hands. You can tell by their wobbly writing that they still have far to go to develop the hand control needed for most schoolwork. Activities with materials that use the small muscles, such as pegboards, beads, and small building toys, give Fives the chance to solve problems and use their eyes and hands together. You will find that most of the art activities in the Creative Activities section of this book encourage Fives to develop small-muscle skills, too.

Many activities in the sections for large- and small-muscle development include ideas for the adult to help children learn words and other thinking skills as they enjoy physical activity. Physical activities are learning activities, and you have to plan for them as carefully as you do for other learning. Every new thing Fives learn to do with their large and small muscles builds their feelings of confidence and pride in what they can do for themselves.

Materials and Notes

Large Muscles

balance beams

low basketball hoop

tricycles

climber with slide

wagons

balls

- Younger Fives and older Fives do not differ greatly in the large-muscle activities they enjoy. You will probably be able to use many of the open-ended activities in this section for both age groups. When you try any activity, watch carefully to see that the activity is fun and challenging without being frustrating. If these things are true, then the activity is right for the children.

- Fives will practice running, climbing, balancing, jumping, and many other large-muscle skills on their own. Just give them lots of time and space to do this in their own special way. Then you can add the activities in this book to what they do by themselves.

- Avoid having Fives compete with one another. Instead, encourage each child to do his or her own best, and to face the challenge of getting just a little better.

- To insure safe large-muscle activities for your Fives, be sure to read "Outdoor Play" in the Planning for Fives section of this book.

- Give parents ideas for safe large-muscle activities for children to do at home. Talk about how things in the home, such as large boxes, blankets, and balls can be used in many fun ways.

- Remember that Fives still need supervision when doing active play. Remind parents that although their children may seem to be very competent, they still need a safe place to play and some supervision.

Activity Checklist

Large Muscles

Large-muscle activities with Fives include experiences in which the arm, leg, and body muscles are used and strengthened. Large-muscle activities for five-year-olds include climbing, running, throwing, balancing, pedaling wheel toys, pumping on a swing, and many others. Equipment should encourage these skills so that Fives are safely challenged. In addition, some Fives will be interested in working on some of the skills required for organized sports, such as kicking a ball into a goal for soccer or shooting baskets for basketball. But understanding all the rules for these types of sports will be beyond the abilities of most five-year-olds.

Check for each age group

	60–66 months	66–72 months
1. Adult supervision is provided for large-muscle activities, both indoors and outdoors.	❐	❐
2. Large-muscle activities are scheduled regularly, with at least one hour in the morning and one hour in the afternoon for a full-day (8–10 hour) program.	❐	❐
3. Children are allowed free choice of activities during most of the large-muscle activity time, with daily opportunities to take part in adult-directed play if children are interested.	❐	❐
4. A safe, fenced, open space is provided for large-muscle play outdoors except when weather is very bad. Safe, open space with suitable equipment is provided indoors during bad weather.	❐	❐
5. Safe, sturdy, developmentally appropriate large-muscle equipment (riding toys, wagons, slides, climbers, low basketball hoops, balls, jump ropes) is available for children's daily use.	❐	❐
6. Duplicates of popular large-muscle toys are available. When sharing is a problem, a waiting list or other system is used so that the problem is handled fairly.	❐	❐
7. Surfaces in large-muscle play areas are suitable for different types of play (smooth areas for running and wheel toys, cushioning under climbing equipment).	❐	❐

Activity Checklist

8. Different play areas are organized so that one type of play does not interfere with another. ❏ ❏

9. Adult talks to children and is involved with them during large-muscle time. ❏ ❏

10. Adult suggests some organized group games for any interested Fives to play. ❏ ❏

11. Children are encouraged to develop skills that will be used in sports, such as kicking the ball into the goal for soccer or dribbling the ball for basketball) but playing of sports, with complex rules and skill requirements, is not emphasized. ❏ ❏

12. Adult encourages new skills and the combination of different skills, such as kicking a ball and then running to a base, when children seem ready. ❏ ❏

111

Fives can

- enjoy playing with other children
- use their imaginations

Box Play

Bring in a few <u>appliance boxes</u> from a local store. Put them outside on a dry, soft area for free play. Let Fives have fun using them in their own way for climbing, rolling, tumbling, pushing, or hiding. Ask them to tell you about what they are doing.

What are you and Max doing with the boxes, Lois?
Did you build a house? No?
Oh, yes. I see. You made a garage for the bikes.

Be sure to have enough boxes so that children will not be crowded when they play. Talk about rules for taking turns and using boxes safely if needed.

 outdoors   5–30 minutes   1–3 Fives per box

112

Fives can

- run changing direction
- follow simple directions

Change Speed and Direction

Play movement games with your Fives in which they have to change their speed and direction. Try some of these ideas:

- Run to the tree and back, then walk very slowly to the fence.
- Walk around the table, then walk back fast.
- Crawl across the room slowly, then crawl back fast.
- Zigzag to the door, then tiptoe back.
- Run fast, walk slow, run fast, walk slow.
- Roll slowly, then fast.

Give children the chance to take turns giving some of the directions for how to move.

 in or out   3–10 minutes   1–20 Fives

113

Fives can

- catch a ball with two hands
- play well with three or four other children

Catching Balls

Stand four or five feet away from your five-year-old. Tell him you are going to throw him a small ball and ask if he can catch it. Gently toss a small ball. After he catches the ball ask him to throw it back to you. Encourage a few other Fives to join in the catching game. Have them stand in a circle or square to take turns catching and throwing.

You caught the ball, Jimmy.
Now throw it to the next person.
Whoops! You threw it so high.

Use balls of different sizes and weights with this activity. If children have difficulty catching the small ball, use a larger one or move closer together. Keep all the balls in a balls activity box to take outdoors.

 in or out   5–20 minutes   1–8 Fives

114

Fives can

- catch a bounced ball
- take turns
- enjoy circle games

Bouncing Ball Circle Game

Stand with eight to ten children in a circle with 6' of space between each child. Form the circle where the ground is smooth. Use a 12" rubber or plastic ball. Let the children know that they will be bouncing the ball around the circle. Tell the child next to you to get ready to catch. Then bounce the ball to the child so it hits the ground about halfway between the two of you. When she catches the ball, tell her to bounce it to the next child in the circle. Continue so that the ball goes around and around the circle Try these ideas:

- Everyone can move back a step if the game is too easy.
- Have a child call out another child's name and bounce it across the circle to that child.
- Use balls of different sizes.

 in or out   4–15 minutes   8–10 Fives

115

Fives can

- move in many ways
- play simple games
- take turns

How Many Ways Can You Go Over and Under?

Have two children (or adults) hold the ends of a jump rope so it is about waist high for the other children. Place one or more big mats under the rope so that if children trip or fall while playing this game, they will not be hurt. Challenge the Fives to go over or under the rope in as many ways as they can.

Move the rope to higher and lower levels every so often to give the children different challenges as they play.

Encourage the children to describe the ways they moved.

Jerry, you went over the rope when it was really high. How did you do it? Yes, you did fly like Superman!

 in or out   3–20 minutes   1–20 Fives

116

Fives can

- pump on swings by themselves

Swinging

Have a swing set with low, safe swings for your Fives to use. Be sure the swings are out of the way of other activities. If there are no swings on the playground, take the children to a park where there are safe swings.

Allow the children to use the swings freely as long as their swinging is safe. Watch to see who can manage swinging all by themselves.

You're as high as the sky, Leroy. It looks like you are on your way to the clouds!

 outdoors   3–20 minutes   1 child per swing

117

Fives can

- control different muscles at will
- know names of many body parts

Relax!

Have Fives lie down on their backs, with each child in his own space. Ask the children to think about the part of their body that you name. First have them tighten that body part as hard as they can. Watch to see if they can do this. Then tell them to relax that part of their body. Do this for hands, fingers, feet, toes, back, stomach, legs, neck, shoulders, face, and arms. See if the children can suggest which parts of the body to tighten and relax next.

Tighten your hand. Make a hard, hard fist.
Now relax your hand. Make it as floppy as you can.
Shake it around and see if it flops.
Just let your hand hang and take a big rest.

This activity is great after very active play.

 in or out   3–15 minutes   1–20 Fives

118

Fives can

- run well
- kick a ball
- follow directions

Goal Kicking

Set up a goal outdoors for your Fives to kick balls into. Use a soccer goal with a net or a big box will do, too. Set the goal up in a clear fenced open space. Have one big soccer-sized ball for each child who will play. Have a waiting list for balls if lots of children want to take part. Show children how to kick the ball across the field and then make a final kick into the goal when they feel they are close enough.

You kicked that ball hard, Emma. It's almost to the goal.

Try some of these ideas:

- Mark lines about 5', 8', and 10' from the goal where children can stand and kick toward the goal.
- Have two goals at opposite ends of the space. Let children kick from one goal to the other.

 outdoors   5–20 minutes   1–4 Fives

119

Fives can

- copy movements
- know about many animals

Guess Which Animal Moves Like This?

Put pictures of several familiar animals into a feelie box or bag. Have a child close her eyes, reach in, and pick one out. Ask her to tell you about the animal she chose. Then see if the child can show you how it moves.

Then everyone can move the way the child does. See if someone else can show you a different way that same animal moves and copy that child's movements, too.

Andre showed us how the lion puts his paws out to swipe and claw. Can anyone think of another movement the lion does? Yes, Mari knows that lions stretch and yawn!

Leave the feelie box and animal pictures out for children to use on their own.

 in or out   4–15 minutes   1–8 Fives

120

Fives can

- move in many ways
- understand words for different movements

How Many Ways Can We Cross the Playground?

Ask an interested child to show you how many ways he can move across the playground. Watch as he shows you his different ways and talk about what he is doing. Join in and copy how he moves if you wish. Invite other children to join the game.

Wow! Edmund raced across the playground.
Catia, you're going so slowly that I can hardly see you move.

Encourage lots of ideas by making suggestions about moving fast or slow, high or low, frontward or backward, noisily or quietly. Try this game inside and see how many ways the children can think of to move across the room or down a hallway.

 in or out   5–15 minutes   1–16 Fives

121

Fives can

- kick a ball
- catch a big ball
- throw a ball

Kicking a Rolled Ball

Tell the child that you are going to play a ball-kicking game with her. Have her stand facing you on smooth ground and tell her what will happen.

Lisa, I am going to roll the ball to you.
Try to kick it back to me.

Gently roll a big ball toward her feet and see if she can kick it as it moves. Have fun catching the ball and trying again.

Try these ideas, too:
- Organize outfielders to catch the ball once it has been kicked, and a catcher, to get the ball if the kicker misses. Children can take turns playing all positions.
- Have pairs of children roll balls to one another to kick.

 outdoors   5–20 minutes   # 1–8 Fives

122

Fives can

- ride a tricycle and other wheel toys well

Tricycles, Plus!

Put out bicycles with training wheels for your Fives to ride, in addition to tricycles, big wheel toys, scooters, and wagons. Let children choose the toys they wish to ride and then practice at their own skill level.

Talk about how to share the wheel toys so that everyone gets a chance to ride. Use a sign-up sheet and timer if there are not enough wheel toys for all who wish to ride.

You are not interested in using the wagon, Dennis?
Robin has the blue bike now, but you can sign up to use it.
Let's see how many people are ahead of you.
Do you want help writing your name?
What else will you do while you wait for your turn?
Great! We will call you when Jasmina is finished riding.

 outdoors   5–20 minutes   # 1–10 Fives

123

Fives can

- ride a tricycle and other wheel toys well

Riding Track

Mark off a long track where your Fives can use their riding toys. You can have a paved or dirt track built on the playground or mark a track with plastic streamers or used tires. Be sure the track is wide enough for wheel toys to pass each other safely and is not in the way of other activities. Provide various wheel toys for your Fives to use on the track.

I see you are giving Jeremy a ride on the back of your trike, Sheila. It looks like there is a traffic jam here. How can you untangle all the trikes?

 outdoors   5–20 minutes # 1–10 Fives

124

Fives can

- run well
- begin to understand what time is and what clocks are for

Laps on the Track

On some days, use the trike track as a running track. Do not bring out the wheel toys. Instead, encourage children to run along the track. You can use a stopwatch to time how fast each child runs and let them know if they ran faster or slower than the last time they ran. Show them the numbers on the stopwatch. Teach your Fives how to use it to time their friends, and then help them read what it says.

Did you stop the watch, Shavan? It says that Jinsy ran around the track in 55 seconds. That's faster than she ran the last time. How slowly can you go this time, Jinsy?

Encourage children to figure out many ways to get around the track, and talk about which ways are faster or slower, harder or easier.

 outdoors   5–20 minutes # 1–10 Fives

125

Fives can

- move in many ways
- follow simple directions

Quiet-Moving Game

Use a whispering voice to invite your Fives to play a quiet-moving game.

The bookmobile is here. Let's be mice and move so that no one can hear us.
Who can move so that we cannot hear any footsteps or voices?

Remember to move quietly yourself. Then creep or tiptoe quietly with your Fives from one place to another. Use this game when children must move past quiet areas, such as another classroom, or just for a fun change of pace.

 in or out   1–3 minutes # 1–20 Fives

126

Fives can

- walk on a narrow balance beam
- walk on balance board forward, backward, and sideways

Walking on a Line

Use 1"-wide masking tape to make a long path on the floor for your Fives to follow. Put in corners, curves, or even small loops. Have the path end at some special place, such as the sink, the bathroom, or the cubbies. Challenge children to walk along the line without stepping off. See if they can walk along the line sideways and backward, too. Have them experiment to see if it is easier to walk fast or slowly on the line. Join in and have fun as everyone tries to stay on the line.

Have children experiment to see how many different ways they can move along the line.

Jerry is crawling along the line. How will you move on the line, Harriette? Are you going to try it with your eyes closed?

 indoors   1–5 minutes # 1–20 Fives

Activities for Physical Development

127

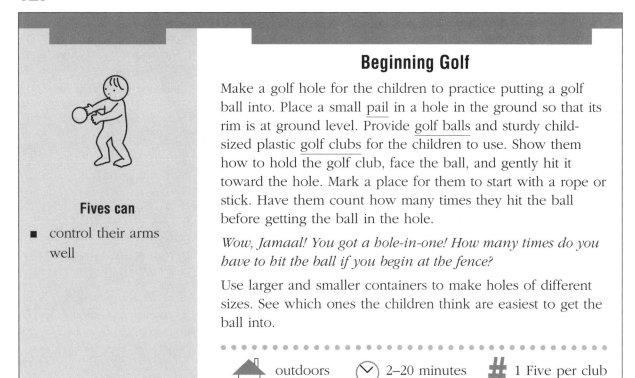

Fives can

- control their arms well

Beginning Golf

Make a golf hole for the children to practice putting a golf ball into. Place a small pail in a hole in the ground so that its rim is at ground level. Provide golf balls and sturdy child-sized plastic golf clubs for the children to use. Show them how to hold the golf club, face the ball, and gently hit it toward the hole. Mark a place for them to start with a rope or stick. Have them count how many times they hit the ball before getting the ball in the hole.

Wow, Jamaal! You got a hole-in-one! How many times do you have to hit the ball if you begin at the fence?

Use larger and smaller containers to make holes of different sizes. See which ones the children think are easiest to get the ball into.

🏠 outdoors   🕐 2–20 minutes   # 1 Five per club

128

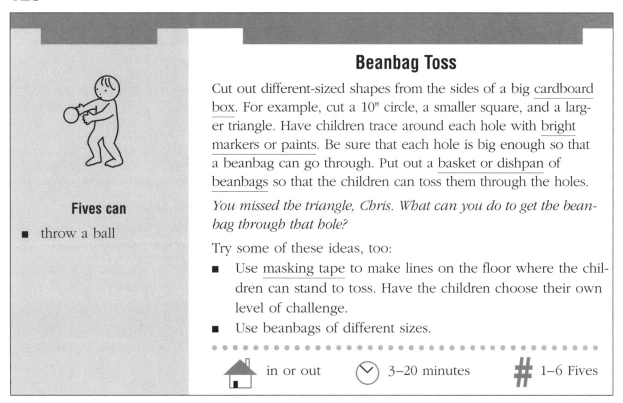

Fives can

- throw a ball

Beanbag Toss

Cut out different-sized shapes from the sides of a big cardboard box. For example, cut a 10" circle, a smaller square, and a larger triangle. Have children trace around each hole with bright markers or paints. Be sure that each hole is big enough so that a beanbag can go through. Put out a basket or dishpan of beanbags so that the children can toss them through the holes.

You missed the triangle, Chris. What can you do to get the beanbag through that hole?

Try some of these ideas, too:

- Use masking tape to make lines on the floor where the children can stand to toss. Have the children choose their own level of challenge.
- Use beanbags of different sizes.

🏠 in or out   🕐 3–20 minutes   # 1–6 Fives

129

Fives can

- follow simple directions
- move in many ways
- understand words for different movements

Red Rover

Have all interested Fives stand on one side of the room or playground. Call to them from the other side and say:

Red Rover, Red Rover, everybody run over!

Have them follow your direction and run across the play area. Try some of these ideas: jump, walk backward, hop, twirl, tiptoe, skip.

Let children take turns thinking of a way for the group to move and then call out their own directions. Also use directions that ask for just a few children at a time, such as calling for all children with red pants to run over, all children with mittens to jump over, and so on.

Red Rover, Red Rover, everyone with sneakers tiptoe over!

 outdoors   5–20 minutes   2–20 Fives

130

Fives can

- walk on a balance board forward, backward, and sideways

Balancing Acts

Set up very low balance beams of different widths for your Fives to use. Have one that is very wide, made of a 12"-wide board and others that are 6", 4" and 2" wide. Secure these to blocks of smooth wood so that they are 3" to 6" off the ground. Place them on a steady surface with grass or mats on the sides of each so there will be cushioning if children fall.

Encourage the children to walk on the balance beams in many ways. See which they can balance on alone. Encourage friends to help one another on the narrow beams.

Enrico, you can walk backward on the wide balance beam! How can you get to the end of the narrow beam?

 in or out   2–20 minutes   1–10 Fives

131

Fires can

- jump over a knee-high obstacle with both feet together

Hurdles to Jump Over

Make a hurdles course for interested Fives to use. First mark off a big track on a soft surface, such as grass or sand. Then place hurdles (12" or lower) on the track for the children to jump over as they run. You might use vinyl-covered foam blocks as hurdles or low ropes with flags attached so that children can easily see them. Take care not to use a hurdle that might hurt or cause falls. If you make the track indoors for bad-weather play, place carpet or mats around the hurdles.

Show your Fives how to run and jump the hurdles. Help them take turns running so that they do not crowd each other.

Jimmy is halfway around now. See, he is running past the oak tree. Do you think it's safe to start, Dianna?

 in or out   5–20 minutes   # 1–10 Fives

132

Fires can

- march
- follow simple directions

Move and Stop

Play some lively music for any Fives who are interested in marching. Tell them that in this game they should march when they hear the music, but stop when the music stops. After they have marched a bit, turn the music off and see if the children remembered to stop. Make a fun game out of marching and stopping.

Children can move and stop to some of these actions, too:
- clapping
- hopping
- stamping
- shaking hands or whole body

 in or out   4–20 minutes   # 1–20 Fives

133

Fives can

- move in many ways
- understand place words, such as *in front of, under, behind, on top of*

Plastic Hoop Places

Give each interested five-year-old a large plastic hoop to use for this game. Tell the children to position themselves by following the directions. Then ask them to

- balance on tiptoes in front of their hoops
- stand on top of their hoops
- run around their hoops
- shake their hoops over their heads
- hop over their hoops
- skip around their hoops

Encourage children to be creative in the ways they follow your directions. Use other place words, too. Show the children what you mean if they do not understand your directions. Allow children to give the directions, too.

 in or out   5–20 minutes   1–20 Fives

134

Fives can

- throw a ball
- dribble a ball with direction

Outdoor Basketball

Set up a basketball hoop outdoors for your Fives to use. Secure it to a steady surface about 4' off the ground. Provide several basketballs (real or lighter in weight) for the children to use as they try to shoot baskets in their own way.

Nicky, you made a basket. Wow! Susie made a basket, too! How many balls have you gotten through the hoop, Sandy?

Bring out different-sized balls for the children to use with the basketball hoop. Talk about the sizes of the balls and which ones are easier or harder to get through the hoop.

Put up a second hoop that is higher or lower than the first, so that everyone can be challenged and successful.

 outdoors   3–20 minutes   1–4 Fives

Activities for Physical Development

135

Fives can

- throw a ball
- cooperate with a few friends in play

Basketball Indoors

Put a big basket or box in a big clear space. Give your Fives a few small, soft foam balls to toss into the box. You may also be able to find a real basketball hoop that is made especially for indoor use with foam balls. Have fun throwing the balls in different ways or from different directions. Try some of these ideas:

- Raise the box on a table or chair.
- Throw the ball to a friend who throws it into the basket.
- Try larger or smaller soft balls.
- Throw the ball with your eyes closed.
- Throw the ball while standing with your back to the box.
- Stand closer or farther away when throwing the ball.
- Stand behind a line made of tape to throw the ball.

 in or out   3–20 minutes   1–4 Fives per basket

136

Fives can

- jump over a knee-high obstacle with both feet together
- enjoy pretending

Jumping on Stepping Stones

Use masking tape to make a path of stepping stones that your Fives can follow by jumping from stone to stone. Make tape squares on the floor that are large enough and spaced so that children can safely jump from one to the other. Explain safety rules for using the stones, such as "Only jump to an empty space." Have just a few children use the stones at a time. Avoid lining up all the children to wait a turn.

Have fun as you and your Fives pretend that there is water all around the stones and try not to fall in. Encourage the children to think of their own pretend reasons for staying on the stones as they move.

As children become more exact jumpers, use smaller squares or squares that are farther apart.

 indoors   2–6 minutes   1–6 Fives

137

Fives can

- work with a few friends
- enjoy building with different materials

Tents

Provide materials for your Fives to make tents to crawl in and play under. Encourage them to figure out how to use the things to make tents in many different ways. (See Ways to Make Tents on page 168.) Allow children to use soft toys, dolls, blankets, and books under each tent to add to their play. If the tents are popular, set up several or use a waiting list so that each child can get a turn to play.

Brian, you seem to have a problem getting this part of the tent to stay up. Look over here. Do you see anything that you could use? Mark has an idea. Do you want to work together?

Store tent-making materials in a tents activity box for the Fives to use on their own.

 in or out   2–30 minutes   1–4 Fives per tent

138

Fives can

- jump and hop
- play simple group games

Leapfrog

Explain the way to play leapfrog to any Fives who are interested. Tell them to make a line and then squat down on their hands and knees. Be sure they tuck their heads into their arms so that they are like small balls.

Help the child at the end of the line to place her hands on the back of the child in front of her and then to leap over, like a frog. She should continue until she is at the front of the line. Then the next child at the end becomes the leaper, and so on, until all children have had a chance.

It helps if children have their shoes off for this game, so that no one gets kicked by hard shoes. Guide the children so that they jump carefully and do not hurt each other.

 in or out   5–15 minutes   2–20 Fives

139

Fives can

■ cooperate with a small group of friends

Creating Obstacle Courses

Provide <u>materials</u> for your Fives to use to make their own <u>obstacle course</u>. Include some of these things:

■ tunnels or tents to crawl through
■ masking tape to mark stepping stones or lines
■ mats or big pillows to roll over
■ hoops to jump through or in and out of
■ boxes or milk crates to step over
■ smooth boards to make into low slides

Allow three or four children to arrange these in their own way, and then everyone who wishes can try out the challenge. Supervise carefully to be sure things are safe. Talk with the children about how to solve safety problems.

This looks pretty wobbly. What could you do to make it safe?

 in or out   5–30 minutes   1–10 Fives

140

Fives can

■ bounce a tennis ball with one hand, catch with two

■ throw a ball overhand 12'

Bouncing Balls Against a Wall

Show your five-year-olds how to throw balls against a blank wall and then catch them as they bounce back. (You can also secure a large sturdy board to a fence to be used as a bouncing wall.)

Let the children try different kinds of <u>balls</u> to see how they bounce differently.

The tennis ball bounced high, didn't it, Ray?
What happened when you threw the beach ball?

 outdoors   2–20 minutes   1–4 Fives

141

Fives can

- play circle games
- understand more complex directions

Duck-Duck-Goose

Before playing, show and tell children what to do. Have all interested Fives sit down in a circle in a big, clear space. Choose one child to walk around the outside of the circle and gently touch each child as she passes, saying "Duck" each time she touches a person. When she chooses a person to be the chaser, have her touch the person and shout "Goose!" Then have her run around the circle, with the child chasing. Have her stop running when she reaches the spot where the child was sitting. If she is caught, that's fine—have her take the other child's place. The chaser then becomes the chooser and the game starts again until everyone has been chosen.

If there are too many children, play with smaller groups and use a waiting list.

 in or out   8–20 minutes   2–20 Fives

142

Fives can

- understand words for different movements
- follow simple directions

Movement Path

Allow each child or a small group of friends to use 1" masking tape to create different movement paths on the floor. Their paths can be straight, zigzagged, full of loops, or any other creation they can think of. When a path is finished, ask the child to tell others how to move on the path. For example, one path might be just for hopping on one foot, and another might be for walking backward.

Tell me about your path, James.
How should we move on your curvy path? Can you show us?

Pull up the tape at the end of the day or leave it for children to play with for a few days. Outside, children can use chalk to make movement paths on sidewalks or even use a stick to make a path in the dirt.

 in or out   2–15 minutes   1–20 Fives

143

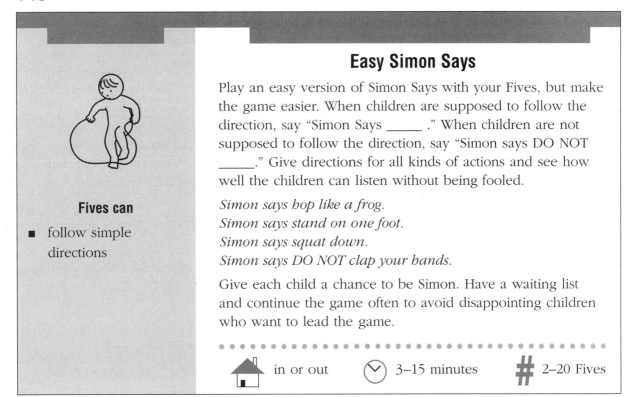

Fives can

- follow simple directions

Easy Simon Says

Play an easy version of Simon Says with your Fives, but make the game easier. When children are supposed to follow the direction, say "Simon Says _____ ." When children are not supposed to follow the direction, say "Simon says DO NOT _____." Give directions for all kinds of actions and see how well the children can listen without being fooled.

Simon says hop like a frog.
Simon says stand on one foot.
Simon says squat down.
Simon says DO NOT clap your hands.

Give each child a chance to be Simon. Have a waiting list and continue the game often to avoid disappointing children who want to lead the game.

in or out   3–15 minutes   2–20 Fives

144

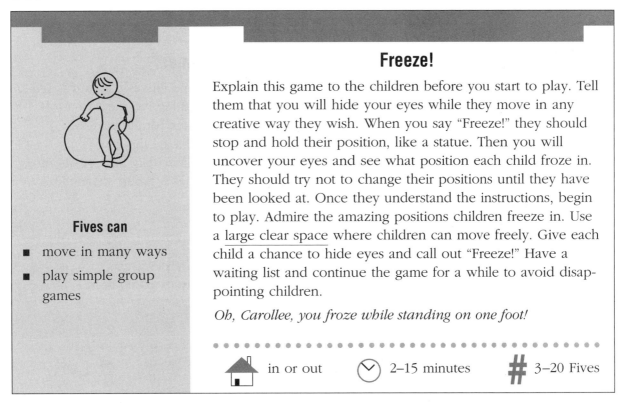

Fives can

- move in many ways
- play simple group games

Freeze!

Explain this game to the children before you start to play. Tell them that you will hide your eyes while they move in any creative way they wish. When you say "Freeze!" they should stop and hold their position, like a statue. Then you will uncover your eyes and see what position each child froze in. They should try not to change their positions until they have been looked at. Once they understand the instructions, begin to play. Admire the amazing positions children freeze in. Use a large clear space where children can move freely. Give each child a chance to hide eyes and call out "Freeze!" Have a waiting list and continue the game for a while to avoid disappointing children.

Oh, Carollee, you froze while standing on one foot!

in or out   2–15 minutes   3–20 Fives

145

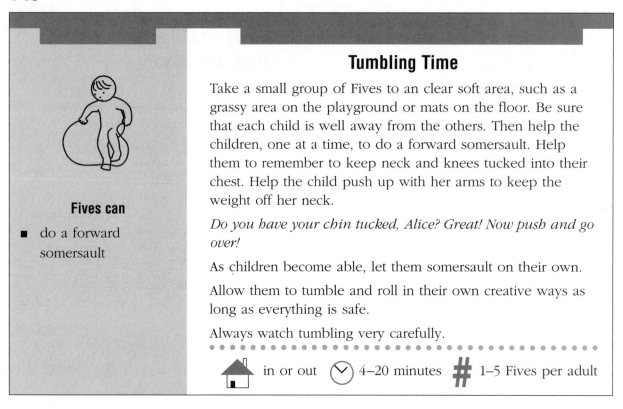

Fives can

■ do a forward
 somersault

Tumbling Time

Take a small group of Fives to an clear soft area, such as a grassy area on the playground or mats on the floor. Be sure that each child is well away from the others. Then help the children, one at a time, to do a forward somersault. Help them to remember to keep neck and knees tucked into their chest. Help the child push up with her arms to keep the weight off her neck.

Do you have your chin tucked, Alice? Great! Now push and go over!

As children become able, let them somersault on their own.

Allow them to tumble and roll in their own creative ways as long as everything is safe.

Always watch tumbling very carefully.

🏠 in or out   🕐 4–20 minutes   # 1–5 Fives per adult

146

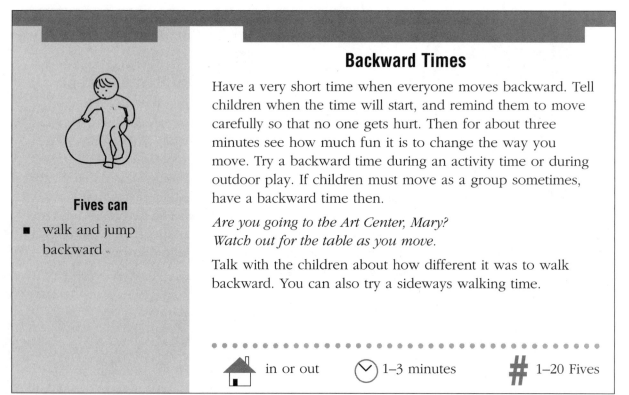

Fives can

■ walk and jump
 backward

Backward Times

Have a very short time when everyone moves backward. Tell children when the time will start, and remind them to move carefully so that no one gets hurt. Then for about three minutes see how much fun it is to change the way you move. Try a backward time during an activity time or during outdoor play. If children must move as a group sometimes, have a backward time then.

Are you going to the Art Center, Mary?
Watch out for the table as you move.

Talk with the children about how different it was to walk backward. You can also try a sideways walking time.

🏠 in or out   🕐 1–3 minutes   # 1–20 Fives

147

Fives can

- build with blocks and other materials
- walk on a balance beam

Creative Playground Equipment

Put out things Fives can use to build their own movable playground equipment. Try long, smooth wooden boards, sturdy cardboard boxes, milk crates, sturdy blocks, a small ladder, wooden or metal triangles to make ramps. Include some mats to put under parts that are off the ground. Let the children set them up in their own creative ways. Supervise carefully to be sure everything they build is safe to use. When things are not safe, have the children figure out why and then how to build something safer.

Amos, do you think this is safe? Let's check it out to see if your bridge is sturdy enough to walk on. Yes, it's wobbly here. How can you make it steadier?

 outdoors   3–30 minutes # 1–6 Fives

148

Fives can

- kick a moving ball
- cooperate with a friend in play

Kick to a Partner

Ask a pair of children to stand facing each other and tell them to get ready to kick a ball back and forth. Have the first child kick a soccer or kick ball toward her friend's feet and see if the friend can kick it back. If they are successful, see how many times they can make it go back and forth. Count the number of times they pass the ball to each other.

Get it, Lisa! Great! Here it comes again.
Wow! That's five . . . six . . . seven.

Try these ideas too:
- Organize catchers to get the ball if the kicker misses. Have children take turns playing all positions.
- See if two children can walk or run across the playground, kicking the ball to each other as they go.

 in or out   3–20 minutes # 1–12 Fives

149

Fives can

- throw a ball over-hand 12" or more

Throw at the Target

Set out a basket of bright tennis balls. Put up a big circle or rectangle target for children to throw at and see if they can hit it. You can make a target on a big sheet of easel paper or cardboard and hang it outdoors on the side of the building, on a tree, or on the side of a storage shed.

Use short pieces of rope to mark where children can stand when they throw—at about 3', 5', 8', 10', 12', and 15' from the target. Allow the children to begin at the closest line and move back each time hitting the target is too easy.

The children can help you measure where the lines should go, and you can even label them with the distance from the target. Talk with the children about distances as they play.

 outdoors   2–15 minutes   1–4 Fives

150

Fives can

- jump well
- follow simple directions
- understand a little about measurement

Standing Broad Jump

Make a 6' ruler out of strips of cardboard. Mark off every foot and inch. Place this ruler along a grassy area outdoors or a carpeted area indoors where it will be safe for children to jump as far as they can. Show the children how to stand next to the beginning of the long ruler and then jump as far as they can. Let the children try. You can point out how far each child was able to jump. Encourage children to compete with themselves, not against others.

Laura, you jumped a whole foot farther this time than last time. Do you think you can do it again?

Children may not be very exact about using the correct jumping-off place. That's OK as long as children are stretching and using their muscles.

 in or out   1–20 minutes   1–6 Fives

151

Fives can

- jump well
- follow simple directions
- understand a little about measurement

Running Broad Jump

Have the children try running up to the starting point on the 6' ruler used for the standing broad jump and then jump as far as they can. Don't worry if they run past the starting place when they jump. It's hard for children to be exact when they are running. Just laugh and enjoy how they try.

Show the children how far they jumped by using the ruler as a measure.

Help the children figure out which kind of jump (standing or running) helps them go farther.

Can you jump farther with the standing jump or the running jump? Let's try both and measure to see, Daniel.

 outdoors   2–15 minutes   1–6 Fives

152

Fives can

- hit a stationary baseball with a bat

Beginning Baseball

Set up an easy-to-hit baseball game that uses a lightweight plastic baseball and bat so that the children can practice batting. You will find directions for making two easy-to-hit baseball games on pages 168–9, or you can buy one from a school supply or toy store.

Swing hard, Karen. Reach out with the bat.
Great! That looks like a home run!

One child can play alone or friends can take turns being fielder and batter. Be sure children understand rules for safety and that no one stands too close to the batter. If needed, put out a bench or chair to sit on for those who are waiting, or use a sign-up sheet so that children can play elsewhere while waiting a turn.

 outdoors   1–15 minutes   1–3 Fives

153

Fives can

- roll a ball
- cooperate with a friend

Bowling

Make a bowling activity box with a set of plastic bowling pins and a lightweight bowling ball. Have the Fives use these in a narrow area (bowling lane) that you can separate from the rest of the room with bookcases, cubbies, or other room dividers. Then the ball will not escape.

Have several masking-tape lines where the children can stand to bowl. Allow them to choose the place where they can bowl most comfortably.

Show the children how one person can bowl while a friend catches the ball, returns it to the the bowler, and resets the pins. Children can change places.

 in or out   3–20 minutes   1–4 Fives

154

Fives can

- jump over a knee-high obstacle with both feet together
- cooperate with friends in play

The High Jump

Have a very lightweight dowel (1/4" in diameter and 4' long) for your Fives to jump over. Place mats on one side of the dowel where the children can land without getting hurt. Hold the dowel out at different heights for the children to jump over. If you wish, you can measure the height of the dowel with a yardstick and tell children how high they jumped.

Show the children how to hold the dowel steady for their friends to jump over.

You held the dowel so still for Sabrina to jump over, Matthew. Let's measure to see how high she jumped.

 in or out   3–8 minutes   1–5 Fives

155

Fives can

- dribble a ball with direction
- take turns in a small group

Basketball Dribble Down the Lane

Set up this activity so that children can play on a smooth sidewalk or in a clear area indoors. Make a clear path or lane that is at least 10' long and 4' wide. If needed, mark where the path is with a rope or masking tape. Use a basketball and show children how to keep bouncing (or dribbling) the ball as they move forward down the path. Let children take turns trying to dribble the ball down the lane.

Whoops, Mary. The ball got away from you! Do you want to try again?

To add more challenge, make the lane longer or narrower. You can also use different-sized balls and see which the children find easiest and hardest to dribble.

 in or out   8–15 minutes   1–6 Fives

156

Fives can

- kick a ball
- enjoy experimenting

More Exact Ball Kicking

Make big round targets on a building (not near windows or doors!), on a tree, or on the side of a storage shed. Place some targets high and some low. See if your Fives can kick a soccer or kick ball to hit the targets. Encourage them to experiment and notice how to make the ball go high, low, left, right, or straight.

Paul, you kicked the ball very high. Can you kick it so it hits the lowest target?

You can use short pieces of rope to mark where children can stand when they kick—at about 3', 5', 8', 10', 12', and 15' from the target. Encourage the children to begin at the closest line and move back each time hitting the target is too easy.

 outdoors   8–20 minutes   1–4 Fives

157

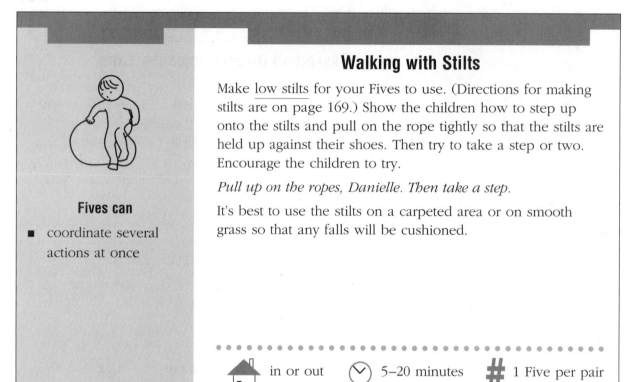

Fives can

- coordinate several
  actions at once

Walking with Stilts

Make low stilts for your Fives to use. (Directions for making
stilts are on page 169.) Show the children how to step up
onto the stilts and pull on the rope tightly so that the stilts are
held up against their shoes. Then try to take a step or two.
Encourage the children to try.

Pull up on the ropes, Danielle. Then take a step.

It's best to use the stilts on a carpeted area or on smooth
grass so that any falls will be cushioned.

🏠 in or out   🕐 5–20 minutes   # 1 Five per pair

158

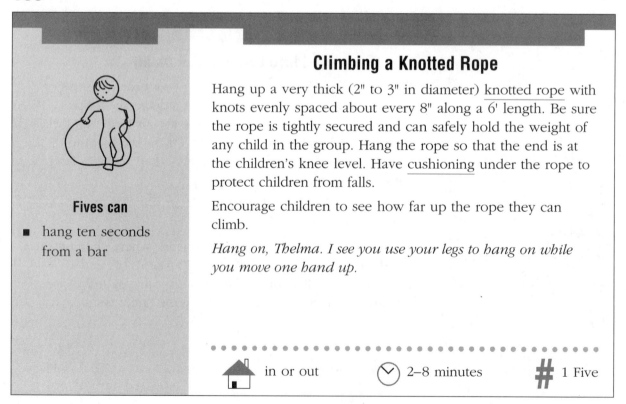

Fives can

- hang ten seconds
  from a bar

Climbing a Knotted Rope

Hang up a very thick (2" to 3" in diameter) knotted rope with
knots evenly spaced about every 8" along a 6' length. Be sure
the rope is tightly secured and can safely hold the weight of
any child in the group. Hang the rope so that the end is at
the children's knee level. Have cushioning under the rope to
protect children from falls.

Encourage children to see how far up the rope they can
climb.

*Hang on, Thelma. I see you use your legs to hang on while
you move one hand up.*

🏠 in or out   🕐 2–8 minutes   # 1 Five

159

Fives can

- follow more complex directions
- cooperate with friends
- take turns

Relay Race Practice

Teach interested Fives how to run a relay race. Explain how the team lines up, waits for the people in front to run, and then runs when their turn comes. Walk children through a race. Make a line where they wait. Have a clearly marked place that they must touch before running back. Stand next to the group and help each child know when his turn comes. Then urge all children to run as fast as they can. Appreciate each child's trying.

Here comes Sonia! Run, Sonia! Great! Now touch Aaron's hand! Go, Aaron! Go down and touch the wall.

Have a relay group compete against themselves, not another team. Use a stopwatch to time the group and let them know how well they did each time they try.

 in or out   5–12 minutes   2–20 Fives

160

Fives can

- ride bicycles
- take turns
- coordinate several actions at once

Bicycles

Discuss with parents that children will be practicing bicycle riding in your program. Provide several small-sized bicycles with training wheels removed. Have safety helmets that riders *must* use. Talk about bicycle safety and make safety rules with your Fives. Then let children use the bicycles and practice riding at their own level. You may help a child get started by holding her up and running alongside, but this is optional. Supervise carefully. Use a waiting list and timer if necessary. If you do not have bicycles, have special bike-riding days when children can bring bikes from home to use.

Note: Do this activity only if you have a large, clear, safe space where bike riders will not interfere with other activities.

 outdoors   10–30 minutes   1–4 Fives

161

Fives can

- begin to jump rope by self
- coordinate several actions at once

Jumping Rope

Provide sturdy individual-sized jump ropes for your Fives to use as they teach themselves to jump. Let them experiment and practice until they coordinate their movements and find success. Encourage the progress each child makes and help them get through the frustrating time of learning.

Have children jump where there is a smooth, clear surface and plenty of space so that the rope does not hit obstructions. Talk with your Fives about making sure each child has her own space to practice.

You managed six jumps before you got caught that time, Marta!
Are you going to try some more? I'll count for you if you want.

 in or out   8–30 minutes   1–10 Fives

162

Fives can

- dribble a ball with direction
- coordinate a sequence of actions

Basketball Dribble and Shoot

Once your Fives can dribble a ball with some control and can shoot the ball at a low basket, see if they can begin to put these two skills together in a sequence. Encourage them to dribble the ball to a place where they want to shoot from, and then to stop and shoot.

Allow children to experiment freely as they try to make the sequence go smoothly. Encourage them to watch others, too.

Look at Michael, Jeri.
See how he stops and looks at the basket before he shoots?
Whoops, he missed! Let's see if he makes it the next time.

 in or out   8–15 minutes   1–8 Fives

163

Fives can

- do a variety of large-muscle activities
- enjoy challenging themselves

Kindergarten Olympics

Organize a Kindergarten Olympics in which each child competes against himself to see how well he can do. Decide with the children which activities they want to have in the Olympics. Make a score sheet for each child like the one shown on page 171.

Then set up the different activities. Have children complete three tries for each and help them record how they did. Olympics can be held in one day, but you will need lots of parents to help with timing, measuring, or counting with the children. Olympics held over several days can cover one or two activities each day.

Encourage children to watch how others are doing, but have other activities for children to do, too.

 in or out   10–120 minutes per day   1–20 Fives

Ways to Make Tents

- Put a blanket or sheet over a table.
- Set up a child's bed-tent on an old mattress in a corner of the room.
- String a rope between two trees outdoors and then throw a sheet or blanket over the rope.
- Get a real tent at a yard sale or at a thrift shop and set it up for the children to use.
- Cut large openings in the ends of a large box and lay it on its side. Throw a blanket or sheet over it.
- Make a house shape with large snap-together plastic panels. Put a blanket over the top.
- Throw two or three blankets over a small climber.
- Tack old blankets or sheets around the platform of a climber so that children can hide and play underneath.
- Ask the children for more ideas on how to make tents.

Easy-To-Hit Baseball Games

Hit the Ball off the Pipe

1. Attach a plastic plumber's pipe that is 24" high and 2" wide to the center of a sturdy board that is about 8" wide by 4' long. Use screws to attach the pipe securely.

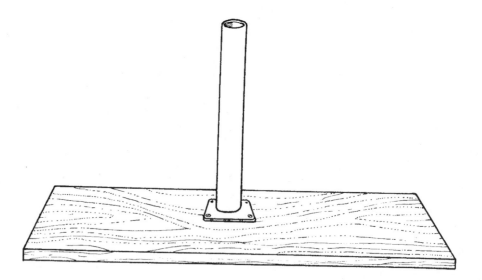

2. Child can place a lightweight plastic baseball on top of the pipe, stand on the opposite end of board, and then hit the ball off the pipe with a bat.

3. Use in an out-of-the-way place.

Activities for Physical Development

Hit the Hanging Ball

1. Thread some sturdy cord through a lightweight plastic baseball with holes in it. Make a knot in the cord so that the ball will not fall off.

2. Hang the ball in an out-of-the-way place so that it is about 2½' from the ground, or waist-high for most of the children. For example, hang it from the limb of a tree in a corner of the playground, or from an overhang of the building where not many people play.

3. Allow a child to bat at the ball to see if she can hit it.

Making Stilts

Wooden Block Stilts

1. Use smooth pieces of wood that are about the size of medium rectangular unit blocks.

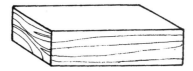

2. Glue sandpaper to the top side of the block.

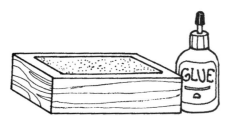

3. Drill a hole through the side of the block.

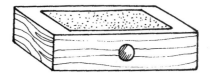

4. String about 36" of sturdy clothesline or jump rope through the hole and tie the ends to make a loop.

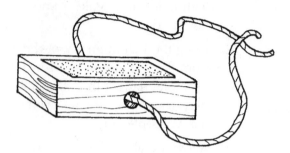

5. Stand on the blocks while holding on to the rope to hold the blocks next to your feet. Take a few steps, keeping the rope tight to hold the blocks on.

Tin Can Stilts or Plastic Bucket Stilts

(Make two of each type.)

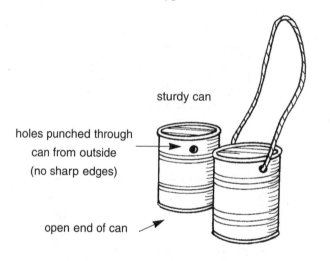

sturdy can

rope long enough for children to hold onto while standing straight, knotted inside can

holes punched through can from outside (no sharp edges)

open end of can

child's sturdy sand bucket, handle removed

holes punched through bucket

Sample Olympics Scoresheet

Name _____   Date _____

	1st time	2nd time	3rd time
Jump rope: How many times did you jump without missing?			
Standing broad jump: How far did you jump each time?			
Running broad jump: How far did you jump each time?			
Basketball shoot: Did you make a basket?			
Standing on one foot with eyes closed: How long did you stand?			
Ball throw: How far did you throw the ball each time?			
Rope arm hang: How long did you hang on each time?			
Running 50 yards: How long did it take each time?			
Skipping 50 yards: How long did it take each time?			
Ball dribbling: How many times did you bounce the ball each time?			

Materials and Notes

Small Muscles

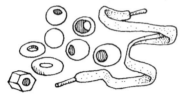

small beads to string

marbles of different sizes

10- to 20-piece puzzles

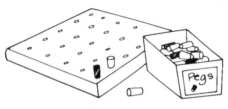

pegs and pegboards

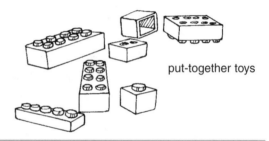

put-together toys

- A Small-Muscle Center should be set up so Fives can use the toys and materials on their own. Be sure to read "Making Activity Centers" in the Planning for Fives section of this book.

- Store each toy with many pieces in its own sturdy box, dishpan, or plastic container. Put a picture/word label showing the toy and its name on the box. Put six or seven different sets at a time on low shelves and change them often.

- If there are problems with sharing, have more than one set of the most popular small-muscle toys. Do not store them as one very big set. Instead, store them as two or more sets, so that one or two children can play with each.

- Check often for broken or lost pieces. Lost pieces frustrate children and keep them from finishing an activity with success.

- Make careful cleanup of the Small-Muscle Center an important part of your daily schedule with the children. Challenge children to find every small piece of the various materials and put them into the proper container. Make this clean-up time fun by showing delight with each small piece they find.

- Many activity ideas can be used with either younger or older Fives because they are open-ended and can challenge children with a wide range of abilities.

- Give parents ideas about how they can help their children practice using their small muscles at home (putting tops back onto jars, breaking eggs while helping to cook, putting pillow cases on pillows, folding laundry).

Activity Checklist

Small Muscles

Small-muscle activities with Fives include experiences in which children refine the control of hands and fingers, usually with eye coordination. As eye-hand coordination improves, Fives enjoy being independent as they dress themselves, buttoning buttons and zipping zippers. Fives build with toys that have small pieces, are able to use scissors to cut out simple shapes, and can usually handle fragile things without harming them.

Check for each age group

	60–66 months	66–72 months
1. Small-Muscle Center is set up with space for at least five children to use at a time.	❏	❏
2. Small-Muscle Center is available for long periods daily for children's free choice.	❏	❏
3. Center is stocked with a variety of safe small-muscle toys.	❏	❏
4. Small-muscle toys organized by type are stored in containers that have picture/word labels and are accessible to children on low shelves.	❏	❏
5. Small-muscle toys are changed regularly.	❏	❏
6. Duplicates of popular toys are available or a fair system, such as a waiting list, is used for sharing.	❏	❏
7. Materials are available for children of differing abilities.	❏	❏
8. Adult introduces new small-muscle materials to children and actively supervises the center.	❏	❏
9. Toys are clean and in good repair.	❏	❏
10. Children are encouraged to do small-muscle activities throughout the day during other activities, such as managing their own meals and snacks, sharpening pencils, and doing art or carpentry activities.	❏	❏

164

Fives can

- use toys with many small pieces

Lots of Put-Together Toys

Have many different types of put-together/pull-apart toys. Store all sets in their own labeled containers. Put six or seven sets out on a low shelf in the Small-Muscle Center for your Fives to choose when they are interested. Change some of the sets that are out on the shelves every week. Leave the most popular sets for children to use every day.

Some put-together/pull-apart small-muscle toys that Fives enjoy are
- Lego® or other put-together building bricks
- Blocks that stick together with plastic bristles
- Building logs
- Blocks that snap together

 in or out   5–30 minutes   1–2 Fives per set

165

Fives can

- coordinate eyes and hands well
- play well with a few friends

Pegs and Pegboards

Have several different types of pegboards with pegs. For example, have big wooden pegs, thin wooden pegs, and brightly colored plastic pegs, too. Use a separate plastic container to store the pegs for each type of board.

Talk with the children about the colors of pegs they use, the number of pegs, and the designs they create. Encourage friends to work together on a peg designs using a big pegboard.

Tell me about your peg design, Marwan.
Oh, yes. I can see that you are sorting the different colors into different rows.

Change the types of pegs that are out on the shelf often.

 indoors   5–20 minutes   1 child per board

166

Fives can

- coordinate eyes and hands well
- follow simple patterns

Pegboard Patterns

Make simple pegboard patterns for any interested children to follow. Trace an outline of the pegboard on a piece of paper. Then draw little circles where all of the holes are. Make ten copies of your pegboard drawing so that you can make ten different patterns. Color in the little circles to make simple patterns. For example, on one sheet, color in a straight line of yellow circles and a line of blue ones. On another sheet, color in circles with red to make a red *X* across the board.

Keep the patterns very easy until you see how the children do. Then make harder patterns for them to follow if the first are too easy. Cover the patterns with clear contact paper or laminate them. Keep the patterns in a container with the pegboards and pegs.

 in or out   3–30 minutes   1–3 Fives per board

167

Fives can

- coordinate eyes and hands well
- play well with a friend
- follow simple patterns

Pegboard Pattern Sharing Box

Show children how to make pegboard patterns using a paper outline of the pegboard and crayons or watercolor markers. Then let them design their own patterns. They can make a pattern with pegs on the pegboard first and then copy it or design the pattern on the paper first and see if they can follow it.

Have them put their names on their patterns and then put them into a pegboard pattern sharing box. (You can help children with their names if they cannot write yet.)

The children can then look through the patterns, see who designed them, and work on the ones they like. Talk with the children about the colors and designs in the patterns they make and use.

 in or out   3–30 minutes   1–6 Fives

Activities for Physical Development **175**

168

Fives can

- coordinate eyes and hands well
- play well with a friend

Geoboards

Make a few geoboards for your Fives to use. (Directions for making geoboards are on page 195.) Put the boards out on a low shelf in the Small-Muscle Center. Place a container full of colorful rubber bands next to each board.

Show interested children how to stretch a rubber band around a few nails to make a shape. Then let each child use the board and rubber bands in her own creative way. Add geoboard patterns for children to follow as they play.

This pattern looks like a rubber star, Jasmine!
How many rubber bands did you have to use?

 indoors   4–20 minutes   1–2 Fives per board

169

Fives can

- string small beads

Stringing Buttons

Collect many colorful buttons of different sizes and shapes. Ask the children's parents to help add buttons to the collection. Store the buttons in one or more plastic containers with lids so that they do not spill out. Add some sturdy shoelaces that will fit through the holes in the buttons. Allow children to string these in their own creative ways.

See if children discover that the buttons can be strung so they look different on the string. For example, if a button is strung using two of its holes it will lie flat.

Which buttons do you like best, Charles?
Why do you like them?

Keep these materials in a stringing buttons activity box.

 indoors   3–15 minutes   # 1–6 Fives

Fives can

■ begin to tie simple knots

Tying Knots with Help

Show your Fives how to tie a simple knot as you name the steps. Then give them lots of chances to practice. You can

■ provide thick, brightly colored cord so that they can make knot bracelets

■ have short ribbons in the pretend play area to tie on dolls' clothes and into hair

■ let children tie the knots when you are binding the books they make

■ let children add strings or ribbons to packages they wrap

Encourage the children to work with a friend when tying knots. One child can hold the string in place so that the other can make the next knot.

 in or out 1–6 minutes 1–10 Fives

Fives can

■ stack many inch cubes to make towers

Inch-Cube Towers

Put out a set of inch cubes in a labeled dishpan or box. Set the box out on a low open shelf or table for the children to choose freely. Be sure that the space for playing with the cubes has a steady surface. As they play with the cubes, see how many cubes they can stack to make a tower. Count the cubes with the child as he balances them. Talk about the different ways children use the small blocks.

Henry, what are you making with the cubes?
A tiny bridge? That bridge is getting taller!
Oh! It collapsed! Now what will you do?

Encourage children to make many creative cube designs.

 indoors 2–15 minutes 1–3 Fives per set

172

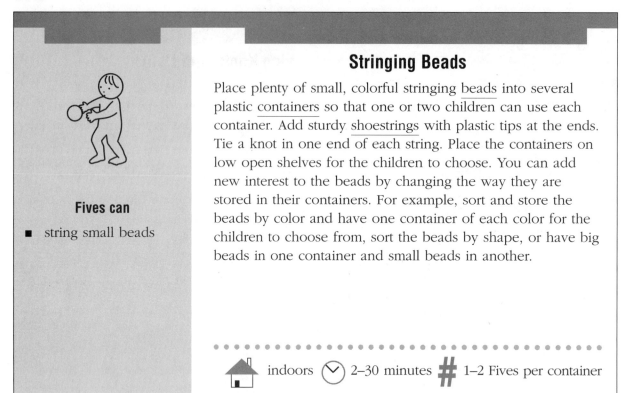

Fives can

- string small beads

Stringing Beads

Place plenty of small, colorful stringing beads into several plastic containers so that one or two children can use each container. Add sturdy shoestrings with plastic tips at the ends. Tie a knot in one end of each string. Place the containers on low open shelves for the children to choose. You can add new interest to the beads by changing the way they are stored in their containers. For example, sort and store the beads by color and have one container of each color for the children to choose from, sort the beads by shape, or have big beads in one container and small beads in another.

indoors   2–30 minutes   1–2 Fives per container

173

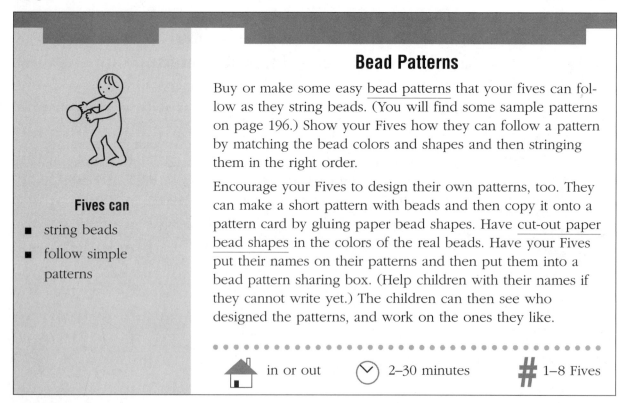

Fives can

- string beads
- follow simple patterns

Bead Patterns

Buy or make some easy bead patterns that your fives can follow as they string beads. (You will find some sample patterns on page 196.) Show your Fives how they can follow a pattern by matching the bead colors and shapes and then stringing them in the right order.

Encourage your Fives to design their own patterns, too. They can make a short pattern with beads and then copy it onto a pattern card by gluing paper bead shapes. Have cut-out paper bead shapes in the colors of the real beads. Have your Fives put their names on their patterns and then put them into a bead pattern sharing box. (Help children with their names if they cannot write yet.) The children can then see who designed the patterns, and work on the ones they like.

in or out   2–30 minutes   1–8 Fives

174

Fives can

■ do puzzles well

Puzzle Place

Set up a place in the Small-Muscle Center just for puzzles. (You'll find ideas for the puzzle place on page 197.) Put out a few easy puzzles and a few hard ones on a low shelf where the children can easily see what the puzzles look like. Keep the rest stored away. Change the puzzles often. Be sure to have a low table or clear floor space, out of traffic, for putting puzzles together.

Observe children doing puzzles and give help if a child wishes. Use words to help the child see the next step, or work together to finish the puzzle. Do not make a fuss if children do not finish a puzzle. Be sure puzzles are put away properly.

I bet we can work together to finish this puzzle, Aaron. I'll do a piece, and then you do a piece.

 in or out   2–20 minutes   1–7 Fives

175

Fives can

■ do puzzles with more than four pieces

Floor Puzzles

Place one or two large floor puzzles on the puzzle shelf for Fives to choose. Show children a clear floor space nearby that is out of traffic so that they can work on these big puzzles by themselves or with a friend.

The children can make their own floor puzzles by gluing or drawing big pictures onto large sheets of cardboard and then cutting each one into five or six pieces. You may have to help with the cutting.

Try outlining your Fives onto sheets of cardboard. They can color the outline the way they want. Then you can cut these pictures into a puzzle. (Be sure to let each child choose whether to cut their picture up into a puzzle or to leave it whole.) Add these puzzles to the puzzle place.

 in or out   2–10 minutes   1–4 Fives

Fives can

■ control hand and finger movements quite well

Peel-and-Stick Sticker Fun

Have lots of different colorful peel-and-stick stickers that your Fives can peel off by themselves and stick onto things they want to decorate. Keep these in a container with paper for the children to use when they are interested.

Show them how to bend the backing of the sticker so that an edge comes loose. Then they can grasp the sticker and pull it off.

Marcia, what are you making with all these bird stickers?

You can look for free stickers that come in junk mail. Ask parents to bring in any stickers they find, too.

 in or out   2–12 minutes   1–6 Fives

177

Fives can

■ coordinate eyes and hands well

Lock Boards

Make several lock boards for your Fives to use. (You will find directions for making lock boards on page 198.) Have different-sized locks with their keys on the boards. Be sure the keys to the locks are securely attached to the boards. Also try easy-to-use combination locks with numbers or letters that must be lined up. Write the combinations onto the board next to the lock.

Show children how to work the different kinds of locks and then let them try on their own. Talk about why people use locks and give help as children ask.

You can't find the right key for that lock, can you, Jimmy? Try each key, one at a time, until you find the right one. Which one do you want to try first?

 in or out   3–15 minutes   1–2 Fives per board

178

Fives can

- use fingers and hands quite well

- experiment and talk about their discoveries

Tweezers-and-Tongs Activity Box

Collect different-sized tweezers and tongs, from small to quite large. Place them in a container with many objects of different sizes. Include tiny dried beans, small plastic toys, wooden 1" blocks, and beads of various sizes. Let the children experiment using the tweezers and tongs to pick up the objects. Talk about which tools are easiest to use to pick up the different objects.

Dick, what things are easiest to pick up with the biggest tongs?

Let children use these tools for real activities, too. For example, have tweezers in the Science and Nature Center to pick up small pebbles or leaves.

 in or out   3–20 minutes   1–3 Fives

179

Fives can

- trace around shapes

Tracing with Stencils

Provide stencils of various shapes for your Fives to trace around. Have paper and pencils or watercolor markers for the children to use as they trace. Keep these things together in a stencil activity box or in a container on a low shelf in the Writing or Art Center. Then the children can choose this activity when they wish.

Talk with the children about the patterns and designs they make using the stencils.

You traced lots of different shapes on top of each other, didn't you, Jeremy? What did you trace first?

 in or out   2–15 minutes   1–6 Fives

Activities for Physical Development

Fives can

- coordinate eyesand hands well

- control hand and finger movements quite well

Marble-Rolling Game

Place eight to ten large marbles in a plastic container or box with a large cutout paper or cloth circle. Put the circle out on a flat surface. Show children how to roll the marble gently so that it rolls onto the circle and then stops before it goes out. Let the children play to see how many marbles they can get onto the circle. Children can play this game with a friend— one child can roll the marble and the friend can catch those that go too far.

How gently can you roll the marble, LaMont?
Great! It stopped so near the circle.

It's best for children to play the marble-rolling game in a corner so that marbles that go too far can be caught by the walls or furniture.

 in or out   2–20 minutes   1–4 Fives

181

Fives can

- print own name, but not always clearly

Practice Printing Names

Give your Fives many chances to practice printing their own names. Write their names clearly for them to see. Then encourage them to copy what you have written when they are interested.

Encourage children to write their own names on waiting lists, on their own artwork, on masking tape to show things that belong to them, on signs, and in chalk on a sidewalk.

Have sheets of paper with children's names for children to use when practicing.

 in or out   3–10 minutes   1–20 Fives

182

Fives can

- control hand and finger movements quite well

- play well with another child

Rolling Small Cars

Have a box of small toy cars on a shelf in the Small-Muscle Center for the children to use to play a rolling game. Show them how they can sit at a table and gently roll a car across the table so that it goes close to the opposite edge without rolling off.

Encourage friends to play together, taking turns rolling and catching.

Your Fives can try these games, too:
- Roll the cars into different-sized boxes.
- Roll the cars so that they stop close to a masking-tape line.
- Roll the cars so that they stop on a paper parking lot.

 in or out   2–20 minutes   1–6 Fives

183

Fives can

- string small beads

- want to take home things they have made

Beads-and-Strings Activity Box

Make a beads and strings activity box that has beads of different kinds and other objects with holes, such as cut-up plastic straws or cardboard shapes with holes punched in them. Add strings with a knot on one end and a firm masking-tape tip or covered wire for stringing. Do not use food, such as macaroni or cereal; it cannot be kept sanitary, and the children may want to eat it.

Let the children string things in their own creative ways. Whenever possible, let them keep their creations.

You put just a few things on your string, Sabrina. How did you choose what to use?

 in or out   3–20 minutes    1–4 Fives per box

Fives can

- string small beads

Making Jewelry Kids Can Keep

Make a jewelry-making activity box that has big darning needles, sturdy yarn, and things to string. Show children how to thread a needle and tie a big knot at one end. You may have to tie a sturdy object at the end of the yarn so that things do not fall off as the child works. Show children how to gently push the needle through the things they want to string. When done, you can help the child tie the string to make a necklace or bracelet. Try these things to string:

- colorful fall leaves
- aluminum foil scraps
- buttons
- plastic foam peanuts or disks
- cardboard scraps the children have decorated

 in or out   5–30 minutes   1–8 Fives

185

Fives can

- use pencils and crayons quite well

Tracing Paper Fun

Provide tracing paper and crayons or watercolor markers for your Fives to use. Show them how they can put flat things under the paper and see the outline. To make tracing easier, show the children how they can hold the paper in place with masking tape.

Allow children to use the tracing paper freely. They may want to try to trace a picture they created, their names, other words and letters, shapes, or even pretty leaves. Encourage children to experiment to find out what can be traced.

Where did you find the leaf you are tracing, Brittany?
It looks like a maple leaf.

 in or out   3–20 minutes   1–8 Fives

186

Fives can
- catch a bounced ball

Bounce and Catch Little Balls

Have a collection of colorful 1" bouncy balls for your Fives to bounce and catch. Show the children how they can sit on the floor, drop the ball, and then catch it as it bounces. Hard floors are better for bouncing than carpeted floors, and this game is best in a corner where the balls will be less likely to roll away. Here are some challenges for your Fives to try:
- Bounce the ball and clap before catching it.
- Drop the ball so that it lands in a small box or can.
- Bounce the ball and pick up a jack before catching the ball.

Encourage your Fives to think of other creative ways to bounce and catch the little balls.

 in or out   2–15 minutes   1–8 Fives

187

Fives can
- do puzzles well
- cooperate with friends

Jigsaw Puzzles

Place two or three 25- to 100-piece jigsaw puzzles on the puzzle shelf for Fives to choose. Start with puzzles that have fewer pieces and offer harder puzzles as children become more able to handle the challenge. Have a low table nearby where children can work on these for more than one day without being disturbed. Tell children that these puzzles can be worked on with friends until they are finished.

Show children how to begin by finding all the pieces that have a straight edge to make the puzzle's border. Then they can use the rest of the pieces to fill in the center. Show them how to look at the picture on the box to see where different colors go.

 indoors   2–20 minutes   1–4 Fives

188

Fives can

- coordinate hand and arm movements quite well

- use simple tools

Pencil Sharpening

Put up a wall-mounted <u>pencil sharpener</u> where children can reach. Be sure that it is <u>not</u> where people will bump into it. Introduce this tool to the children, talking about safety and proper use. Encourage children to sharpen pencils as needed.

Our pencil points are really worn down, Debby.
Would you like to sharpen them this morning?

Show children how to empty the wood shavings from the sharpener. Talk with the children about the inner parts of the sharpener and what they do.

Have small <u>hand-held pencil sharpeners</u> for children to use, too. Talk about which type of sharpener is easier to use.

 indoors 2–5 minutes 1 Five at a time

189

Fives can

- control hand and finger movements quite well

Fishing Game

Make a magnetic fishing game with several fishing rods and lots of pretend fish. Tie a sturdy <u>18" string</u> to the end of a <u>12" dowel</u>. Attach a <u>magnet</u> to the other end of the string. Cut out large fish from colorful <u>construction paper</u> or <u>cardboard</u> and attach a metal <u>paper clip</u> at the mouth of each. Show your Fives how to put the fish on the floor, hold the rod steady, move it gently until the magnet attracts the paper clip, and then bring in the fish. Allow the children to experiment in their own ways to be successful fishermen. Talk about the different things they do to catch the fish.

Emma caught a fish! She held the line with her hand to keep it steady.
Show me how you caught so many fish, Paul.

 in or out 2–15 minutes 1 Five per rod

190

Fives can

- safely cut with a sharp kitchen knife when supervised
- follow directions for cooking

Practice with Knives

Set up and closely supervise many cooking experiences, such as those shown on page 199, in which children cut things up themselves. Use sharp paring knives with sturdy handles. Place red plastic tape on the upper side of the handle and tell children to be sure they can see the tape when cutting. Be sure children are never crowded and work in a place that is out of traffic when cutting. Pre-cut hard foods so that each piece has a flat side. Explain serious cutting rules to all children:

- Watch what you are cutting. Keep your fingers safe.
- Use a cutting board. Hold the food with its flat side down so that it does not wobble.
- Use knives only when an adult is nearby.
- Keep away from others who are cutting.

 in or out   5–20 minutes   1–5 Fives

191

Fives can

- use more complex put-together toys

More Complex Put-Together Toys

Add to the Small-Muscle Center more complex put-together toys. Let your Fives experiment freely with them. Provide help if needed with toys such as the following:

- colorful plastic gears
- Lincoln Logs®
- Tinkertoys®
- blocks with grooves to put together and roll marbles
- plastic or metal construction sets with parts that bolt or screw together

 indoors   5–30 minutes   1–6 Fives

192

Fives can

- control hand and finger movements quite well

Pickup Sticks

Place a set of pickup sticks in the Small-Muscle Center. Show your Fives how to hold up a small bunch of the sticks and then drop them. Show them how to pick up as many sticks as they can without moving any others. Help each child learn to first pick up the sticks that are not near any others and then to carefully try to pick up those that are touching.

Which stick will you pick up first, Thomas?
Look carefully. Which one is far from the others?

Don't worry if children move the sticks as they play. The real challenge is for the children to see how careful they can be.

 in or out   3–15 minutes   1–2 Fives per set

193

Fives can

- use simple tools

Using Classroom Tools

Make classroom tools, such as the tape dispenser, stapler, staple remover, scissors, or cassette player available for your Fives to use. Explain how each is used and stored. Emphasize any safety rules that are required.

Encourage children to help to figure out any problems that may come up when these tools are being used.

Janice says the stapler isn't working.
Does anyone know why?
Do you know how to check to be sure there are staples in it?

 indoors   2–10 minutes   1–10 Fives

194

Fives can

- use and enjoy simple computer or video games

Computer Games

If you wish to have computer or video games, set them up in a quiet out-of-the-way space where one or two children can play. Teach children how to use the equipment carefully. Allow children to use computers for no more than 15 to 20 minutes at a time. If necessary, use a timer to remind children to move on to another activity.

Choose computer/video games for your Fives that are challenging but not too difficult. Be sure the games help children learn in other areas while encouraging small-muscle skills.

 indoors   1–20 minutes   1–2 Fives

195

Fives can

- lace shoes
- begin to tie shoes

Shoe-Tying Activity Box

Make a shoe-tying activity box containing a pair of clean, low-cost sneakers and lots of brightly colored shoelaces. Have colorful laces with sparkles or pretty designs and sturdy tips for the children to use. Be sure the children know how to lace. Then teach your Fives to tie.

To teach children to tie, first do all the steps to tying as they watch. Talk about what you are doing for each step. Next, let the child do the last step. Once he can do it, see if he can do the last two steps, and so on until he can do all steps. Leave the activity box on a low shelf for children to practice when they wish.

Watch carefully, Byron. I cross the two loops.
Now can you take over?

 in or out   3–15 minutes   1–2 Fives per box

196

Fives can

- control hand and finger movements quite well
- use some real tools

Plumber's Pipes and Wrenches

Go on a pipe hunt with the children. Look for pipes under sinks and in other likely places. See if there are any pipes outdoors that go into the building. Talk about how pipes carry water, natural gas, heat, and other things.

Place a collection of plastic plumber's pipes in a large box that has a picture/word label. Include pipes of different sizes. Have pipes that are curved, straight, and flexible. Add several lightweight wrenches. Show the children how to use the wrenches to connect or loosen pipes. Let them use these materials freely. Talk with children about the work plumbers do.

Children can pour water through the pipes to see if their connections are tight, or they can roll marbles or small balls or cars through the pipes.

 in or out   5–30 minutes   1–4 Fives

197

Fives can

- control hand and finger movements quite well
- use some real tools
- do long-term projects

Simple Sewing

Plan very simple sewing projects, such as sewing a dress for a doll or a small treasures bag. (Directions for these two projects are on pages 201–203.) Provide large needles, thread, scissors, and cloth for the children to use. Then help them learn to fold, thread needles, cut, and do a simple running stitch. If necessary, have the child staple the edges that need sewing so that they stay together. Staples can then later be removed. Supervise well and talk about safety rules for using needles and scissors.

Help children understand how valuable their creations are even if they might not look perfect. Since this is a long-term project, have a safe place to store the child's work and encourage children to continue work on their projects.

 in or out   10–30 minutes per day   1–6 Fives

Fives can

- control hand and finger movements quite well

Spinning Tops

Make a tops activity box for the Small-Muscle Center. Place tops of different sizes and colors, tops made of wood and of plastic, and dreidels in a labeled container. Show interested Fives how to hold the top and give it a spin while releasing it onto a smooth surface. Allow children to practice as much as they like. Explain that it takes lots of practice to make the top spin.

Show delight as the children think of their own ways to use the tops collection.

Amos, you are spinning the top on its side.
It went around very fast.
Zina, you lined all the tops up from big to small.

 in or out   1–15 minutes   # 1–3 Fives

Fives can

- control hand and finger movements quite well
- play simple games with others

Marble Game Activity Box

Make a marble game activity box for your Fives to use. Include 12 big marbles and a circle (2' across) cut out of plain fabric. Show your Fives how to spread the circle out on the floor in a quiet corner, place the smaller marbles in the center, and then roll a large marble into the group of smaller ones to scatter them. Then they can keep rolling the large marble to hit the smaller marbles to knock them out of the circle.

One child can play alone or two friends can take turns. Point out that the way to do well at the game is to carefully aim the big marble, rather than to just roll hard. Then let children experiment with rolling and aiming in their own ways.

You hit it, Adele! You aimed very carefully.
Which marble will you try for next?

 in or out   2–15 minutes   # 1–3 Fives

200

Fives can

- wrap and unwrap things
- play cooperatively with friends in a small group

Wrapping Practice

Have pretty, leftover gift wrap and tape for children to use to practice wrapping things. Encourage them to wrap up creations that they have made to take home or to wrap make-believe presents as they take part in pretend play.

Show children how to work with a friend to hold the paper in place so that the tape can be put on.

You're having trouble holding the paper, Kenneth. How can you solve this problem?

Children can color plain paper to make their own gift wrap to use, too.

 in or out   2–15 minutes   1–2 Fives

201

Fives can

- control hand and finger movements
- follow easy directions
- do long-term projects

Telephone-Wire Jewelry

Ask your local telephone company for leftover colorful strands of plastic-covered wire. These are usually in a big cable. Just cut off the plastic covering of the cable and pull out the brightly colored wires. Cut the wires into 6" to 12" pieces and place them in a container for the children to use. Show your Fives how to twist the wires together to make rings, bracelets, necklaces, and anything else they can think of.

Daniel, you have blue wire with white stripes and some yellow wire. What do you plan to make with it?

Provide a safe, organized place for the children to store work in progress. Encourage children to return to their work at another time.

 in or out   2–30 minutes per day   1–8 Fives

202

Fives can

- control hand and finger movements
- follow easy directions
- do long-term projects

Embroidery

Have large darning needles, colorful yarn or embroidery thread, a loosely woven, light-colored material (such as burlap), and embroidery frames for the children to use to create a stitched picture. First have the children make a simple line drawing on the material with a colored marker. Then help them secure the material onto the embroidery frame. Show them how to outline their picture with stitches—help them thread the needle, make a knot in the yarn, and go up and down through the fabric to sew. Remind children to keep the material tight in the frame and to avoid going around the edges of the frame when sewing.

Have a safe place for children to store projects so that they can work on them for several days.

 in or out   10–30 minutes per day   1–6 Fives

203

Fives can

- control hand and finger movements quite well
- follow directions

Stringing Tiny Decorative Beads

Have a collection of tiny decorative beads for your Fives to string onto very thin wire. The beads and wire may be found at hobby stores or in the crafts departments of variety stores. Put the beads into shallow containers that will not tip over easily. Show children how to slip the first bead onto the wire and twist the end of the wire around it so the first bead will keep the rest from slipping off.

Let children string the beads in their own creative ways and keep what they made. Encourage children to store works requiring more time and continue them later. Talk about the patterns and colors of their creations.

I see you picked out all red and yellow beads, Don. What are you planning to make?

 in or out   5–30 minutes per day   1–10 Fives

204

Fives can

- cooperate with a friend
- control hand and finger movements quite well

Building Simple Card Houses

Show children how to make a simple card house out of three playing cards. Have interested children work with friends to balance one card on top of two others that are held up vertically. Provide a whole deck of cards so that children can see how big a house they can make.

Let children experiment to find out how to place the cards to make a more sturdy house. Talk with the children about their experiments with fragile structures.

Andrew, you and Jenny used three cards to make a triangular base for your house. How did that work out? Was the house sturdy?

 indoors   4–30 minutes   # 1–10 Fives

205

Fives can

- copy folding a paper square on a diagonal
- follow more complex directions

Simple Origami (Japanese Paper Folding)

Practice doing a few simple origami projects so that you can help your Fives learn to do them, too. (Directions for making a Japanese paper doll and a paper glider are on pages 204–205.) Use large paper squares. Help children practice making very straight folds and pressing down along fold lines to make them sharp. Show the children how to do each project one step at a time. Show them the illustrated folding instructions you are following if possible.

Encourage children to try the paper folding over and over. Once they have mastered a paper-folding project, encourage them to teach it to their friends.

Find out how to make newspaper hats, too, and teach the project to interested children.

 in or out   5–30 minutes   # 1–4 Fives

How to Make Geoboards

1. Cut a piece of 1" thick plywood into 7" squares. Sand all edges and corners until they are smooth.
2. Follow the pattern below and hammer 25 nails ½" deep into each plywood square. Use sturdy 2" nails with smooth, flat heads.

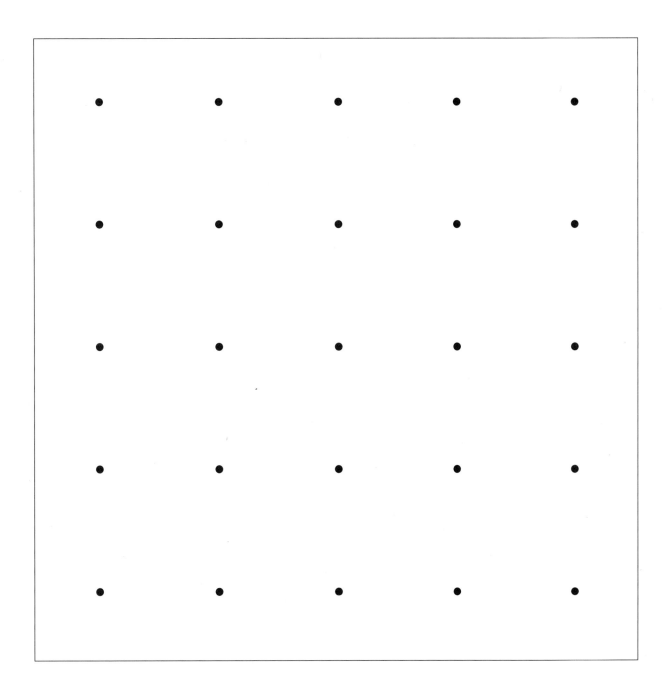

If you don't have any plywood, hammer a few nails into a stump or big log outside. Have fun making designs on it with rubber bands.

Sample Bead Patterns

1. Copy bead patterns onto cardboard cards. Use the real beads you have as a guide for drawing.

2. Color beads to match the beads you have. Use only two, three, or four colors in one pattern. Have some patterns with just one color, too.

3. Show children how to copy the pattern by first putting beads on the cards, then stringing them in the right order.

4. Show children how to string the pattern again.

5. Try making your own patterns, too.

6. Encourage children to use two patterns at one time. They can string one of the patterns, then the other and repeat the two designs in their own way.

7. Be sure to encourage Fives to make up their own patterns, too.

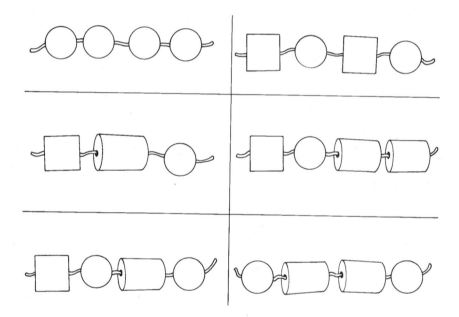

Puzzle Place Ideas

- Before you put puzzles out on the shelf, mark the back of each piece with the puzzle's name. Then you can tell which pieces go with each puzzle.

- Set puzzles out on a low open shelf. Make sure the shelf is not cluttered with other toys and that the puzzles are not piled on top of each other.

- If you have problems with pieces getting mixed up or lost, store each puzzle on its own tray. Be sure the tray is big enough to hold the puzzle frame and all the pieces when they have been dumped out. Show the children how to keep the pieces on the tray as they work.

- Be sure to have a flat, open space near the open shelf where the children can work on their puzzles. A low table or rug out of traffic works best.

- Have several different kinds of puzzles for the children to do. Choose puzzles that have different textures and numbers, colors, and sizes of pieces. Be sure children are challenged by the puzzles they try.

- Change the puzzles you have out for the children to choose. Do not keep all the puzzles out at the same time.

- Encourage children to finish one puzzle before starting another, but do not make a fuss if a child becomes frustrated and does not want to go on. Instead, work together to put the puzzle away, helping the child do as much as he can by himself.

- Help children learn how to do harder puzzles. Teach them the different ways to solve the various types of puzzles.

- Puzzle racks make it hard for children to see and choose puzzles. Use them for storing extra puzzles that are not out for the children to use. Separate easy from hard puzzles and label each rack.

- Puzzles for Fives should:
  - have 10–30 pieces; jigsaw puzzles with 25–100 pieces can be used with older Fives
  - be colorful
  - be interesting for children to look at
  - be sturdy
  - be of different textures (wood, rubber, plastic, thick cardboard)
  - be challenging but not too difficult

Lock Board Ideas

1. Hammer two or three very large, sturdy staples into a board. You can get these at a hardware store. Or use hasps that open and close.

2. Put pictures under the hasps so that the children will see them if they get the lock open. A small unbreakable mirror under one hasp is also fun.

3. Put different-sized padlocks on the staples or hasps.

4. Put the keys to the padlocks on a key ring. Attach the ring to a sturdy string and fasten it to the board so that the keys won't get lost.

Put the Lock Board in a safe place where it can't tip over, or nail it to the end of a bookcase or cabinet where the children can easily reach and play with it.

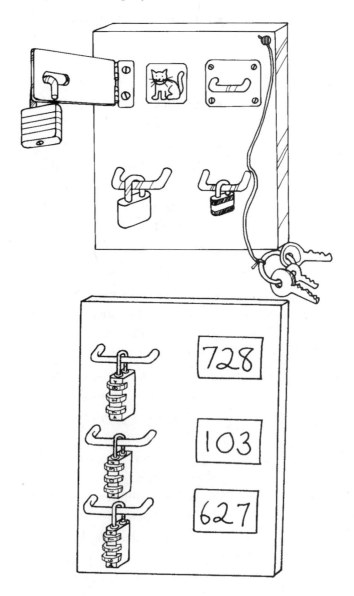

Recipes to Use for Cutting Practice

Fruit Salad

1. Copy this recipe on large pieces of cardboard to make recipe cards.
2. Put each card in a row on a low table or counter from left to right.
3. Put each bowl of fruit in front of its card.
4. Have each child start on the left and take the right amount of fruit to put into his own cup.

FRUIT SALAD

2 apple slices ①

3 banana slices ②

3 pineapple chunks ③

2 orange sections ④

4 raisins ⑤

Stir and eat. ⑥

This recipe is from *Cook and Learn* by Beverly Veitch and Thelma Harms. Menlo Park, CA: Addison-Wesley Publishing Company, 1981.

Vegetable Soup

1. Ask each child to bring a raw vegetable from home.
2. Talk with the children about the vegetables they brought in.
3. Set up an area where the children can safely wash, peel, and cut up all the vegetables. Be sure the area is uncrowded, and the cutting surfaces have been sanitized. Use a waiting list if children are worried about getting a turn.
4. Provide cutting boards and sharp paring knives for the children to use. Supervise cutting carefully.
5. Pre-cut hard vegetables, such as potatoes or carrots, so that each large piece has a flat side. Help children to remember to place the flat side down so that it does not wobble.
6. Have children place all their cut-up vegetables into a crock pot. Add a large can of tomato juice. Add chicken or beef stock, too, if you wish.
7. Plug the crock pot in and set it on the high setting. Talk about how the soup smells as it cooks.
8. Eat the homemade soup for a snack when the vegetables are soft.

Applesauce

1. Let each child help peel, core, and cut up apples into small pieces. Use sharp paring knives and cutting boards.
2. Have the children put all the apple pieces into a crock pot. Then they can add enough water to cover the apples one fourth of the way. You may add a little cinnamon or nutmeg.
3. Slowly cook the apples until they cook down into applesauce. Children can mash the cooked apples to make the sauce smoother.
4. Eat the applesauce at snack time.

Sewing a Simple Dress for a Doll

1. Fold a rectangular piece of cloth in half.

2. Place a doll on the cloth so that its neck is on the fold.

3. Draw lines along the sides of the doll at least 2" from the doll's body. (Lines can be closer to the sides of smaller dolls—the point is to have enough cloth to fit around the doll once it has been sewn.)

4. Cut along the lines.

5. Mark where the doll's head is so that you can cut a hole in the fold for the doll's head to go through. Cut the hole.

6. Turn the dress inside out. Then begin at the bottom of the dress and sew up each side. Stop before reaching the top to leave holes for the arms.

7. Turn the dress right side out. Put it on the doll. Tie the dress around the doll's waist with a ribbon or a strip of cloth.

Activities for Physical Development

Sewing a Small Treasures Bag

1. Fold a 10" × 20" piece of cloth in half. Fold the cloth so that it is inside out.

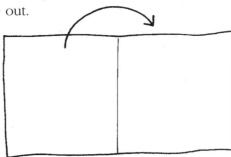

2. Sew up the two sides, leaving the top open. Then turn the bag right side out.

3. Cut four to six evenly placed holes in the cloth about 1" from the top.

4. Weave a ribbon or a long narrow strip of cloth through the holes. Tie the ends of the ribbon together.

5. To close the treasures bag, pull the ribbon tight, gathering the top.

Simple Origami (Japanese Paper Folding)

Note: The folding required for origami is easier when children can use larger pieces of paper than are usually available for this craft. Use a paper cutter to cut off the edge of 8½" × 11" paper so you have 8½" by 8½" squares.

Japanese Doll

1. Use a square piece of paper. Fold it in half once and once again so that it is creased into quarters. Then unfold it.
2. Take each corner and fold it into the center. Crease the folds so that they are sharp.
3. Turn the paper over. Fold the four new corners into the center, creasing folds so that they are sharp.
4. Turn the paper over. Fold the corners into the center, creasing the folds again. You may want to tape down the corners so that they remain fixed in the center.
5. Turn the paper over. Choose one of the four diamonds to be a face for the doll. Draw the face and place the face diamond at the top.
6. To make the doll's arms and legs, put your finger under the center tip of the other three diamonds and push under, away from the center, to open up the diamond and then flatten it down into a rectangle. Color the doll to make clothes.

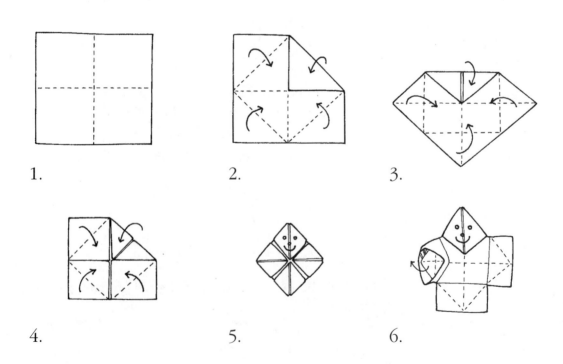

1.   2.   3.

4.   5.   6.

Paper Glider

1. Fold a paper rectangle in half lengthwise. "Iron" the fold with your fingers.
2. Open the paper and draw a fold line down the center.
3. Fold bottom corner up to touch center line. Repeat with other corner. Press folds.
4. Fold up outside edge to touch center line. Repeat with other side. Press folds.
5. Again, fold up outside edge to touch center line. Press fold. Repeat with other side.
6. Fold in half backwards. Press folds down tight.
7. Open sides to make wings.
8. Hold glider by underside and fly!

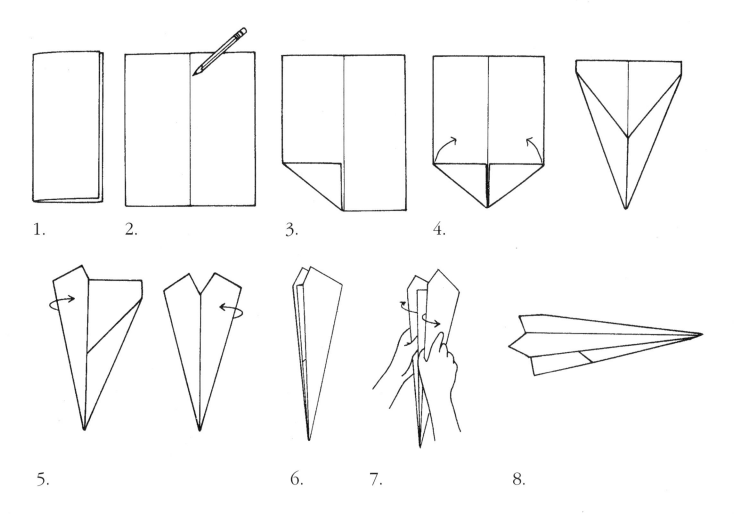

1.   2.   3.   4.

5.   6.   7.   8.

Activities for Physical Development

Active Learning
for Fives

Creative Activities

Index

of Creative Activities

Here's Why

Art and carpentry, blocks, dramatic or pretend play, and music give Fives chances to express their ideas using interesting materials that show clear results. Fives need to have many creative materials every day to use in their own ways so that their skills can develop.

Drawing and talking are two ways a young child develops understanding. Both are ways to show what the five-year-old knows and is interested in. It takes a lot of practice before a child learns to control his hands and focus his ideas well enough to draw things we can all see. When children are allowed the time and practice to teach themselves to draw, they benefit most. Fives are usually able to draw and paint many recognizable things—people, houses, animals. They will also want to tell you about their pictures. Many other art materials challenge and delight them, including clay, fabric, and yarn. Fives enjoy working on some group art projects as well as doing their own work. They like to make real things they see around them, such as candles and flags, as well as things that give them the freedom to imagine. Display the drawings and other artwork Fives make so that they know how proud you are of what they can do by themselves.

Creative activities besides art are also important. Both music and dramatic play help to build memory for words and ideas. Fives love to sing along with familiar songs. They also enjoy pretending about the things they see happening around them, as well as things they hear and read about. Pretend play materials are needed both indoors and outdoors for active Fives.

When Fives play with blocks, they become aware of differences in shape, size, and weight. They learn about balance as they build a big tower. Block play can also be a form of pretend play. Block play is a good way to learn how to share and how to play near others without bothering them.

Fives enjoy all the creative activities. They like the fact that they can do things themselves. They also enjoy the messy, active, noisy way the arts work. You can help them learn many other skills as they work with the activities in this section.

Materials and Notes

Art and Carpentry

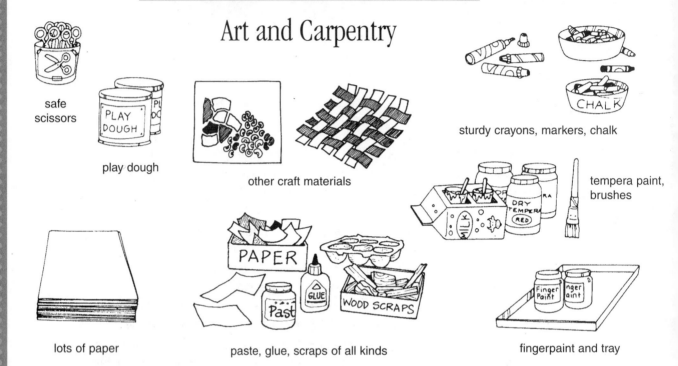

safe scissors

play dough

other craft materials

sturdy crayons, markers, chalk

tempera paint, brushes

lots of paper

paste, glue, scraps of all kinds

fingerpaint and tray

- Make sure all the art materials you use are nontoxic.

- Have art activities out for Fives to use every day.

- Put up lots of the children's artwork to look at. Change the display often.

- Encourage parents to hang up their children's work at home. Let them know that Fives enjoy being respected for what they can do. Drawing also gets children ready for writing later on.

- Offer Fives lots of art experiences, such as carpentry, mosaic, weaving, clay, and so on.

- Let the children use art materials in their own way. Do not have Fives copy things you have made.

- Do not have Fives color in coloring books. Coloring does not help them develop drawing and thinking skills.

- Cover tables with newspaper or a heavy plastic dropcloth where watercolor markers, clay, glue, or other messy materials are being used.

- See Art Center Ideas on page 247 and recipes on page 260.

Activity Checklist

Art and Carpentry

Art for Fives includes providing things for them to look at, as well as art materials for them to use. Interest in handling art materials usually is well established by age five. This is the time the child can use drawing materials, finger paints, and play dough with greater control. Fives enjoy scribbling and drawing designs but also start to draw recognizable faces, shapes, and pictures of other things they are interested in. They also enjoy new challenges using new materials, such as sewing, carpentry, and wood/glue sculpture.

Check for each age group

	60–66 months	66–72 months
1. A variety of drawing materials are available daily for free choice.	❐	❐
2. Some additional nontoxic art materials are out daily for independent use, including several colors of paint, play dough, or pasting.	❐	❐
3. Art materials are organized for easy, independent use by the children.	❐	❐
4. A low, sturdy table and easel are used for art activities.	❐	❐
5. Children are offered art materials but are not forced to use them. Alternate activities are available.	❐	❐
6. Children are encouraged to handle and explore materials and create as they wish.	❐	❐
7. Art materials and activities that require more adult help and supervision are often available, such as potters' clay, carpentry, weaving, sandcasting, and finger painting.	❐	❐
8. Adults and children talk about the shape, color, and textures of things and about what the child is making with the art materials.	❐	❐
9. Children help with cleanup and care of materials.	❐	❐
10. Children's artwork is displayed where children can see it.	❐	❐
11. The art display is changed often.	❐	❐
12. Artwork is sent home with each child.	❐	❐

206

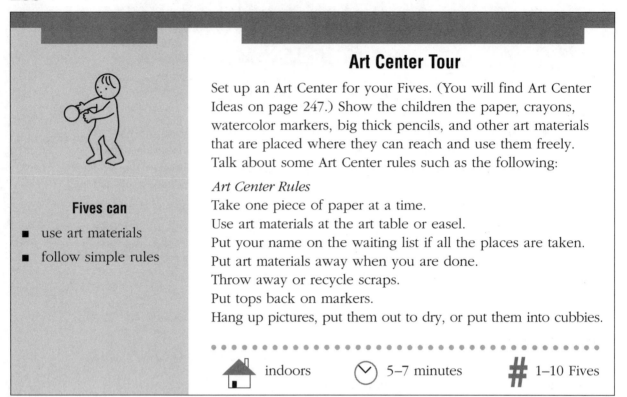

Fives can

- use art materials
- follow simple rules

Art Center Tour

Set up an Art Center for your Fives. (You will find Art Center Ideas on page 247.) Show the children the paper, crayons, watercolor markers, big thick pencils, and other art materials that are placed where they can reach and use them freely. Talk about some Art Center rules such as the following:

Art Center Rules
Take one piece of paper at a time.
Use art materials at the art table or easel.
Put your name on the waiting list if all the places are taken.
Put art materials away when you are done.
Throw away or recycle scraps.
Put tops back on markers.
Hang up pictures, put them out to dry, or put them into cubbies.

indoors   5–7 minutes   # 1–10 Fives

207

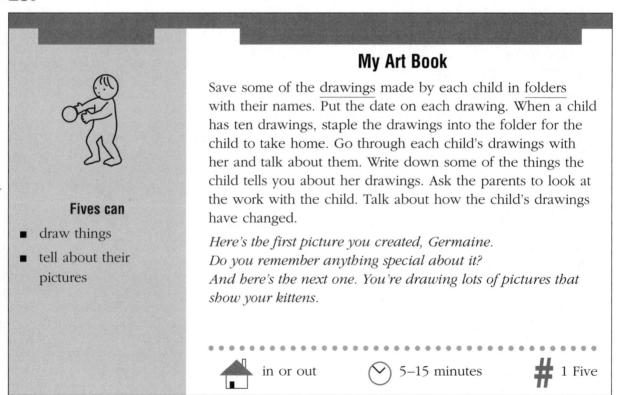

Fives can

- draw things
- tell about their pictures

My Art Book

Save some of the drawings made by each child in folders with their names. Put the date on each drawing. When a child has ten drawings, staple the drawings into the folder for the child to take home. Go through each child's drawings with her and talk about them. Write down some of the things the child tells you about her drawings. Ask the parents to look at the work with the child. Talk about how the child's drawings have changed.

Here's the first picture you created, Germaine.
Do you remember anything special about it?
And here's the next one. You're drawing lots of pictures that show your kittens.

in or out   5–15 minutes   # 1 Five

208

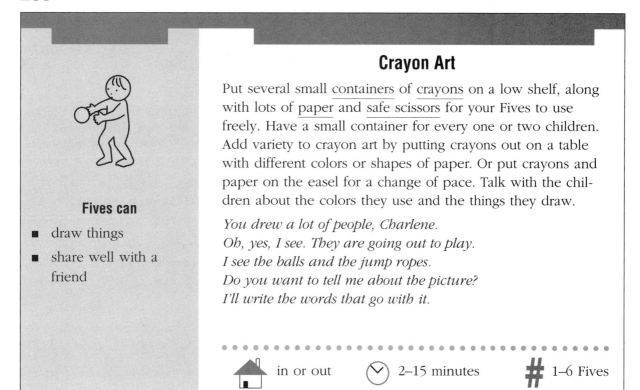

Fives can

- draw things
- share well with a friend

Crayon Art

Put several small containers of crayons on a low shelf, along with lots of paper and safe scissors for your Fives to use freely. Have a small container for every one or two children. Add variety to crayon art by putting crayons out on a table with different colors or shapes of paper. Or put crayons and paper on the easel for a change of pace. Talk with the children about the colors they use and the things they draw.

You drew a lot of people, Charlene.
Oh, yes, I see. They are going out to play.
I see the balls and the jump ropes.
Do you want to tell me about the picture?
I'll write the words that go with it.

🏠 in or out   🕐 2–15 minutes   # 1–6 Fives

209

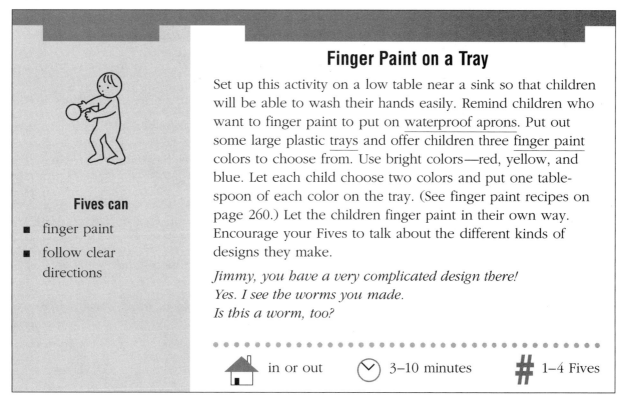

Fives can

- finger paint
- follow clear directions

Finger Paint on a Tray

Set up this activity on a low table near a sink so that children will be able to wash their hands easily. Remind children who want to finger paint to put on waterproof aprons. Put out some large plastic trays and offer children three finger paint colors to choose from. Use bright colors—red, yellow, and blue. Let each child choose two colors and put one tablespoon of each color on the tray. (See finger paint recipes on page 260.) Let the children finger paint in their own way. Encourage your Fives to talk about the different kinds of designs they make.

Jimmy, you have a very complicated design there!
Yes. I see the worms you made.
Is this a worm, too?

🏠 in or out   🕐 3–10 minutes   # 1–4 Fives

210

Fives can

- finger paint
- use hands gently

Finger Paint Prints

Have your Fives finger paint on a tray. Ask each child to tell you when she has made a design that she wants to print onto paper. When the child is ready, have her wash and dry her hands thoroughly. Then put her name on the back of a piece of paper, or have her write it if she wishes. Help her lay the front of the paper onto the paint, gently smooth her hands over the paper, and carefully lift it off. Hang up the print, or place it on a flat surface to dry.

Are you ready to make a print of your design now, Charlotte? OK. Let me know when you want to see how to do it.

Encourage children to do the process by themselves once they know how.

 in or out   5–10 minutes   1–4 Fives

211

Fives can

- do lots of artwork
- enjoy seeing their work

Art Gallery

Make special display spaces in the room for art galleries, where Fives can put their favorite artwork. Use a wall, the backs of toy shelves, or doors. Let the children know that they can choose what they want to put up. Have enough space for everyone to use. It's good to have a shelf or windowsill to display play dough or carpentry art.

Let children help hang up their work or choose where it should go. Help the children talk about what they have done so that they know you're interested.

Dennis, do you want to hang this in our art gallery? Where would you like it to go?

Also hang children's work in other places in the room where they can easily see it.

 indoors   1–3 minutes   1–2 Fives

212

Fives can

- use paints with a brush
- have ideas for artwork

Tempera Painting

Set up a low <u>easel</u> with <u>paper</u>, three or four colors of thick <u>paint</u> in <u>cups</u> that won't tip over, and one sturdy <u>brush</u> for each color. (You'll find paint recipes on page 260.) Have a place ready to dry paintings. Remind children to wipe the brushes on the side of the cup to keep paint from dripping, and to keep each brush in its own paint color. Have extra paint ready to replace mixed-up paints. Then let children paint freely. Talk about the colors and designs in their artwork.

Have painting with paper flat on a table, too. Try different sizes of brushes, from thin to thick, to add interest.

 in or out   5–10 minutes # 1–2 Fives

213

Fives can

- clean up after play
- work a clothespin

Hanging Pictures to Dry

Put up a low <u>clothesline</u> or <u>fishnet</u> where Fives can hang their artwork to dry. Have lots of <u>clothespins</u> ready. Show children how to bring wet pictures to the hanging place and get a clothespin. Then you can show them how to squeeze the clothespins open to hold the pictures in place. Be sure that children's names are on their pictures and that there is plenty of room so that pictures don't stick together. A wooden clothes-drying rack can also be used.

Let's check to see if your name is on the painting, Nathan.
You can work those clothespins very well.
How long do you think it will take your painting to dry?

 indoors   1–2 minutes # 1–2 Fives

214

Fives can

- talk about their artwork
- know that what they say can be written and read

Picture Talks

When a child finishes a picture, talk about it with him. Ask questions to see how much he will say. Ask him if he wants you to write down what he tells you and do so only if he wants you to. Enjoy the different kinds of talk you get from different children.

Tell me about your picture, Emile.
It's a monster?
How did you make your monster?
Would you like me to write down what you are telling me so that we can remember it?
You can write your name on it, too.

 in or out   1–3 minutes   1 child at a time

215

Fives can

- follow simple directions
- enjoy play dough

Play-Dough Fun

Have the children help you mix play dough. (See play-dough recipes on pages 261–263.) Before children help, get all the things you will need—flour, salt, oil, color, water, measuring cups, and a big unbreakable bowl. Have your Fives help you measure, pour, and mix. Make one color at a time. When it is done, give each child some dough to use at a table in his own way. See how many things the Fives do with the play dough using just their hands. Help the children remember how they made the play dough. A picture recipe like the one on page 261 can help them remember.

How did you make your play dough, Fred?
Yes, you followed a recipe. How much flour did you use?
What else did you use?

 in or out   10–20 minutes   1–6 Fives

216

Fives can

- draw some recognizable figures
- take care of materials

Watercolor Markers

Have several separate <u>containers</u> with thick and thin watercolor <u>markers</u> for Fives to use on their own. Let them use the markers on <u>paper</u> of different sizes, shapes, and textures. Remind your Fives to always replace the marker caps and not to press too hard. When children have finished their creations, talk with them about their work.

You're using the green marker on bumpy wallpaper, David.
You made a little face with the thin markers, Isabelle.
Tell me all about the picture you made.

 in or out   3–10 minutes   1–6 Fives

217

Fives can

- paste on the right side
- use different colors and textures

Paper Scraps Collage

Collect pretty <u>paper scraps</u> for your Fives to <u>paste</u> onto pieces of <u>paper</u>. Include scraps of construction paper, wallpaper, and gift wrap. Give each child a little paste in a paper cup to use with a stick. Let them paste the scraps they like and make their own designs. Encourage them to talk about the scraps they used and the designs they made when they are finished.

You decided to use only three types of paper in your design, Catrina. Oh, yes. I see how you made it look like a pinwheel here. Are there other parts of the design you want to tell me about?

Try collages made of pretty fabric scraps or even different grades of sandpaper for a change of pace.

 indoors   5–15 minutes   1–6 Fives

218

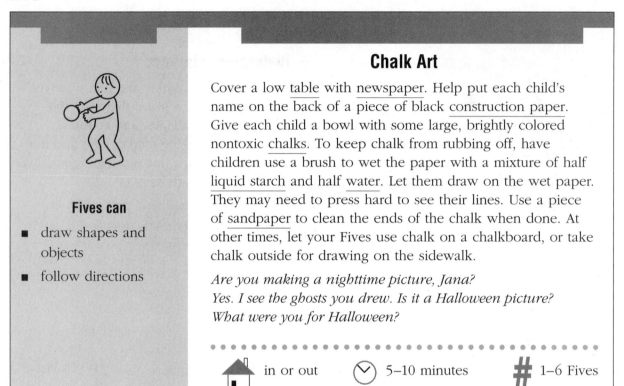

Fives can

- draw shapes and objects
- follow directions

Chalk Art

Cover a low table with newspaper. Help put each child's name on the back of a piece of black construction paper. Give each child a bowl with some large, brightly colored nontoxic chalks. To keep chalk from rubbing off, have children use a brush to wet the paper with a mixture of half liquid starch and half water. Let them draw on the wet paper. They may need to press hard to see their lines. Use a piece of sandpaper to clean the ends of the chalk when done. At other times, let your Fives use chalk on a chalkboard, or take chalk outside for drawing on the sidewalk.

Are you making a nighttime picture, Jana?
Yes. I see the ghosts you drew. Is it a Halloween picture?
What were you for Halloween?

in or out   5–10 minutes   1–6 Fives

219

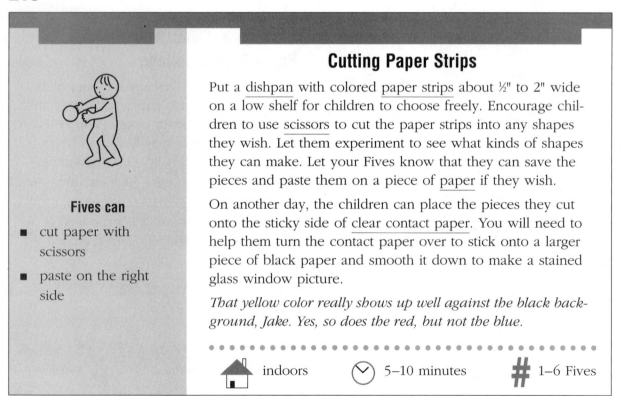

Fives can

- cut paper with scissors
- paste on the right side

Cutting Paper Strips

Put a dishpan with colored paper strips about ½" to 2" wide on a low shelf for children to choose freely. Encourage children to use scissors to cut the paper strips into any shapes they wish. Let them experiment to see what kinds of shapes they can make. Let your Fives know that they can save the pieces and paste them on a piece of paper if they wish.

On another day, the children can place the pieces they cut onto the sticky side of clear contact paper. You will need to help them turn the contact paper over to stick onto a larger piece of black paper and smooth it down to make a stained glass window picture.

That yellow color really shows up well against the black back-ground, Jake. Yes, so does the red, but not the blue.

indoors   5–10 minutes   1–6 Fives

220

Fives can

- paint with a thin brush
- use size words

Painting Little Pictures

Put onto a low table cups of tempera paint in a paint cup holder. Also put out some thin paintbrushes and small pieces of paper. Let your Fives paint little pictures in their own way. Talk about the size of the brushes, paper, and the designs they make.

You're using the the purple paint to make a person, aren't you, Susie? What is your little painting about?

If you wish, have an easel set up nearby and let children choose to paint big, medium, or small pictures.

 in or out   5–15 minutes   1–6 Fives

221

Fives can

- draw with a pencil

Pencil Pictures

Have in a container on the art shelf soft lead pencils that make dark marks for your Fives to use freely. Keep plenty of paper nearby for children to use with the pencils. Make pencil art a special activity by putting pencils out with different shapes of paper. For example, put out pencils to use with long, narrow paper; heart or star paper shapes; or very tiny paper.

You made lots of tiny circles on this paper, Dinah.
Oh, they are bubbles.
That is a tall man on the long paper, Justin.
Yes, I'll help you print the rest of your name, Justin.
You made a good J.

 in or out   2–10 minutes   1–6 Fives

222

Fives can

- use glue in a squeeze bottle
- squeeze out a small amount

Yarn-and-Ribbon Pictures

Have washable white glue in small squeeze bottles for your Fives to use. Put the glue out on a table covered with newspaper. Add yarn and ribbon scraps for the children to glue to pieces of paper.

Remind your Fives that only a little glue is needed to hold things together. Gently help the Fives use the right amount of glue to make things stick.

Good, Sarah. You are using a little dot of glue to make the yarn stick.
When the glue dries, it will stick on the paper.
I think you like the shiny ribbon best, Dale.

 indoors   3–15 minutes   # 1–6 Fives

223

Fives can

- draw a face
- follow directions with several steps

Paper-Plate Masks

Look at some pictures of masks or some real masks with your Fives. Then cut eye holes in paper plates for your Fives to make into masks. Have the children use watercolor markers to color their masks in their own way. Let them staple on yarn for hair. Have each child staple yarn or cloth strips to the plate so that it can be tied. Have a mirror nearby so that children can see themselves in their masks. Talk about the different ways the Fives decorated their masks.

Matthew, you drew a nose and mouth on your mask.
Yours has red hair, Andre. Why do you think people use masks?

Use this activity at Halloween but do mask-making at other times, too.

 in or out   5–15 minutes   # 1–6 Fives

224

Fives can

- tell about their artwork
- be proud of things they make

Show-and-Tell Artwork

Give Fives a chance to tell their friends about the artwork they have done. Have one child at a time show his work to a small group. Keep things short. Ask questions to help the child say a little about the artwork.

Tell us about your painting, Tim.
What did you use to make this picture?
Did anyone else paint today?
Cathy wants to show us her clay work and tell about it.

Then help the children put their work up in the art gallery.

 in or out   2–5 minutes   3–10 Fives

225

Fives can

- use paste and glue
- know opposites

Texture Collage

Put two dishpans with small pieces of textured paper and cloth out on a low table. Have smooth things, such as shiny papers and silky cloth in one dishpan, and rough things, like fine sandpaper, in the other. Give each child some paste and a piece of colored paper.

Encourage children to talk about the smooth things and the rough things as they feel and paste them.

What are you going to paste on first, Ian?
Yes, that sandpaper is rough.
Look at Jessie's creation. Do you want to tell us about the pieces you used?

At other times, try texture collages with soft and hard things or bumpy and smooth things.

 indoors   5–10 minutes   1–6 Fives

226

Fives can

- paint with a brush
- understand size words

Great Big Pictures

Hang very big sheets of paper from a <u>roll of paper</u> on a wall or fence outdoors. Have one sheet for each child. Put out <u>tempera paints</u> in a <u>paint cup holder</u> and encourage children to paint in their own way on the great big paper. Use <u>brushes</u> of various widths, including painters' brushes 1" to 3" wide. Talk about *big, medium,* and *small.* Help the children look at and compare their own designs with those of their friends.

You made great big designs with lots of circles and lines, Ellen. Yes. Your creation looks like a giant or a monster, Jeremy. Tina, you made a tiny painting on the big sheet of paper.

 outdoors   3–10 minutes   1–6 Fives

227

Fives can

- follow directions with several steps
- paint with a thin brush

Watercolor Paintings

Put out <u>watercolor paints</u> with small, sturdy <u>brushes</u> for your Fives to use. Begin with two of the primary <u>colors</u> (red, yellow, or blue). Have <u>margarine tubs</u> filled with clean <u>water</u> and <u>paper towels</u> ready. Wet a piece of <u>white paper</u> for each child to paint on. Show your Fives how to dip their brush into water, swirl it in a color, and paint on the wet paper. Show them how to clean the brush in water, then blot it on a paper towel as they change colors. Talk about how the colors spread out and what happens when colors mix together.

Look, Joel. You're getting orange.
How do you think you made orange?

Add other colors one at a time when the children are able to manage the process. Rinse and blot paints dry when done.

 in or out   5–20 minutes   1–6 Fives

228

Fives can

- use glue in a squeeze bottle
- make creative designs
- follow directions with several steps

Sprinkle Pictures

Show your Fives how to place a piece of paper into a shallow box. Let them squeeze a thin line of white glue onto the paper in a design. Then have them sprinkle sand over the glue and carefully lift the paper so that the extra sand falls into the box. You can put colored sand in empty spice bottles with covers that have holes big enough for the fine sand to pass through. Color the sand by mixing it with a little dry tempera paint powder. You can also have glitter to sprinkle.

You are letting the extra sand roll off the paper.
I see the colors mixed here.

Make sprinkle pictures on paper of different sizes, colors, and shapes.

 in or out   5–10 minutes   1–2 Fives

229

Fives can

- use tape
- take care of materials

Using Tape

Give Fives chances to use tape. Help them use tape to hang up pictures they make, to seal papers they fold, or to attach small pieces of paper to a larger paper in a design. You may need to show the children how to cut the pieces of tape. You can also put lots of short pieces on the edge of a table for them to take.

You're cutting the tape very well, James. Thanks for helping.
Now press the tape down. It's sticking!
What else can you use to make things stick together?
Allison just taped two pieces of paper together like a book.

Also provide colored tapes for children to use in creating tape design pictures.

 indoors   5–10 minutes   1–6 Fives

230

Fives can

- use crayons
- plan designs
- follow directions with several steps

Crayon Rubbings

Have the children choose flat objects such as paper clips, leaves, or coins to make a rubbing. Let them put the objects out on a table that is protected with newspaper. Cover the objects with a piece of paper and tape the paper down so that it won't move. Have the child color over the whole paper with the flat side of a crayon. You may have to remind the child to press hard while coloring. Talk about the shapes that appear like magic.

Look, Ricky! What is this shape?
Color on it some more, then we'll see the whole thing.

Let the children try making other designs by moving things around or collecting other objects.

 in or out   5–20 minutes   1–6 Fives

231

Fives can

- make forms with play dough
- plan a design

Play-Dough Pictures

Give each child a piece of wood or heavy stiff cardboard about 8" × 10". Put out lumps of play dough of different colors. (See the recipe for Self-Hardening Play Dough on page 262.) Let your Fives take the colors they need to make a picture. Explain how to flatten out the play dough on the board to cover a big space and how to press smaller pieces together to make a picture. When the play dough dries, the picture will stick to the backing.

What is up in the sky you made, Jason? Oh, I see, it's an airplane. And this looks like a tree with apples, Adele.
Oh, they are cherries. I love delicious cherries.

Take walks with your Fives and help them remember what they saw to put in their play-dough pictures.

 in or out   5–15 minutes   1–6 Fives

232

Fives can

- string things
- experiment with balancing things

Make a Mobile

Hang up a wire coat hanger as a base for a mobile. Put out a tray of stringing things with holes in them—small foam balls, buttons with big holes, shapes children have made of pipe cleaners. Use easy-to-bend wire or string to attach the shapes to the bottom of the coat hanger. Let your Fives choose what they want to hang on their mobiles. Encourage them to experiment by moving things around until the mobile hangs straight. Then use tape to help things stay in place. Take the mobiles outside and watch them blow and move in the wind.

Juan, the mobile bends down on this side.
What makes it go down on one side?
Can you make your mobile balance so it is straight, Angie?
What do you need to put on the other side?

 in or out   5–20 minutes   1–6 Fives

233

Fives can

- balance and build
- use glue and scissors well

Paper Box Sculpture

Have the children and their parents help you collect sturdy paper boxes of various sizes. Use tape or glue to seal the boxes. White or solid-colored boxes and boxes with pretty pictures work best. Let each child have a small bottle of glue and select the boxes to make a sculpture by gluing the boxes together. They may need to hold some of the boxes together with tape until the glue dries. See if children want to draw on the boxes with watercolor markers or paint the sculpture after it is dry. They can also use collage materials and cut paper shapes to decorate their paper box sculptures.

Paul is cutting a door and windows in his house.
What are you planning to do with yours, Tyler?

 indoors   10–30 minutes   1–6 Fives

234

Fives can

- balance and build
- use glue with wood
- work on a long-term project

Wood-Scrap Sculpture

Collect small wood scraps. (Ask parents to help bring in scraps.) Add spools from thread or other small wooden shapes. Give each child a flat piece of wood at least 8" to 10" to use as a base, and a small bottle of glue at a table covered with newspaper. Let your Fives choose the shapes they need to build whatever they can imagine. Remind them that they need only a little glue to make the wood stick.

Children may find that for some more complicated sculptures they may need to put some pieces together and let them dry. Then they can return to their work the next day. When the glue is dry, the children can rub the sculpture with cooking oil on a cloth, or paint it if they wish.

 in or out   10–30 minutes # 1–8 Fives

235

Fives can

- tell colors of many things
- draw some things we can recognize

Pictures with Seasonal Colors

As the seasons change, have the Fives collect natural things such as leaves in fall, budding branches and bright flowers in spring. Put up a display of these things and of pictures showing what people like to do in that season. Discuss what changes happen at this time of year and decide with the children what colors they see around them. Include these seasonal colors at the painting easel and among the crayons or watercolor markers at the drawing table. Add the children's pictures to the seasonal displays you have in other areas.

Simone thinks we should add orange, brown, and red for fall colors.
Brian said there is still some green on the trees.
Are there other colors we should use for fall?

 indoors   5–15 minutes # 1–6 Fives

226

236

Fives can

- tell the color of many things

- understand the words *light, medium,* and *dark*

Shades of Colors

Put out a tray with a cup of white tempera paint and a cup of bright blue paint at a table for color mixing. Have a 6-muffin tin or some paper cups, a few plastic teaspoons and some coffee stirrers on the tray. Ask your Fives whether they can make different shades of blue in the different cups by mixing different amounts of the white and blue in each cup. Put out white paper and brushes so that children can use the colors they mixed.

Charles has made a very light blue.
How did you make that color?
Yes. You used lots of white and just a little blue.

Next time, put out white and red, white and purple, or white with any other strong color.

 in or out   5–15 minutes   1–6 Fives

237

Fives can

- cut and paste simple shapes

- work carefully with small things

Making a Mosaic

Cut paper strips 1" to 1½" wide of different textures and colors. Have the children cut these into small squares and rectangles. Put out paste or glue and construction paper squares 5" × 5". Show the Fives some things made of tiles— small mosaic pieces, the floor in the bathroom, or the kitchen countertop. Ask parents to send in any mosaic pictures they might have. Make sure to explain that a mosaic has small pieces put very close together to make one big picture.

Andre has made a red and blue mosaic with lots of squares.
What shapes and colors did you use, Todd?

Later, the Fives can glue real mosaic tiles on a piece of thin plywood or masonite.

 indoors   5–15 minutes   1–6 Fives

Fives can

- follow directions
- copy adult actions

Table Washing After Art

Fill a bucket about 1/3 full of water. Put in a sponge that fits a child's hand. Show the children how to wring the sponge close to the top of the bucket so that the water goes inside and does not splash around. Then show them how to wash the spots off the table. After they wash the whole table clean, show them how to wash, rinse, and wring out the sponge. Then show them how to pick up all the excess water with the almost dry, clean sponge. If the children do this carefully with long strokes, the table will look bright and shiny when they are finished.

Remind children to wash their hands at the sink after finishing table washing. Table washing can also be done after snack and lunch time.

 in or out   3–5 minutes   1–4 Fives at a time

239

Fives can

- follow directions
- copy adult actions

Sweeping Up After Art

After an art activity, when there are scraps of paper and other art materials on the table and floor, have children help with cleanup. First, have the children put the bigger pieces in the wastepaper basket. To sweep the floor, help them draw a chalk circle about 1½' in diameter to give them a target area into which to sweep. The children should use brooms with broomsticks cut down to a size that is easy and safe for them to use. Adult-sized brooms are dangerous because children can't control the long broomsticks.

After the dirt is swept into the circle, it is easier to sweep it into a dustpan with a brush and put it into a nearby wastepaper basket.

 in or out   3–5 minutes   # 1–2 Fives

240

Fives can

- enjoy new challenges
- ask for help when needed

Computer Art

Find an art program for your classroom computer that lets the children do freehand creative drawings. Show the children individually what they need to do to get the program started. Stay with them until they feel comfortable with computer art and are making a drawing. They may need to scribble again, just as they did when they first learned to draw. As children become more skillful, let them help others to learn about computer art.

Display the computer art drawings along with other artwork in your classroom.

 indoors   5–20 minutes   1 Five at a time

241

Fives can

- understand opposites
- understand the words *same* and *different*
- hammer a nail

Experimenting with Hard and Soft Woods

Put out pieces of various kinds of wood—hard wood like oak and soft wood like pine, wood with knots and smooth wood, coarse and fine grain, solid wood and plywood. Ask your Fives to scratch pieces of soft wood and hard wood with nails. Talk about which type of wood is easier to mark with a nail. Then have the children try to hammer a nail into each piece of wood. Encourage them to find out which one is easier to drive a nail into. Also let them experiment to find out if it is hard or easy to hammer into the plywood and the knot.

Andy, what did you learn about the oak? How is it different from the pine? Which do you think would be harder to saw?

Always supervise carpentry carefully. See the carpentry card on page 251 for more ideas.

 outdoors   10–30 minutes   1–4 Fives

242

Fives can

- follow simple safety rules
- enjoy a challenge
- learn to saw

Sawing Wood

Talk about sawing wood with your Fives, using the carpentry card on page 256. Put out a box of soft wood pieces about 6" long and no more than 2" wide for sawing. Have a C-clamp or a vise on the carpentry table to hold the wood for sawing. Have a crosscut saw 12" to 15" long for the Five who is going to saw. After the child chooses his wood, help him fix it tightly in the vise or C-clamp and show him how to keep his other hand far from the saw. Help get the sawing started so that there is a little groove in the wood. If the saw sticks, show the child how to rub it lightly with soap.

You're working hard, Peter, to make the teeth of the saw cut the wood. That's sawdust on the ground. Where did it come from?

 outdoors   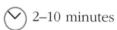 2–10 minutes   1 Five at a time

243

Fives can

- follow directions
- enjoy a challenge

Drilling Holes in Wood

Show your Fives the carpentry card on page 255 and talk about how to use a drill. Then help one child attach a piece of soft wood to the carpentry table with a C-clamp so that it sticks out away from the table. Have a brace and bit drill or a hand drill for the child to use that makes a hole about 1/4" to 1". Have the child mark the wood where she wants to drill the hole. Help her tap a thick nail in that place to make a little hole and then pull the nail out. Show the child how to use the little hole to keep the drill steady at the beginning and then start to turn the drill. If you use a brace and bit drill, help children work together so that one person holds the brace steady as the other turns the drill.

 in or out   10–30 minutes   1–2 Fives

244

Fives can

- follow directions
- enjoy making something to use
- hammer a nail

Making a Sanding Block

Set out small blocks of wood that can fit in a child's hand with pieces of three grades of sandpaper—fine, medium, and coarse. Cut the sandpaper into lengths that can fit around the block with a 1" overlap where the two ends meet.

Show children the carpentry card on page 252. Have your Fives try each grade of sandpaper and choose the one they want for their sanding block. Then have them wrap the piece around the block tightly and use a hammer to nail the sandpaper in place with short nails. Encourage children to use their personal sanding block to sand wood pieces smooth.

Good Julie. You remembered to sand with the side that has no nails! What would happen if we left wood rough? Yes, you could get splinters.

 in or out   10–30 minutes   1–4 Fives

245

Fives can

- follow simple safety rules
- hammer a nail

Hammer and Nails

Put out two medium-sized claw hammers, 10 to 13 ounces in weight, on a carpentry table. Have several different lengths and thicknesses of nails with heads separated in different small boxes. Collect soft wood pieces with the grain running the length of the piece to prevent splitting. Include a tray of things that are easy to hammer onto wood, such as bottle caps, leather, and fabric scraps. Ideas for setting up a carpentry center and for carpentry projects are on pages 248–258.

You used bottle caps for wheels on your car, Paula.
Jesse made an airplane. How did you attach the wings onto the body?

 in or out   5–30 minutes   1–2 Fives

246

Fives can

- hammer a nail
- plan and carry out a project

Nail-Head Designs

Put out a large assortment of nails with heads of different sizes—roofing nails with large heads, box nails, common nails, and brass nails. Put out fairly thick pieces of wood for children to use as a base for their nail designs. Have children use pencils or markers to draw a design on their piece of wood. Then encourage them to use nails to outline or fill in their designs in their own creative ways. Remind children that they can vary the design by pounding in the nails so that they are different heights.

Yes Alice, you made a nails rainbow.
How many rainbow stripes are there?

 in or out   5–30 minutes   1–4 Fives

247

Fives can

- hammer, saw, and drill
- make something with wood

Carpentry Display

After a carpentry piece is finished, ask the child to tell you about it. Print what he says on a piece of paper and have the child sign his name. Ask the child to put the carpentry piece on the display table with the story nearby. Let everybody know about the carpentry display.

What did you make, Aaron?
How many pieces of wood are there in Jerry's airplane?
Yes, you may take yours home today, Rebecca.
We'll do more carpentry tomorrow.
Pat, what will you make when you get your turn?

 in or out   2–5 minutes   1 Five

248

Fives can

- tie knots
- work a long time on a project

Keys Wind Chimes

Collect keys that are no longer needed from parents and also from a key-making shop. Show children how to secure the keys onto a coat hanger or piece of wood with 8" to 10" pieces of string or picture wire. Have tape ready for children to use to hold keys in place as they balance their creations. Have children place their wind chimes in a breeze to see what kinds of sound they make.

While the key collection builds, you can use the keys to do sorting games and to talk about different kinds of keys—car keys, house keys, golden keys, small keys, and so on. Make sure the children know that the keys in the wind chimes are old keys that are no longer in use and that they must be sure not to play with the keys people still use.

 in or out 10–20 minutes 1–5 Fives

249

Fives can

- enjoy trips
- plan an activity

Special Art Show

Take your Fives to see an art show. Look for art shows in a museum, art gallery, high school, or shopping center. Then plan an art show with your Fives for their families and friends. Talk with them about:

- where the art show should be held
- what work they will show
- what they will do as guides when people come

Make a special occasion of the art show. Have refreshments for the visitors. Let the children help choose the things to be displayed, put pictures in paper frames, and arrange the display. Take photographs of their art show that you can put in a book for the Book Center. Make sure everybody has some work displayed in the special art show.

 in or out 10–60 minutes 1–20 Fives

250

· Fives can

- cut well with scissors
- make a face

Paper-Bag Puppets

Put small paper bags, colored paper shapes, yarn of different colors, watercolor markers, paste or glue, and scissors out on a table covered with newspaper. Encourage the children to use their own ideas as they make their own creative paper bag puppets. Talk about all the ways your Fives create eyes, ears, hair, a tongue, teeth, or whatever they want.

When the paper-bag puppets are finished, see if any children want to have a puppet show with their friends.

Melissa, your puppet has all kinds of spots.
Would you like to tell me about your puppet?
Tony made a puppet with red hair.
What did you make, Karen?

 in or out   5–30 minutes   1–8 Fives

251

Fives can

- follow directions
- plan what they want to create

Hand-Shaping Play Dough

Have your fives follow a recipe for making play dough. Recipes for play dough are on pages 261–263. After your Fives have made different colors of play dough, ask them what shapes they can make using only their hands. Encourage them to experiment to find out.

You rolled the play dough into a ball, Chris.
Oh, yes. I see. There's the bigger ball, and you made lots of tiny ones.
Miriam, it looks like you made a long thin snake.
Oh, it's a rope! Do you know how to attach another piece to make the rope longer?

Challenge your Fives to make as many shapes as they can think of with the play dough, using only their hands.

 in or out   5–25 minutes   1–8 Fives

252

Fives can

- use fingers well
- work with small things

Play-Dough Beads

Let a few Fives help you make jewelry modeling dough using the recipe on page 263. Then show your Fives how to make a bead with the dough by pushing a round toothpick through the center of a ball of dough while it is still soft, so that each bead has a stringing hole when it dries. Make sure children move the toothpick around so that the hole will be big enough. Let beads dry for two to four days till very hard. Then provide paint or thin markers to decorate the beads after they are dry. Children can string finished beads with fishline or strong packing string.

Who are you making the necklace for, Nathan? Your big sister, Ellen? She will really like it. Your necklace has lots of shapes in it. Can you tell me about them?

 in or out   10–30 minutes   1–6 Fives

253

Fives can

- use fingers well
- plan and follow a pattern

Sewing a Design

Have your Fives draw a simple design with pencil on a piece of loosely woven, easy-to-sew cloth. Stretch the cloth in an embroidery hoop or tack it down on a wood picture frame so that the design is in the center. Help the children thread some big needles with brightly colored cotton or wool yarn. Add beads, buttons, and other stringing things for the children to use. Remind them to sew only inside the hoop, never around the edge of the hoop.

What are you sewing, Karl? A house with a chimney?
Yes, you can work more on your design later, Adele.
You can keep it safe in your cubby till then.

 in or out   5–20 minutes   1–6 Fives

254

Fives can

- work on a long-term project
- work with play dough

Making Clay Forms

On a covered table, give each child a piece of wood or masonite 8" × 11" to work on. Give each one a lump of self-hardening or oven-hardening clay that you can get at a craft store. Be sure the clay is not too soft or too hard. Let the children work with the clay as they wish. If they want to to take home a completed piece, follow the directions that come with the clay so that the piece can harden.

Dick made a bowl that he wants to take home. Who remembers where we put clay creations so that they can dry safely?

When the children are finished working with the clay, show them how to scrape the clay off the boards and put them away for next time.

 in or out   5–30 minutes   1–8 Fives

255

Fives can

- work on a long-term project
- use fingers well
- work carefully

Clay Coil Bowls

After your Fives have had many chances to work with play dough and clay, see if they want to try to make a coil bowl. Show them how to make a snake and how to wind it around to make the bottom of the bowl. Then they can build up the sides, coiling the snakes one on top of the other. When the coil bowl is finished, the children can smooth the inside and outside to keep the coils together.

Do you know why this is called a coil bowl?
Is there anything else that is coiled like this?
Yes, Brett. A rope can be coiled. So can a wire spring.

Place coil bowls in a safe place to harden. Be sure children can identify their own work.

 in or out   5–30 minutes   1–8 Fives

256

Fives can

- work on a long-term project
- use fingers well
- follow directions
- weave

Paper Weaving

Cut 3/4" × 11" strips out of various types of paper—shiny, colored, bumpy, crepe, tissue. Help your Fives staple the strips close together on a piece of 1" × 8" stiff paper so that they hang straight down. Explain that this is called the "warp." Then show them how to weave a strip of paper over and under the warp strips. These strips are called the "woof." Help children make a frame for their weaving when they are finished by stapling the woven strips to stiff paper strips on the remaining three sides.

On another table close by, have pieces of loosely woven fabric with a magnifying glass so that the children can see how cloth is woven the same way.

 in or out   5–30 minutes   1–6 Fives

257

Fives can

- work on a long-term project
- use fingers well
- follow directions

Yarn Weaving

Make a frame of cardboard or other stiff material. Attach thick colorful yarn pieces to make a warp by stapling or tying yarn on the top and bottom. Let the children choose strips of yarn, fabric, and ribbon to weave into the warp. Yarn is easier to weave if it has a piece of tape on the end to hold onto.

When your Fives are finished with the weaving, help them put a second frame on top and glue it to the yarn and the bottom frame. When the children are experienced weavers, you may want to get frames and materials for making pot holders.

Kenny has used lots of bright, shiny ribbons.
I think I have some feathers if anyone wants to weave them into their work.

 in or out   5–30 minutes   1–6 Fives

258

Fives can

- draw with watercolor markers
- plan and create a design

Cloth Flags

Display flags of different countries and books about flags. Talk about the different designs flags have—stripes, stars, big patches of color.

Cover a table with newspaper. Give each child a piece of sturdy cardboard or wood 8" × 11" or larger. Help children tape a piece of white cloth onto the wood or cardboard piece to hold it in place. Encourage children to use bright-colored watercolor markers to draw designs on their flags. When they are finished, help the children tack or tape their flags onto thin dowels or other thin wood pieces.

Why do you think people have flags, Nicky?
Where have you seen flags, Kristin?
David has a flag at his home.

 in or out   5–20 minutes   1–8 Fives

259

Fives can

- use scissors and collage materials
- work together
- plan and create a design

Fancy Hats

On a table, put out strips of colored paper 3" to 4" wide and 11" long, paper plates, yarn, and collage paper pieces, tape, glue, watercolor markers, and scissors. Encourage the children to cut, decorate, and make hats in different ways. For example, they can measure one another's heads and make a wide band to decorate as a hat. Or some may want to decorate hats made of paper plates tied with yarn.

Give the children a chance to wear their hats and show them to the group before they take them home. Ask them to tell how they made their hats.

Raynika, how did you to make this fancy part here? Was it hard or easy to do?
You made two hats, Wolfgang. They look really different.

 in or out   5–30 minutes   1–8 Fives

260

Fives can

- use scissors, glue, and other art materials
- make believe
- plan and create a design

Fancy Costumes

Help your Fives make costumes. Use large paper bags or large sheets of butcher paper with arm and head holes cut out as a base to decorate. Encourage your Fives to make hats, other head covers, and masks also. They can use collage materials, watercolor markers, and scissors to make their costumes.

You're going to be a cat, Vanessa?
What will you need? Ears, a tail, and whiskers?
Here are lots of things to use. Maybe you'll want to make a cat mask, too.

This is a good activity for Fives to do when they are planning to act out a story for others.

 in or out   5–30 minutes   1–6 Fives

261

Fives can

- build and balance
- use glue, scissors, and other art materials

Big Paper Box Sculptures

Collect large paper boxes including shoe and boot boxes, packing boxes, and gift boxes. Close the boxes with glue or tape to make them strong. Encourage your Fives to build large structures by gluing the boxes together. They can make many different types of things, including houses, animal sculptures, spaceships, or anything they can imagine. Paint can be used on the finished buildings and other things glued on to make them more complete.

Denise is using her princess costume because she and Cathy built a castle!
Paul is making a lion to guard the castle.

 in or out   5–30 minutes   1–4 Fives

262

Fives can

- plan a project
- cooperate with friends to do a group project
- work on a long-term project

Play-Dough City

Talk with your Fives about the things they would find in a town and city. Then put a large piece of plywood or masonite on a covered table as a base for a play-dough city that the children can make. Have bowls with balls of self-hardening play dough in many colors. (See page 262 for recipe). Add other things children can use for buildings, etc., such as cardboard tubes, wood pieces, and paper boxes.

First have children cover the plywood with play dough to make grass, roads, and lakes. Help everyone take part in designing how the town should be arranged. Then they can add tunnels, bridges, buildings, and more.

Eli wants to make a playground. What can he use to make slides and swings and trees?

 in or out   20–30 minutes   1–4 Fives

263

Fives can

- plan a project
- cooperate with friends to do a group project
- work on a long-term project

Wood-Scrap Mural

Put a large flat piece of plywood on a table covered with newspapers. Nearby put a box full of wood scraps of various sizes and shapes. Give each child a small bottle of glue to work on the mural. Talk about working together on a mural that will be put on the wall in the classroom. As children finish, let others come to work on the mural and add their ideas.

Blake is connecting two sculptures with a long piece of wood. Oh, its a bridge. There's lots of space here. What could go in that space?

When the mural is dry, it can be finished by rubbing with nontoxic vegetable oil on a cloth or by painting with tempera paint.

 in or out   10–20 minutes   1–3 Fives

264

Fives can

- plan what they draw
- make something to use

Picture Place Mats

Put out white paper 8½" × 11" or 11" × 14" and thick and thin watercolor markers with many bright colors. Have the children draw a picture on the paper. Tell them they can make a place mat, and explain what a place mat is.

When a child has made a picture he wants to use, cover the picture with clear contact paper or laminate it so it will be protected when used as a place mat. Some children may want to make place mats for friends or family members as well.

Carla made a picture with lots of flowers and trees.
Sandy made an abstract design with stripes and lots of color.

 in or out   10–20 minutes   1–8 Fives

265

Fives can

- draw people and animals
- cut with scissors

Puppets on a Stick

Put out small pieces of paper of various colors, watercolor markers, and tongue depressors to make puppets on sticks. Encourage your Fives to draw people, animals, and imaginary creatures and then cut them out. Show children how to glue each figure onto a tongue depressor or ice cream stick to be used as a puppet.

After children have made several puppets, they might want to make up a puppet play. A stand for the puppets can be made from an egg carton turned upside down with slits cut in the egg compartments for the sticks to fit into.

 in or out   5–30 minutes   1–8 Fives

266

Fives can

- name body parts
- handle fasteners

Brass-Fastener Puppets

Have the children look at their own arms and legs. Talk about where the joints are and how many sections they have in their different body parts.

Put out precut paper head, body, arm and leg sections, and hands and feet pieces for children to fasten together with brass fasteners. (See pattern on page 264.) Have paper hole-punchers to make holes for the fasteners to go through. Show children how to fasten the pieces together to make a movable puppet. Then encourage your Fives to use markers and other materials to decorate their movable people.

If some children wish, they can design and cut out their own pieces, too. Sturdy puppets made of cardboard can have strings attached to the head and arms to make them move freely.

 indoors　　　 5–15 minutes　　　# 1–6 Fives

267

Fives can

- follow directions
- adhere to safety rules, with guidance

Making Candles

Look at the recipe for making candles with your Fives. (See page 265.) You can copy it onto a big piece of posterboard and display it where the children will be working on their candles. Talk with them about the steps they will follow to make their own candles. Discuss why it is important to be safe around hot water and wax. Have them figure out some safety rules to follow so that no one gets hurt, such as a rule that says only one child can work with the hot wax or a rule about where people who want to watch can safely stay.

Set out the things children will need as you help them follow the recipe. Walk each child through the process.

 in or out　　　 10–20 minutes　　　# 1 Five

268

Fives can

- use watercolors
- draw designs

Magic Wax-Resist Pictures

Put out white and other light-colored <u>crayons</u> to draw pictures on white pieces of <u>paper</u>. Be sure the children press hard as they draw so the crayon is quite thick on the paper. Then have the children paint over the drawings with <u>watercolors</u>. The crayon drawings will stand out against the watercolors in the background. Black watercolor paints make the crayon show up best.

The white drawings really look bright against the colored background. Why do you think the watercolors didn't cover the crayon drawing?

You can show children how oil and wax resist, or do not mix with one another, by pouring water and oil together and watching what happens.

 in or out   5–20 minutes   1–8 Fives

269

Fives can

- choose things they like
- plan designs

Sand Casting

Explain to your Fives about what they will do to make a sand casting. Use a picture/word recipe like the one on page 266. Then have each child put 1" of damp sand in the bottom of a small, flat <u>cardboard box</u>. Put out a tray of pebbles, shells, and other <u>natural things</u> that the children have collected. Let each child choose some of these and place them on the sand with the prettier side down. For every box, have the child help you mix <u>plaster of Paris</u> with <u>water</u> in a <u>cottage cheese container</u> until it is as thick as sour cream. Then have the child pour it over the design in the sand. While it is still wet, press into the plaster a piece of <u>paper</u> with the child's name and a loop of <u>string</u> to use as a <u>hanger</u>. When the plaster is dry, have the child lift it out and brush off the extra sand.

 in or out   5–20 minutes   1–4 Fives

270

Fives can

- plan a project
- follow directions with several steps

Leaf Casting

Explain this process to children before they do the activity. Make a picture/word recipe for them to follow. Then help them as needed while they work as independently as possible.

Collect fresh leaves to use in plaster casting. Spread oil over the side of the leaves that have bigger ridges and markings. Place the other side of the leaf on a piece of wax paper or on the sand in a sandcasting box. Mix plaster of Paris and water till it is like sour cream. Pour over and around the oiled leaf. When the plaster is dry, pull the leaf off. The plaster cast will look just like the leaf.

 in or out   5–10 minutes   1–2 Fives

271

Fives can

- use a computer responsibly when taught how

Advanced Computer Art

As a child develops drawing on the computer, help him advance to the next step. Show him how to access other parts of the art program to make more complex pictures.

You can add the story the child tells you about his picture on the computer so that he sees how you use the various keys to make letters and words. Show him how to print his name so that he can sign his drawing.

Jimmy, you can use the shift key, here, to make the uppercase J. Then let go to make the rest of the lowercase letters.
Oh, OK. You want your whole name in uppercase letters.

 indoors   5–20 minutes   1 Five

272

Fives can

- use fingers well
- work with play dough
- work on a long-term project

Potters' Clay Forms

On a covered table, give each child a piece of wood or masonite 8" × 11" to work on. Give each one a lump of potters' clay that is not too soft or too hard. Let the children work with the clay as they wish. If they want to keep a completed piece to take home, it will have to be dried and then fired in a kiln. Thick pieces will have to be scooped out so that they won't explode during firing.

Geoff, you made a bowl to fire in the kiln.
Do you want to paint it with glaze before it is fired?

When the children are finished working with the clay, scrape the clay off the boards and put them away for next time. See page 259, "Working with Potters' Clay," for information on preparing and firing clay pieces.

 in or out   5–30 minutes   1–8 Fives

273

Fives can

- behave well in public
- match things to pictures

What's in a Hardware Store?

While children are doing lots of carpentry work, take a field trip to a hardware store. Have enough adults so that children can move around the store in small groups of four to six children. Give each child a clipboard with a picture-word checklist showing things that are in a hardware store. A sample checklist is on page 267. Have each child find the different things on the checklist as the group goes around the store together.

Yes, Steve. That's where the different sizes of nails are kept.
You can check that on your list.
I see something else you can check off, Judy.
Does anyone else see it?

Be sure to read about trips on page 32 before arranging with a hardware store to visit.

 indoors   10–40 minutes   4–20 Fives

274

Fives can

- hammer and saw well
- follow a plan
- work on a long-term project

Making a Napkin Holder

When your Fives can <u>hammer</u> and <u>saw</u> well, show them the instructions for making a napkin holder. (See page 257.) Put out <u>soft wood</u> about 4" wide and between 5" and 6" long, with the grain running the length of the wood so that it won't split when nailed together. Also have some shorter pieces of the same width. Have <u>nails</u> that are about ¾" to 1" in length to hammer the wood pieces together.

Show the children with pieces of wood how the three pieces will go together. Explain where the napkins will go and show them how to measure and mark the wood, following each step shown on the card.

Give your Fives lots of time and help to complete the holder. Parents might enjoy coming in to help.

 in or out   10–60 minutes   1–2 Fives

275

Fives can

- hammer, saw, and drill well
- follow a plan
- complete a long-term project

Making a Wooden Boat

When your Fives can <u>hammer</u>, <u>saw</u>, and <u>drill</u> well, have <u>pieces of wood</u> and ½" to 1" <u>dowels</u> ready to make boats. Show your Fives the carpentry card on page 258. Talk about how to follow each step shown on the card.

Give your Fives a lot of time to work on their boats. Let them work on them a little at a time. After a child completes her boat, let her try it out in the water table to see how it floats.

See if children who have already completed the project would like to help others who are just getting started.

 in or out   10–25 minutes   1–2 Fives

Art Center

- Put easy-to-use art materials on low shelves for Fives to use freely every day: crayons and watercolor markers, lots of paper, safe scissors, collage materials, and paste or glue. Keep the materials in good shape.

- Show children where art materials are stored by putting picture/word labels on the shelf so that they can put things back.

- Store art materials in many small containers instead of one big one. Giving one or two children a small container of art materials to share cuts down on fighting.

- Let children use art materials in their own way. Don't show children something you have made to copy.

- Let Fives use play dough to make their own original forms without cookie cutters. Then they will see the many shapes they can make with their own hands and imaginations.

- Have art materials that need more help from you ready to bring out when you are free to watch them. Don't have all the children work with them at one time. Add these activities to the many other self-directed activities children can choose to do.

- Make sure that everyone who wants to gets a chance to do artwork. Keep the same special art activity out for more than one day or for as long as it is popular.

- Encourage children to talk about what they have made. Show them you enjoy their artwork with your interest. Mention colors, shapes, and materials they have used to make the work.

- Protect the floor, tables, and walls in the Art Center. Art materials are messy and accidents can easily happen.

- Have clean-up things, such as sponges, paper towels, and water, ready for children to use. Teach your Fives how to use these things.

- If necessary, cut the handles of paintbrushes to about 6" so that they are easier for Fives to control. Smooth the rough edges.

- Use art materials outdoors as well as indoors, especially for messy or noisy activities such as finger painting and carpentry.

- Put the children's artwork on display low on the walls or on the backs of bookshelves where the children can easily see their work. Change the display often.

Carpentry Center

- If possible, set up the Carpentry Center outdoors, where the noise is not so noticeable.

- If you have to do carpentry indoors, cover the woodworking table with thick carpeting to cut down the noise of hammering.

- You will need a sturdy woodworking table and a cabinet to store tools, nails, wood scraps, and accessories for building.

- The tools you buy should be real tools of the right size, not play tools. The Carpentry Center should have at least the following tools:
  - 2 claw hammers, 10 to 13 ounces in weight
  - 1 10-point crosscut saw 12" to 15" long and less than 12 ounces in weight
  - 1 brace and bit drill that can make holes $\frac{3}{16}$" to 1" in diameter
  - 1 hand drill that makes small holes up to $\frac{1}{2}$" in diameter
  - 1 C-clamp and a wood vise to hold wood for sawing and drilling

  You will also need:
  - Nails of different lengths with flat heads, including common nails and box nails
  - A box of soft wood pieces with the grain running the length of the wood to prevent splitting
  - A box of wood-scrap accessories such as small rug scraps, covered wire, rubber bands, linoleum scraps, spools, and bottle caps to use in building

- If needed, start a sign-up sheet for each tool to prevent competition and conflict over tool use.

- Make sure that the Carpentry Center is closely supervised and never without an adult nearby.

- Make sure that the children know the safety rules:
  1. Work far from other people.
  2. Watch where you are hammering.
  3. Keep your other hand (the hand that is not hammering or sawing) as far as possible from the hammer or saw.

The following pages give the activity cards for some of the carpentry activities.

Carpentry Tools

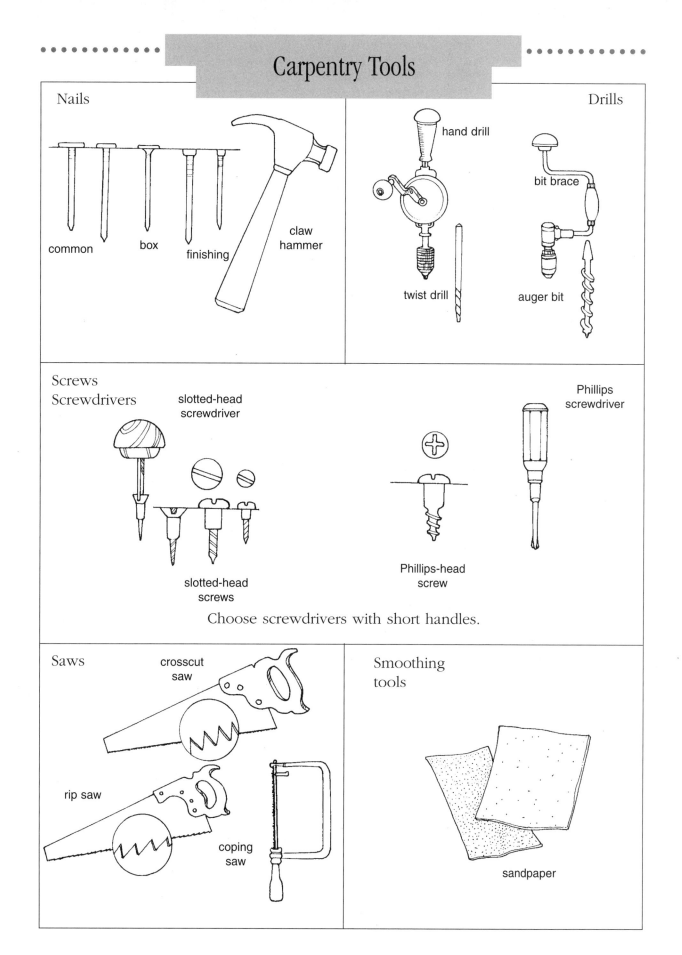

Nails

common   box   finishing   claw hammer

Drills

hand drill

bit brace

twist drill   auger bit

Screws
Screwdrivers

slotted-head screwdriver

Phillips screwdriver

slotted-head screws

Phillips-head screw

Choose screwdrivers with short handles.

Saws

crosscut saw

rip saw

coping saw

Smoothing tools

sandpaper

Setting Up a Carpentry Area

HAMMERING		SAFETY RULES
1. DeShon	7. Chris	1. Give yourself room.
2. Gloria	8. Kim	2. Watch where you work.
3. Carlos	9. Andre	3. Keep your other hand far from the hammer or saw.
4. Brett	10.	
5. Danielle	11.	
6. Billy	12.	

Sign-Up Lists   Safety Rules

Tool Storage Pegboard

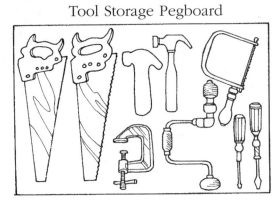

Outline hanging tools to make cleanup easier.

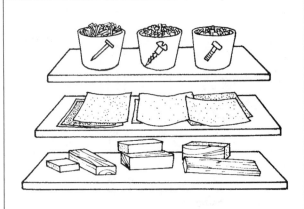

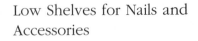

Low Shelves for Nails and Accessories

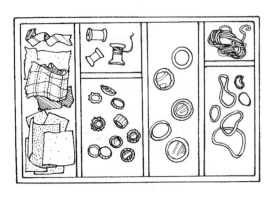

Accessories

Wood Storage

Carpentry Center

Exploring Kinds of Wood

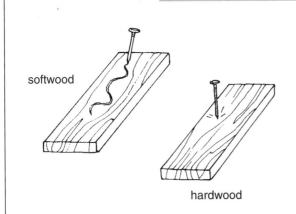

softwood

hardwood

1 Scratch wood with nail.

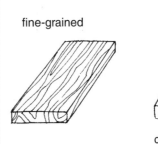

fine-grained

coarse-grained

OIL

2 Rub vegetable oil into surface.

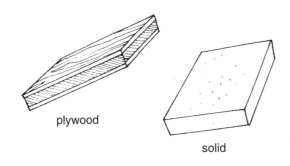

plywood

solid

3 Look at sides.

straight

whorled

4 Look at surface—see grain.

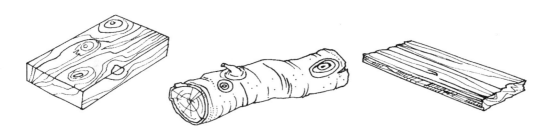

5 Find knots, markings.

6

Making a Sanding Block

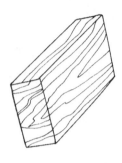

1 Use small block of wood that fits into palm of hand.

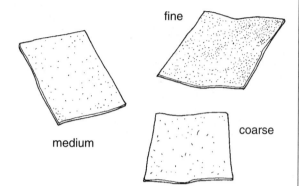

fine

medium

coarse

2 Try each sandpaper—choose grade.

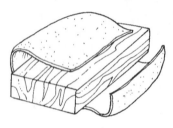

3 Wrap sandpaper around block.

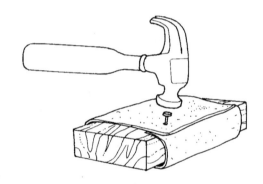

4 Fasten sandpaper with tack.

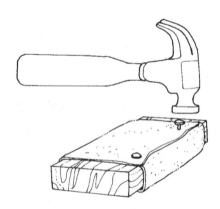

5 Add other tacks to hold sandpaper.

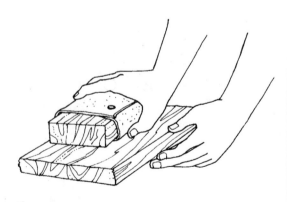

6 Rub sanding block back and forth on wood.

Creative Activities

Making Patterns with Nails

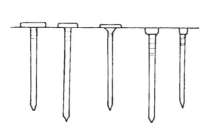

1 Nail heads can make patterns.

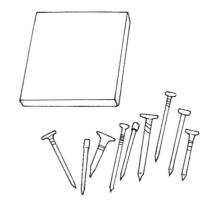

2 Select wood and nails.

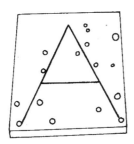

3 Plan patterns.

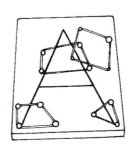

4 Stretch rubber bands.

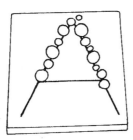

5 Hammer nails carefully to make other patterns.

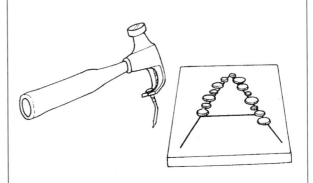

6 If nail bends, use the claw to take it out.

Creative Activities

Nailing Pieces of
Wood Together

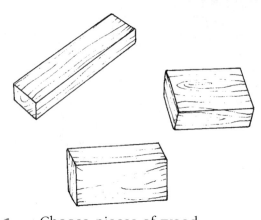

1 Choose pieces of wood.

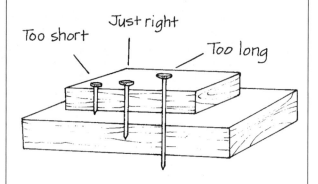

Too short   Just right   Too long

2 Choose nail by measuring.

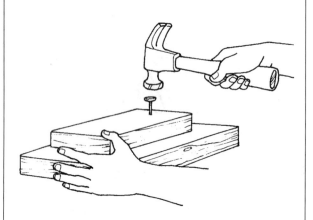

3 Hammer carefully. Hold the wood far from the hammer.

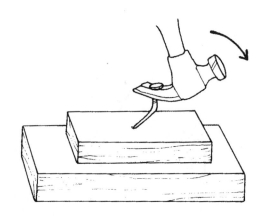

4 Pull out bent nail with hammer claw. Push away from nail.

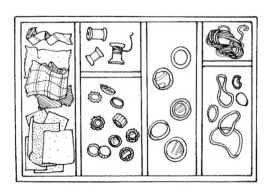

5 Choose accessories.

Drilling Wood

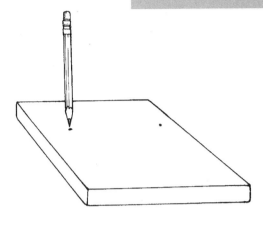

1 Mark wood.

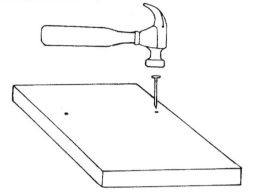

2 Tap holes. Small hole helps steady drill.

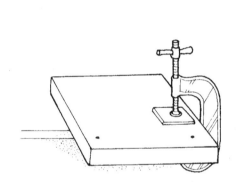

3 Hold wood steady. Attach so hole marks are not over table.

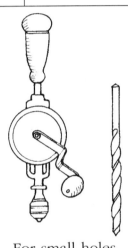

For small holes, use a hand drill.

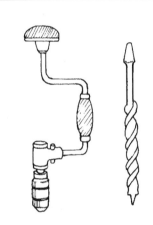

For bigger holes, use a brace and bit drill.

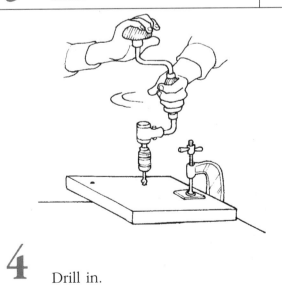

4 Drill in.

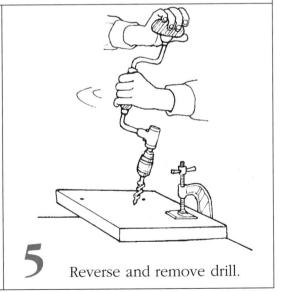

5 Reverse and remove drill.

Sawing Wood

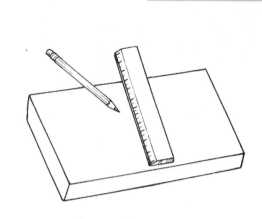

1 Mark wood.

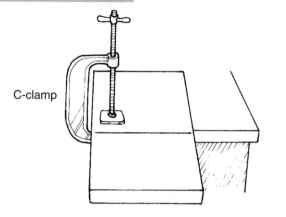

C-clamp

2 Hold wood steady.

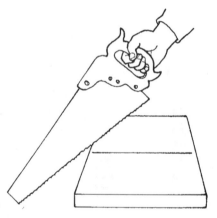

3 Place saw handle close to wood surface. Angle saw to 45°.

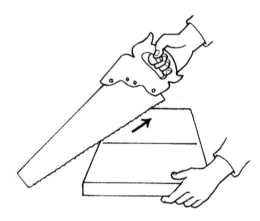

4 Draw sawing blade up to start cut.

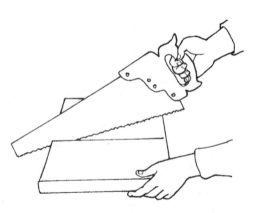

5 Saw by drawing blade up and down.

Creative Activities

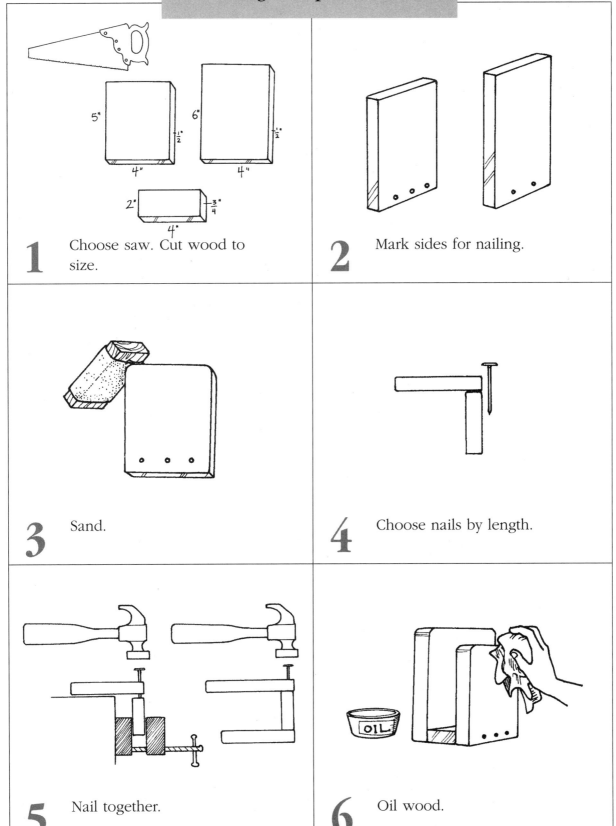

1 Choose saw. Cut wood to size.

2 Mark sides for nailing.

3 Sand.

4 Choose nails by length.

5 Nail together.

6 Oil wood.

Making a Wooden Boat

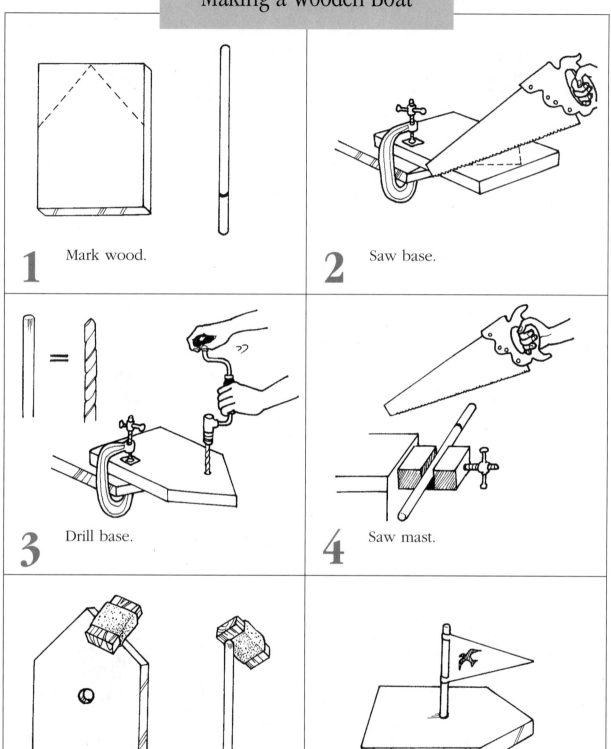

1 Mark wood.

2 Saw base.

3 Drill base.

4 Saw mast.

5 Sand smooth.

6 Push mast into base and attach flag.

Working with Potters' Clay

- Clay is an earth product that can be easily shaped when moist. Clay comes naturally in many colors—gray, red, and tan, among others. We usually see gray clay being used to make pottery, but it is possible to buy clay of other colors.

- Clay must be kept moist while being used to form things. It hardens when it dries out.

- Water can be kneaded into clay that has hardened.

- Keep clay in a plastic bag or a crock so that it won't dry out. A damp cloth should be put over a clay piece to keep it moist while it is being worked on.

- In order to make clay pieces hard and strong, they must be baked in a kiln. This is called firing. To prepare clay pieces for firing, they must be dried.

- Pieces that are very thick should be dried till they can be picked up. Then they should be scooped out with a small metal spoon.

- If any parts of a piece fall off while being dried, they can be put back on by wetting and attaching the ends.

- The child's initials should be scratched in the work while it is still moist.

Glazing Clay Pieces

- Glazes are colors that can be painted on clay pieces after they have been fired once to give them a finished look.

- Glazes are toxic, so they must be supervised very carefully.

- The color of the glaze changes after it is fired. Make sure the child knows what color the glaze will turn out to be.

- Make sure the children wash their hands thoroughly after they glaze clay pieces.

Recipes

(Watch carefully to see that children don't try to eat any of the art materials.)

Brush Paint Recipe

This recipe will help keep down your painting costs because it uses very little dry tempera paint.

1. Mix 1 cup bentonite (an inexpensive clay product that you can get at a pottery supply company) with 2 quarts hot water.

2. Let the mixture stand in a large container with a lid for two or three days. Stir each day. It will be sticky and lumpy to begin with.

3. When the bentonite is smooth and thick, pour it into smaller jars.

4. Add 3 or more tablespoons of dry tempera paint to each jar. Stir.

5. Add more paint if the color is not bright enough. Add more water if the paint is too thick.

6. Pour paint into smaller, unbreakable cups for children to use.

7. Keep jars covered.

Soap Finger Paint

1. Mix 3 cups of Ivory Snow® soap flakes with one cup of water.

2. Beat with an eggbeater until it's thick.

3. Color with a few drops of food color. (You can also try shaving cream as finger paint.)

4. Thin with dishwashing liquid until it is right for finger painting.

5. Add a few drops of food coloring.

Easy Finger Paint

1. Mix 2 cups of flour with ¼ cup of water. Add more water if needed and stir until the mixture is as thick as white glue.

2. Add a few drops of food coloring or ½ teaspoon of tempera paint powder and mix. For a deeper color, add more food coloring or powder.

3. Let each child finger paint with 2 or 3 tablespoons of the mixture on large, sturdy paper, a plastic tray, a cookie sheet, or a tabletop.

Cooked Finger Paint

1. Mix ½ cup flour with 1 cup water. Stir until smooth.

2. Bring to a boil, still stirring. Cook until it is as thick as pudding.

3. Cool.

Play Dough

Play Dough for One Child to Make

1. The child measures and pours into a medium bowl 1 cup flour, 1/2 cup salt, 2 tablespoons oil, 1/4 cup water, and a few drops of food coloring.

2. The child stirs with a large spoon until the ingredients become easier to mix and the food coloring is well-mixed with the other ingredients. An adult can help the child add more water or flour, a tablespoon at a time, until the mixture is firm, not too wet, and sticks together.

3. The child kneads and squeezes the mixture until a smooth dough is made.

1. Flour

1 cup

2. Water

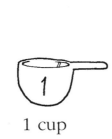
$\frac{1}{4}$ cup

3. Salt

$\frac{1}{2}$ cup

4. Vegetable oil

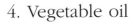

2 tablespoons

5. Food coloring

a few drops

6. Mix.

7. Knead.

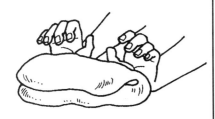

8. Make your own shapes.

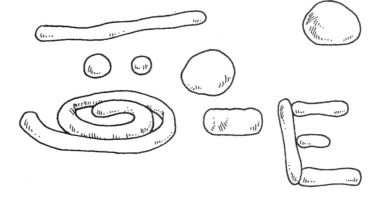

Play Dough for a Group of Children

1. Measure and pour into a large bowl 4 cups flour, 2 cups salt, 1/2 cup oil, 1 cup water, and 1 teaspoon food coloring.

2. Stir with a large spoon until the ingredients become easier to mix and the food coloring is well-mixed with the other ingredients. Add more water or flour, a tablespoon at a time, until the mixture is firm, not too wet, and sticks together.

3. Knead and squeeze the mixture until a smooth dough is made.

Self-Hardening Play Dough

1. Mix 2 cups flour, 1/2 cup salt, and 1 teaspoon of powdered color.

2. Gradually add 3/4 cup water.

3. Mix well and knead till smooth.

4. Add more flour if too wet or more water if too dry.

Jewelry-Modeling Dough

1. Mix 3/4 cup flour, 1/2 cup salt, and 1/2 cup cornstarch in a bowl.

2. Add warm water slowly and gradually until the mixture can be kneaded into stiff dough.

3. Dust with flour to reduce stickiness. Roll into balls for beads, pierce with a toothpick, allow to dry (two to four days), and paint if desired.

4. Food coloring may also be added with water as the mixture is being made.

Pattern for Brass
Fastener Puppets

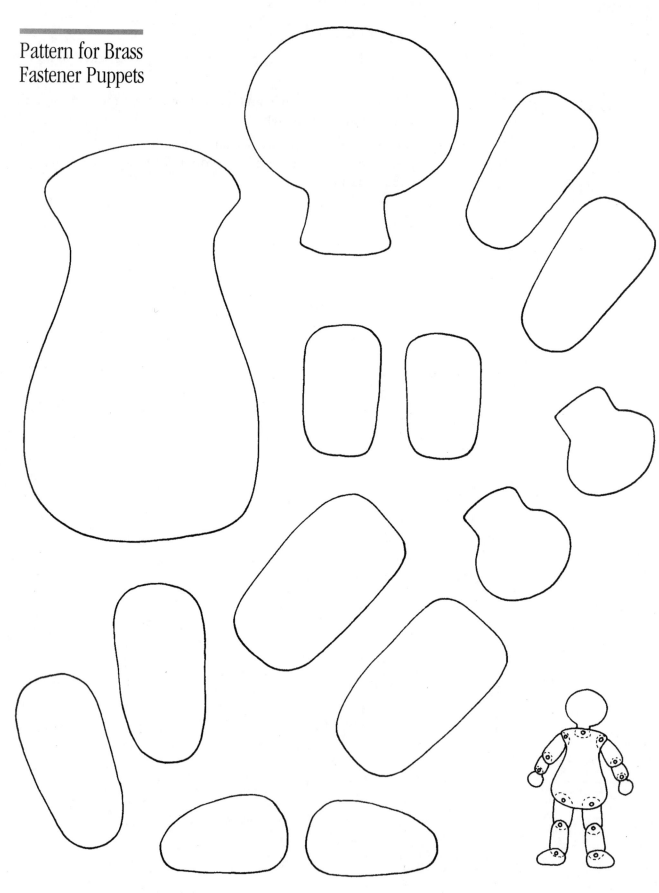

Creative Activities

Recipe for Candle Making

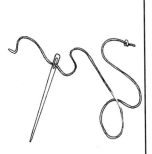

1. Thread needle with wick. Make knot.

2. Poke needle through cup. Pull wick up.

3. Tie wick to pencil.

4. Put cup with wick into another cup.

5. Melt paraffin in pan with water.

6. Add crayon pieces for color.

7. Pour paraffin into cup with wick.

8. Take off cups when solid.

Safety Notes:

■ Don't let the paraffin get too hot because it could catch on fire.

■ Be sure to keep 2" of water in the pan under the melting paraffin at all times. Do not allow the water to boil away.

■ Help children pour the paraffin. Have them use an oven mitt or potholder if the measuring cup handle is too hot.

■ Have a rule that says only one child can work with the hot wax. People who want to watch should remain a safe distance from the hot wax and the child who is working.

■ Supervise very carefully.

Creative Activities

Picture/Word Recipe for Sand Casting

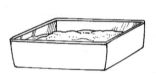

1. Pour sand 1–2" deep.

2. Make design.

3. Measure 1 cup water.

4. Add 1½ cups plaster and stir.

5. Pour gently.

6. Smooth.

7. Attach loop of string.

8. Write name.

Creative Activities

What's in a Hardware Store?

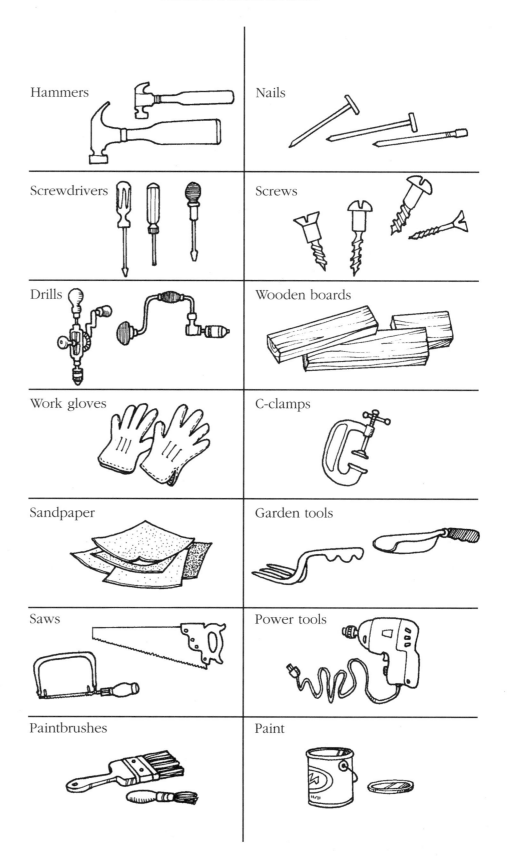

Hammers	Nails
Screwdrivers	Screws
Drills	Wooden boards
Work gloves	C-clamps
Sandpaper	Garden tools
Saws	Power tools
Paintbrushes	Paint

Materials and Notes

Blocks

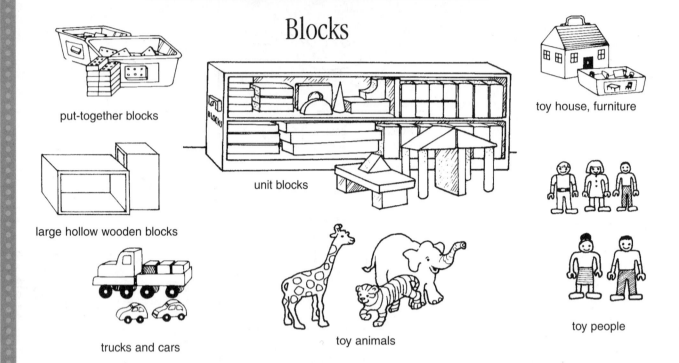

put-together blocks

large hollow wooden blocks

trucks and cars

unit blocks

toy animals

toy house, furniture

toy people

- Encourage both boys and girls to play in the Block Center by having a variety of accessories and blocks.

- Show interest in what your Fives do with blocks. Notice what they build with the blocks and talk with them about their block-building ideas.

- Make sure children understand a few simple rules for using the blocks:
  - Build in the Block Center, but not too close to the shelves.
  - Use blocks gently so that nobody gets hurt.
  - Move carefully around block buildings to protect the work of others.
  - Use blocks that are not being used by others. Ask if you are not sure.
  - Put a "Please Save" sign on any building that is not to be cleaned up.
  - Clean up by putting blocks and toys back in the right places on the shelves.

- Keep the area interesting by often changing or adding to the toys used with the blocks.

- Check blocks and block toys often for sharp edges, rust, or splinters, and remove any that are not safe.

- Many activity ideas can be used with either younger or older Fives because they are open-ended and can challenge children with a wide range of abilities.

- See Block Center Ideas on page 288.

Activity Checklist

Blocks

Block play for Fives includes creating, building, and experimenting with wooden or plastic unit blocks and larger hollow wooden, plastic, or cardboard blocks. Fives use blocks to make buildings, roadways, and other things they see around them and to build structures for pretend play.

Check for each age group

	60–66 months	66–72 months
1. A special area is set up for block play with low open shelves, a flat carpet, and a variety of blocks.	☐	☐
2. Accessories for block play are there to use, such as toy animals and people; small trucks, cars, and other vehicles.	☐	☐
3. Blocks and accessories are safe and in good repair.	☐	☐
4. Block Center is not shared with other activities while blocks are being used.	☐	☐
5. Block Center is large enough for at least four children to play without being crowded.	☐	☐
6. Blocks and accessories are available to children for at least two hours daily in full-day programs and for at least one hour in a half-day program.	☐	☐
7. Block Center is out of traffic so that children can work without interruptions.	☐	☐
8. Blocks and accessories are organized by type and stored on shelves and in containers that are clearly labeled with pictures and block outlines.	☐	☐
9. There are plenty of wooden unit blocks so that children can build large, complex structures if they wish.	☐	☐
10. Adult watches block play and talks with children about their block play to help them learn more, but is careful not to interrupt or take over the play.	☐	☐
11. Some block play is available outdoors with larger blocks and more space.	☐	☐

276

Fives can

- understand where things belong
- help clean up after play

Tour of the Block Center

Set up a Block Center with wooden unit blocks in a variety of shapes. Include some block toys, such as small cars, animals, and airplanes. Be sure to include toy people, too. Add buildings such as houses, barns, and garages as the children are interested. To help children remember where things go, put picture labels and block outlines on the low, open shelves.

When children are new to the room, visit the Block Center with a few Fives at a time. Talk about how the toys in the area are used and cared for. Make sure children know that blocks are to be used in the Block Center. Help children show their friends how they can take blocks off a shelf to build and put blocks away in the right place.

 indoors   5–7 minutes   2–6 Fives

277

Fives can

- follow a few simple rules for getting along with others

Block Center Rules

Have the children help you set a few Block Center rules and write them on a big sheet of paper. Hang them in the Block Center. You will find a list of rules on page 268, but you and the children may want to make up others.

Talk with your Fives about things that make them feel happy and angry when they play with blocks. Talk about how following rules can make block play go better for everyone.

Louise says she feels angry when people kick down her building.
We can be careful of other people's buildings and walk around them so that no one will get angry.

 indoors   5–10 minutes   1–6 Fives

278

Fives can

- build with a friend
- try to get along well with others

Friendly Building

Watch your Fives as they build with blocks. Whenever you see cooperation, being careful of other's buildings, sharing, or other thoughtful acts, let the children know that you noticed how well they handled things.

Talk about what they did and how it made others feel.

Nicky, you walked so carefully.
You really watched out for Robin's tower.

Nicky, did you hear Robin say "Excuse me" so that you would let her reach the shelf?

 indoors   1–2 minutes   1–6 Fives

279

Fives can

- share and cooperate with friends

Spaces to Build

When you have several Fives who want to work in the Block Center, make sure no one builds too near the shelves. Help the children understand why they should leave a clear path to the blocks so that everyone can get the blocks they need without knocking anything down.

Since Fives need lots of room for building, give each child or small group its own space. Use masking tape on the floor to mark spaces if you wish. Remind children to get blocks and toys from the shelves and to be careful of each others' buildings. Encourage children to combine spaces when they want to work together.

You and Rosie are sharing a big space, Brooke.
That's right. You can really build something big, now!

 indoors   2–6 minutes   2–6 Fives

280

Fives can

- use some size and number words
- learn names for some solid shapes

Talk about Block Shapes

As Fives play with blocks, talk about the shapes they are using. Tell the names of the shapes, use words for the block sizes, and say more about how the shapes look. Use words for the solid shapes, too, such as *cylinder, cube,* and *pyramid.*

You used cylinders to hold up your building, Jenna.
And you put some smaller cylinders on the top.

Ask questions to see what the children can say about the blocks.

Can you tell me about your building?
What kinds of blocks did you use?

 in or out   1–2 minutes   # 1–6 Fives

281

Fives can

- sort by shape
- clean up with help

Sorting Game at Clean-Up Time

Make cleaning up blocks into a sorting game. Ask your Fives to find all of each shape and put them onto the shelves in their own labeled spaces. For example, first ask the children to find all the small square blocks and put them away. Next, ask them to find the cylinders. Work on the block shapes until all the blocks have been put away.

Show how delighted you are as the children find the blocks. Give them chances to decide which blocks to find next. You can help find the blocks and put them away, too.

That's great, Juan. You and Henry found all the squares.
Now which shape block should we work on?
OK. Let's find all the long rectangles.

 indoors   5–10 minutes   # 1–6 Fives

282

Fives can

- match block shapes
- copy simple designs
- cooperate with friends

Making Buildings That Are the Same

As a child begins building with blocks, ask if you can try to copy what she is doing. If she says OK, then match each block she uses. Do this for a little while, talking together about the shapes and where they are placed.

Oh, oh! I do not know if I can get my rectangle to balance on top of the cylinder like you did, Theresa.
Wow! I did it!
Now what are you planning to do with that triangle?

Make a game of copying. See if children want to play the block-copying game with each other. But make sure the child who is being copied is asked first and says OK.

 in or out   7–15 minutes   1–6 Fives

283

Fives can

- tell you about their families
- pretend play as they use blocks and accessories

Families

Talk with your Fives about the people in their families. Then put out a dishpan of toy people and a large play house in the Block Center. Be sure to include enough figures to make families of different races with many brothers and sisters, grandmothers, grandfathers, or other relatives. Include figures of people with disabilities, too.

Who do you have in your family, Annie? I see you have two grown-ups here. Is this your mommy? Oh, your grandma and your dad.

Encourage the children to use as many toy people in their block play as they need to show their families.

 indoors   3–20 minutes   1–6 Fives

284

Fives can

- figure out simple problems
- lift hollow blocks

Moving Big Blocks

Take large hollow, wooden blocks outdoors in a wagon with the children's help. Watch and help them decide how many blocks they can load into the wagon and safely move at one time. Talk about how heavy a load they are pulling and how hard it would be to pull up a hill.

Lisa, these blocks are very heavy. I really appreciate your help. John, we got stuck in the mud! What should we do to get out of here? That's a good idea, John. If we dump out two medium-sized blocks, we'll be able to move.

Then let the children build outside with the blocks.

 outdoors   5–10 minutes   1–4 Fives

285

Fives can

- enjoy building with blocks
- pretend in their block play

Road Building

Look at a picture book about building roads with your Fives. Then add toy road-building vehicles such as bulldozers and dump trucks to the Block Center. Have plastic hardhats for children to wear if they wish. Encourage children to build roads with blocks and to use the vehicles as they work.

Be sure to have a dishpan of little cars and plenty of other blocks so that the children can add to their road-building play.

Did the four of you build all these roads?
Where does this road go?
Is this a house? Who lives here?

 indoors   10–30 minutes   1–6 Fives

286

Fives can

- use their imaginations
- build with many types of blocks

Shoe Boxes As Blocks

Bring in some empty shoe boxes and place them in the Block Center. Watch to see how children use these as they play. Encourage your Fives to use the boxes in many ways—to stack, to use as cars or trucks, to load blocks into.

If children are interested, they can decorate the boxes to turn them into accessories for the Block Center. For example, they might want to make a house or car for small dolls. Children may take the boxes to the Art Center where they can use art materials and then return the decorated finished boxes to the Block Center if they wish.

Remove the boxes when children lose interest, and bring something else that is new into the Block Center.

 indoors　　 5–30 minutes　　# 1–6 Fives

287

Fives can

- pretend in their block play
- do creative building with blocks

Trains in the Block Area

Read *The Little Engine that Could* with a small group of Fives. Talk about the details in the illustrations—count how many cars the little engine has to pull, what the tracks are like, where they go, and the buildings.

Add plastic or wooden train sets to the Block Center. Encourage interested Fives to use the trains in their own way. Talk about the "little engines that could." Allow your Fives to add small dolls and toy animals to put on their trains. See if the children build tracks and train stations as part of their play.

Wow! You made the tracks go up a hill. How did you make that hill, Jimmy?

 indoors　　 10–30 minutes　　# 1–6 Fives

288

Fives can

- enjoy pretend play
- cooperate with friends

Hollow Blocks and Dramatic Play Props

Allow your Fives to mix large hollow blocks and dramatic play props for fun pretend play activities. Here are some ideas you can encourage by putting out the props for the children to use with the hollow blocks:

- food cartons, a cash register, and paper bags to make a grocery store
- clothes, paper bags, a cash register, and price tags to make a clothing store
- large toy animals to make a zoo or farm
- doctor kits for hospital play
- play tickets, a coin box, and play money for bus or train play
- a steering wheel for transportation play

 in or out   5–40 minutes   2–6 Fives

289

Fives can

- stack different types of objects
- talk about things they have made

Stacking Things

Put out household things for your Fives to stack. Try margarine tubs with lids, empty cardboard food boxes, small cardboard jewelry boxes, or spools from thread. Keep these things in a labeled box in the Block Center. As children make different kinds of towers, talk with them about the kinds of stacking materials they used.

How many different things did you use to make your tower, Bonita? What is that on the very top? Are some of these things better for building than others?

Make sure that all household things are sturdy and safe and have no rough or sharp edges.

 indoors   5–20 minutes   1–6 Fives

290

Fives can

- pretend in their block play
- share and cooperate with friends

Building a Big House

Work with any interested Fives to build a house that they can pretend to live in. Make an outline with long wooden blocks for the outside walls. Leave an opening for the door. Have the children build up the walls. Help them think of what they need inside the house.

Where is the door to your house?
How many bedrooms do you need?
Elena, what are you working on?

After the children have made the building, let them play in it as they wish. At another time, try building an airport for airplanes or a parking lot for cars as a group project.

 in or out   10–40 minutes   1–6 Fives

291

Fives can

- show things they know about as they build with blocks

Building Zoos and Farms

Look with your Fives at books and pictures of animals in cages, pens, or other fenced-in areas. Talk about the pictures with the children. Put up some of the pictures in the Block Center so that children can look as they build. Put out some toy farm or zoo animals like the ones in the pictures. Add some toy fences, too. See how the children use all these things as they build. Talk with the children about what they are building.

Rasheed, I see you fenced in some lions.
Why do we need to have fences in zoos or on farms?
Do you know anyone who has a fence at home?
Why do people have fences?

Try this activity after children have visited a zoo or farm.

 indoors   3–30 minutes   1–6 Fives

292

Fives can

- understand the words *same* and *different*

Same and Different Blocks

Show your Fives blocks that are different in one way and the same in another way. For example, show a short red rectangle and a long red rectangle. Ask them to tell you all they can about each shape. Then ask them questions to help them tell how the blocks are the same or different from each other.

Are they the same color?
Are they the same size?
Are they the same shape?
Do they both have corners or curves?

Help the Fives compare several different kinds of blocks: cylinder and square, big and little rectangles, and so on.

 in or out   4–8 minutes   1–5 Fives

293

Fives can

- lift large, heavy objects
- stack blocks above their heads

Big Boxes as Outdoor Blocks

Bring in eight or ten big sturdy cardboard cartons or storage boxes for your Fives to use to build outdoors on a dry day or indoors in a large space. Tape the boxes closed with masking tape. Let the children stack them and build with them in many ways. Talk with them about the ways they use the boxes. They can also use these boxes as houses, cars, or boats.

You've stacked five boxes, Carlos.
Are you going to put another on top?
What can you use to help you reach higher?

Check all boxes to be sure they are safe and have no sharp staples. Throw away boxes when they become worn out.

 in or out   5–30 minutes   1–6 Fives

294

Fives can

- use their bodies to lift, stretch, and crawl
- know some words for how they move

How We Move as We Build

Watch your Fives as they build with wooden unit blocks in the Block Center. Comment on how they stretch to stack blocks up high or reach out as far as they can. Talk with the children about the many different ways they move their bodies as they build.

Alicia, you stacked those blocks up above your head. How are you going to take them down?
You really had to stretch and stand on your tiptoes!

At group time, play a game with the children in which everyone acts out familiar movements they make while using blocks, such as taking a block from a shelf, balancing a block on the top of tower, or taking a building apart.

 indoors   2–8 minutes   1–20 Fives

295

Fives can

- use blocks in many creative ways

Build Around Me

Have one child lie down on the floor in the Block Center and have interested children outline his body with blocks. Remind your five-year-olds to be careful as they work. Talk about which blocks work best to outline the different parts of the child's body.

You are using curved blocks to outline Geraldo's head. What will work best to outline his legs, Ashley?

When the outline is finished, help the child get up without knocking the blocks over. Talk about the different parts of the outline.

Encourage children to take turns and cooperate as they outline each other with blocks.

 indoors   5–20 minutes   2–8 Fives

296

Fives can

- write a few letters
- know familiar things in their neighborhood

Making Signs for the Block Center

Display pictures of road signs for your Fives to look at in the Block Center. Include stop, slow, yield, railroad crossing, no parking, and speed limit signs. Talk about the signs with the children. See which ones they know.

You know this sign is a yield *sign, don't you, Kirsty?*
Do you want to make one to put on your road?

Encourage children to make signs for their block buildings. They can use sturdy paper, watercolor markers, ice cream sticks, and masking tape. Help them to write words or write words for them to copy themselves if they wish.

What name do you want to put on your road, Mari?
That's your address! Do you want me to write it so that you can copy it, or shall I write it on your sign?

 indoors   3–20 minutes   1–8 Fives

297

Fives can

- feel ownership
- want to continue working on a project

Saving Favorite Block Projects

Allow your Fives to save special buildings so that they can finish them or share them with others. Help them make signs to put on these buildings so that they do not get cleaned up. Be sure all the children know to look for signs and find out what they say.

This says "Michael and Andrea built this. Please save."
You can help clean up the other buildings, Thomas, but we will save this one for later.

You and your Fives can save block buildings that must finally come down by taking a photograph of the building to display or writing a story the child tells you about the building.

 indoors   2–15 minutes   1–6 Fives

298

Fives can

- show things they know about as they build with blocks
- pretend in their block play

Block Furniture

Put pictures of different rooms in the Block Center. Hang the pictures low so that children can get up close and see. Look at the pictures with the children. Talk with them about the different furniture in the pictures and the kinds of activities people do in each room.

Add blankets and pillows to the Block Center. Have large wooden or cardboard blocks for your Fives to use with these things. See if they use the blocks and accessories to build furniture or pretend rooms.

Annie, you put pillows on these blocks. What did you make? A bed? Who will sleep in the bed?

 indoors   5–30 minutes   1–6 Fives

299

Fives can

- follow simple directions
- take turns in a group
- know most simple shapes

"Which Block?" Shape Game

Sit with a few interested Fives in the Block Center to play a go-and-find-it game. Ask each child to find a block shaped like the one you describe.

Michael, can you bring me a block that is the same shape as our fish tank?
Mei Ling, can you bring me a block that has the same shape as the roll of paper towels?
Do you remember what this block shape is called?

Take turns and let the children tell about a block they want others to find.

 indoors   4–12 minutes   1–6 Fives

300

Fives can

- talk about what will happen
- balance blocks while building
- take turns in a group

What Stacks, What Doesn't?

Build a tower with a few of your Fives using blocks of many shapes. As you add each block, look at the tower and the block you are going to add. Talk about the different ways the block could be added. Help the children guess when a block will balance and when it won't.

Jamal, do you think this cylinder will stay on top of this triangle, or will it fall? Let's try and see. Oh! What happened?

Take turns adding blocks and guessing what will balance.

 indoors   3–12 minutes   1–4 Fives

301

Fives can

- copy simple patterns
- know most simple shapes

Simple Block Patterns

Sort square, triangular, and rectangular blocks into several dishpans with your Fives. Then have one of the children use the shapes to make a pattern on the floor. Ask any interested children to copy the pattern. Talk with them about following patterns.

Emily is putting a square, a rectangle, and a square on the floor. Can you make a pattern just like Emily's?

Encourage children to make their own patterns for you and their friends to follow. See if they can repeat the patterns they have made.

Wow, Annie! You repeated your block pattern four times! And now Tamara is making the same one!

 indoors   3–5 minutes   1–4 Fives

302

Fives can

■ do simple block building

■ share and cooperate with friends

Big Blocks with Boards Outside

Bring big cardboard or hollow wooden blocks outside on a nice dry day. Add some smooth, lightweight boards 3' to 4' long for your Fives to use with these blocks. Watch to see the ways they use these things together. See if the children build bridges, ramps, or seesaws.

Can you go under the bridge, Julia?
I can see that it is safe.

Help children be careful as they move the boards so that no one is bumped. Be sure that blocks or boards won't fall if Fives climb on them or go under or over them.

Have a soft cushioning surface under the blocks and help children figure out what is safe.

 outdoors 5–20 minutes 1–6 Fives

303

Fives can

■ count 10 or more objects

■ know most simple shapes

How Many Blocks?

If a child is interested in numbers, count the number of blocks she uses in her block building. Help the child point to one block at a time as she counts with you. You can count either all the blocks or each block shape that was used.

How many squares did you use in this tower, Lauren?
Can you count them? That's right. Eight.
Oh, there is another one hiding here!
Now how many are there?

 indoors 2–7 minutes 1–2 Fives

304

Fives can

- talk about things they make

Block Photographs

Take photographs of the buildings children have made. Hang them where the children can see. Put the pictures into a Blocks photo album if you wish. Label them to tell who made the building and what it was.

Look at the pictures often with your Fives. Talk with them about the block buildings in many ways. Write down what they say about the buildings and put their stories near the photos. Read their stories to them.

This was a very long, narrow building.
Do you remember who worked on it?
Yes, Laurie. It says, "Laurie and Walter worked on this building together." Can you see what kinds of blocks you used?

 in or out   3–12 minutes   1–4 Fives

305

Fives can

- talk about things they make

- enjoy having you write down and read stories they tell

Block Stories

When a child has built something with blocks, see if he will tell you something about what he did. Ask questions to help him say more.

What did you build, Thomas? Oh, an apartment building.
You live in a building like that, don't you?
Is your apartment somewhere in this building?

Try tape recording or writing down the things a child says about his block building. Put the stories in the Book Center to read or in the Listening Center to play back. You can also write the story down and tape it to the block building as long as the building is left up.

 inside   2–10 minutes   1–2 Fives

306

Fives can

- build well with blocks
- enjoy sand play

Block and Sand Play

Bring unit <u>blocks</u> or smaller blocks to use in the sand table. Let your Fives play freely with the blocks in the sand. Talk with the children about how they can hide or balance the blocks in different ways in the sand. Add animal <u>toys</u> or <u>trucks</u> and see how the children use these, too.

That truck has to plow through the sand to get to the house you made, Peter.
You smoothed the sand so that your tower would balance, Donna.

Remind the children to clean the toys and blocks well before putting them away. Make sure the blocks do not get wet.

 in or out   3–20 minutes   **#** 1–4 Fives

307

Fives can

- show things they know about as they build with blocks

Pictures of Buildings

Put <u>pictures</u> of different types of buildings—small houses, big apartment houses, gas stations, water towers, supermarkets, churches, and others—in the Block Center where children can see and touch. Talk with the children about the shapes they see in each picture. See what they know about the different types of buildings.

Talk with the children about what they build with blocks. See if they try to use any of the ideas they have seen in the pictures as they build their own creations.

What have you built here, Royce?
A supermarket?
Is it like the one in the picture, or did you make a different kind of supermarket?

 indoors   3–30 minutes   **#** 1–6 Fives

308

Fives can

- show things they know about as they build with blocks

Looking at Real Buildings

Take your Fives on a short "Looking at Buildings" walk. Help them see the shapes of different parts of the buildings they find, such as doors, steps, windows, walls, and roofs. Encourage children to feel the buildings, too—to run their fingers along the lines between bricks or feel the corner angles in a wall. As children build with blocks, talk with them about what they have built. See if they tell you about the parts of the buildings that they have created.

You made a sharp corner angle here, Glenda.
What are you working on now?
Oh, steps are tricky to build, aren't they?

You can take photos of some of the buildings your Fives see on their walk to talk and write about later.

 in or out   10–30 minutes   1–20 Fives

309

Fives can

- remember types of buildings
- talk about pretend places

Building a Pretend Place

After children listen to a favorite story, talk with them about how the pretend place in the story looked. For example, if you read "Beauty and the Beast," talk about what the castle looked like. Then encourage the children to build their own versions of the pretend places that were in the story.

I can tell that you two are building a castle, Carrie.
Can you tell me about this part? Oh, yes. I see that it is the tower.
Does anyone live in this part of the castle, Frieda?

Buildings can be created with small blocks on a table or rug or with unit blocks or large hollow blocks indoors or outdoors.

 in or out   5–30 minutes   1–6 Fives

310

Fives can

■ know about different buildings

■ begin to understand maps

Building a Neighborhood

Take your Fives on a walk around the school. Notice the buildings in the neighborhood. Talk about the types of buildings near the school—whether they are tall or short, how many floors they have, what they are used for, and what shapes they have. Take some photos of the school and some of the nearby buildings with an instant camera. Take paper to draw a rough map of the school and the closest buildings.

When you get back, make a map showing where each building is in relation to the school. Glue the photos onto the map and add roads, trees, and other important landmarks the children would remember. Talk about what you are doing as interested children watch. See if children look at the map as they do block building.

 in or out   10–30 minutes   1–10 Fives

311

Fives can

■ show things they know about as they build with blocks

Map of the Block Center

Talk with your Fives about how maps show you where things are. Then after several children have built block buildings, have them help you make a map of the Block Center using markers on a big sheet of easel paper. Draw the furniture in the area first—the shelves and rug. Talk about what you are drawing as you do it, and help the children look from the real things to the map as you work. Then add the children's buildings, talking about where the buildings are in relationship to each other and to where the furniture is. Have the children help you figure out where each building goes on the map of the Block Center.

Where should we put Donnell's building? That's right. It's over by the windows. Here are windows on our map. Should we draw it here?

 in or out   10–30 minutes   1–20 Fives

Block Center

- Find a place for blocks where people do not have to walk through to get to other areas of the room. A corner away from doorways works well.

- Make the Block Center big enough for at least four children to play at the same time with plenty of space to build and move.

- If too many children want to build at the same time, help children use a sign-up sheet so that they will be sure to get a turn. Teach children to go and get the child whose name is next on the list.

- Store blocks and the toys used with blocks on open shelves no taller than the children.

- Label each place on the shelves with a picture of what goes there. Use outlines of blocks or paste cutouts of the blocks right on the shelf. Put the pictures near the front of the shelf and show the block with the long side to the front.

- At clean-up time, the best way to get children to know where the block shapes belong is to start putting a block in the right place and have them copy you.

- Keep small toys and accessories to use with blocks in separate boxes, each labeled with a picture. Have small people, animals, little trucks, and airplanes to use with blocks. Be sure to include enough people for large families and to include figures of different races and ages and people with disabilities. Have a separate, clearly labeled box for each type of toy.

- Put the heavier blocks and toys on the lower shelves so that they will be easier for the children to take out and put back by themselves.

- Have a large flat rug that is good to build on in the Block Center. Remind children to build on the rug. If you do not have a flat rug, show the children how to build on a large, flat board so that their towers will have a steady base.

- Have different kinds of blocks: wooden unit blocks, large cardboard or hollow wooden blocks, and colorful plastic building blocks. Keep all of these organized in their own spaces.

- Have plenty of wooden unit blocks so that children's imaginations can take off. The more blocks are available, the more creative children can be.

- Put up pictures of real buildings to add interest and new ideas. Show pictures of buildings under construction.

- Have wooden or plastic houses, airports, barns, and filling stations near the blocks for the children to use with little toy people and cars. Keep these heavy play buildings on the bottom shelves or on the floor. Older Fives may enjoy making their own buildings in the Art Center.

- Show children how to take the blocks off the shelves carefully and how to put the blocks back without knocking the buildings down. Show children how proud you are when they are careful around blocks.

- Encourage long-term projects. Allow children to come back and finish their buildings later or to save a favorite project for other children and parents to enjoy.

- Have some block play outdoors. If blocks can't be stored outside, take them out in a box and let children play on a rug. Use a wagon to get blocks outdoors. Have the children help take the blocks out and later put them back on the shelves.

Materials and Notes

Dramatic Play

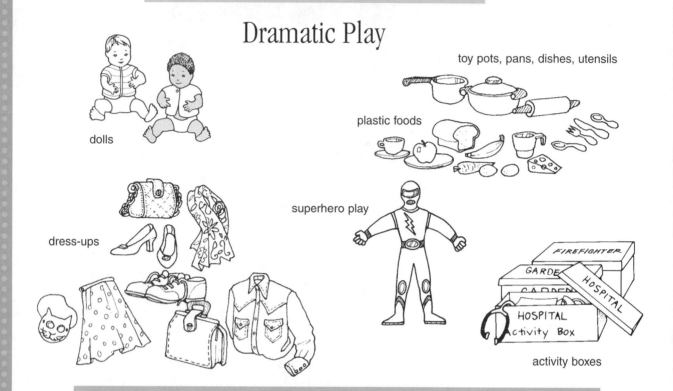

dolls

toy pots, pans, dishes, utensils

plastic foods

dress-ups

superhero play

FIREFIGHTER

GARDE

HOSPITAL

HOSPITAL
Activity Box

activity boxes

- Most of the activity ideas for younger and older Fives can be used with either age group. This is because they are open-ended and can be challenging to children of a wide range of abilities.

- Have many props for Fives to use in their pretend play. Add to these often. Have more than one of the most popular things to prevent fights about sharing.

- Use plastic hats whenever possible and wash all dress-ups weekly. If lice are a problem in your group, omit hats from all activities.

- Encourage both girls and boys to enjoy the Dramatic Play Center.

- Make sure that all toys and props in the Dramatic Play Center are safe and clean for children to use. Shorten dress-ups, disinfect shoes and hats, and wash things regularly.

- Add activity boxes to encourage different types of pretend play. You will find ideas for pretend play activity boxes in the activities in this section.

- Use field trips, books, pictures, and classroom visitors to give children the information they need to pretend about many topics.

- Ask parents to help in collecting things for use in pretend play. Send home lists of the kinds of things you need, such as dress-ups, old pots and pans, or empty food containers from healthful foods.

Activity Checklist

Dramatic Play

Dramatic play for Fives includes pretend play with dolls, stuffed animals, housekeeping toys, community helper props, and other things children use when they act out what they see happening every day. Fives also enjoy props about fantasy or super heroes, characters they learn about. They enjoy acting out familiar stories and making up new ones. Adults can help Fives get new information for play by taking them on field trips, reading books, inviting visitors to talk with children, and providing props for work roles and adventure. Fives enjoy pretend play on their own but sometimes need adult help to solve problems and plan more elaborate pretend play.

Check for each age group

	60–66 months	66–72 months
1. Dramatic Play Center is set up and available for children to choose freely every day.	❑	❑
2. Center has child-sized housekeeping furniture and props for playing house, job/community helper, and fantasy.	❑	❑
3. Props are clearly organized on low shelves and in storage areas of small play furniture.	❑	❑
4. All materials are sturdy, safe, and clean.	❑	❑
5. Children are encouraged to use pretend play materials in their own ways.	❑	❑
6. Additional toys and props are stored but handy so that they are taken out often to be used.	❑	❑
7. Male and female dolls are of different races. Props from many cultures—cooking utensils, pretend foods, dress-ups, and doll clothes—are included for everyday play.	❑	❑
8. Adult helps children elaborate their pretend play by adding new props, reading stories, talking about ideas with children, and taking them on field trips.	❑	❑
9. Adult supervises pretend play by helping children solve problems and guide play so that it does not become dangerous.	❑	❑
10. Props for pretend play are used outdoors as well as indoors.	❑	❑

312

Fives can

- cooperate with friends in pretend play
- pretend about familiar experiences

Play House

Set up a simple playhouse in a corner of the room. (See Dramatic Play Center Ideas on page 312.) Include child-sized-furniture, such as a table and chairs; a low, open shelf; a doll bed; and a pretend stove and sink. Add dolls; pots and pans; and unbreakable plates, cups and silverware. To help Fives at clean-up time, put picture/word labels of toys on the shelf and on other places where things go.

Let your Fives play freely in this playhouse. Talk with the children about their play and join in if you wish.

You are putting on some fancy clothes, Dennis.
What are you going to do?

Be careful. Do not take over the play or interrupt the way it is going unless things are getting out of control.

 indoors   5–30 minutes   1–6 Fives

313

Fives can

- pretend about familiar experiences

Feelings Pantomime

Find a variety of photographs that show different emotions. At group circle time, give each of your Fives a different picture, placed face down.

Ask each of your Fives, one at a time, to act out his feeling card without using words. Let the other Fives guess what the feeling is.

That's right, Mary. It looks like Domingo is pretending to cry.
What do you think his feeling card is?
Yes. It must be very sad.
Can you show us your card, Domingo?
Yes. It's a little boy crying, just like you!

 indoors   2–3 minutes   2–20 Fives

314

Fives can

- cooperate with friends in pretend play
- pretend about things they know

Telephone Play

Have several real or toy telephones in the Dramatic Play Center. Let the children play with these freely. Encourage Fives to talk to each other on the telephones. Enjoy their telephone conversations.

Hi, Raymond. Who are you talking with on the phone? With your girlfriend? What did she say? She wants you to pick her up at her house right now!

Set up an office, a store, or a beauty shop in an area next to the Dramatic Play Center. Encourage children to talk to each other by telephone as they order materials or make appointments.

 indoors   1–5 minutes   1–4 Fives

315

Fives can

- use realistic props in their pretend play
- cooperate with friends in pretend play

Taking a Business Trip

See if any children in your class have parents who take business trips. Have them tell about how parents get ready to travel. Add a business trips activity box to the Dramatic Play Center with a small suitcase, a cosmetics kit, map, used airline ticket, and other traveling things. Allow your Fives to use these things in their own creative ways.

Jose, I need to go to Orlando for business tomorrow. What do I need to pack? You're right. I need to pack my toothbrush.

Children can role-play going to the airport, going to the hotel, calling home and talking to the children, and coming back home again. Also try going on a pretend trip to visit relatives. You may be surprised by how much your Fives can add to this activity!

 indoors   2–5 minutes   1–5 Fives

316

Fives can

- cooperate with friends in pretend play
- use realistic props in their pretend play

Changing Baby

Make a changing baby activity box with squares of cloth for doll-sized diapers, a few newborn-sized rubber pants, and empty baby powder and lotion bottles. Look at all the things in the box with your Fives. Talk about what each thing is and what it's for. Show the children how you diaper a baby doll. Then put the box out for the Fives to use on their own. Children can use masking tape to hold diapers on babies.

How often do you need to change your baby, Sandy?
A hundred times? Your baby must wet a lot!

This is a good activity to try when one of your Fives has a new baby brother or sister. Talk about what changing baby is really like at home!

 in or out   5–20 minutes   1–4 Fives

317

Fives can

- pretend about familiar experiences
- plan a pretend play activity

The Birthday Party

Plan a pretend birthday party with your Fives. Talk with them about what they need in order to get the Dramatic Play Center ready for the party. Let them do all the decorating! You can help by asking questions and making a list of things to do.

How many people are coming to the party?
Who is making the cake?
What decorations are you using?
What do you want to do at the party?

Your Fives can help you think of more things that need to be done. Encourage some children to pretend to be guests by making a present, wrapping it, and coming to the party.

 indoors   2–30 minutes   2–6 Fives

318

Fives can:

- cooperate with friends in pretend play

- pretend about familiar experiences

- use realistic props in their pretend play

The Bakery

Take your Fives to visit a bakery. Talk with them about the different things people do who work in the bakery. When you get back to the classroom, help your Fives set up a pretend bakery using cookie sheets, bakers' aprons and hats, and play-dough food children make or pretend props you already have in the classroom. You can help the planning by asking questions.

Where should we put the bakery?
Next to the shelf over there?
What kinds of things does your bakery sell?
Great, I love bagels. Can I buy some?
Are there paper bags for the things people buy?

Children can take turns baking, selling, and buying.

 indoors   3–15 minutes   2–5 Fives

319

Fives can

- cooperate with friends in pretend play

The Sick Doll

During group time, explain to your Fives that one of the dolls in the Dramatic Play Center has the chicken pox. Talk with your Fives about how to make her feel better.

Isabelle is very sick. She has the chicken pox.
Do you remember when you had chicken pox?
How did you feel? What happened?
What can we do to make Isabelle feel better?
That's a good idea, Dori. We can put lotion on her spots.
Can we do anything else?

Help your Fives set up a sick room for the doll in the Dramatic Play Center. Put the materials to make get-well cards in the Art Center. Encourage children to check on the doll's condition throughout the day.

 indoors   2–20 minutes   2–5 Fives

320

Fives can

- use realistic props in their pretend play

Cooking Spaghetti

Put a large cookpot, a long spoon, oven mitts, a bundle of white yarn cut in 12" lengths, a colander, and tongs in the Dramatic Play Center. Add empty spaghetti boxes and an empty can of grated cheese. Put a menu for a spaghetti dinner on the kitchen table. Watch your Fives to see how many different ways they pretend to cook, serve, and eat spaghetti!

I see you are putting the noodles in a soup bowl, Yoshiko.
Oh, yes, it is soba.
I eat soba when I go to the Japanese restaurant.
Do you have soba at home?

Show children pictures of many different ways that noodles can be used in foods.

 indoors   5–20 minutes   2–6 Fives

321

Fives can

- pretend about familiar experiences

Afraid of the Dark

Bring a small stuffed dog (or other animal) to group time. Tell your Fives that Tiger, the dog, is scared of the dark and needs their help. Encourage children to talk about what they think will make Tiger stop being afraid. You may need to ask some questions to get your Fives started.

Do any of you have a little brother or sister who is scared of the dark? What did your mommy or daddy do?

When group time is over, return Tiger to the Dramatic Play Center. Watch your Fives as they play to see if they try to help Tiger get over his fear of the dark. Don't be surprised if some of your Fives put Tiger in the dark to make him scared!

 indoors   2–5 minutes   1–20 Fives

322

Fives can

- use less realistic props in pretend play

Transportation

Find a large, narrow cardboard box, (such as an empty refrigerator box) and put it on the playground. Tell interested Fives that this box is for transportation. Let them decide what kind of transportation they want it to be and play in their own way.

What kind of transportation should this box be?
It does look like a train. It's long and narrow.
What do we need to add to make a train?

Your Fives may want to paint their train, add wheels and seats, and add a smokestack, or they may want to use the box in many different ways. Leave the box project on the playground to play with until your Fives are tired of it or it falls apart.

 outdoors   10–30 minutes   2–6 Fives

323

Fives can

- cooperate with friends in pretend play

- use realistic props in pretend play

Gas Station

Make an activity box your Fives can use to play gas station, including pieces of hose 1 to 2 yards long, with nozzles attached, sturdy plastic fix-it-tools, signs showing different brands of gas, and a money box for change. With the children, look at a book that shows things that happen at a gas station. Ask questions to help your Fives say what they know about gas stations.

What do we buy at gas stations?
What else happens at the gas station, Tanya?

Attach the hoses to a box or to the fence outside to show the children where they can bring riding toys to be fixed or filled up. Add a tire gauge so that children can check the tire pressure and a pretend air hose for tires that are low.

 in or out   5–30 minutes   1–6 Fives

324

Fives can

- copy adult work
- cooperate with friends in pretend play

Carpenters

Read a book about carpenters with your Fives. Visit a building that is being built if possible. Talk about the work carpenters do. Then collect things children can use as they pretend to be carpenters. Set up a carpenter shop outdoors with some small hammers, large pieces of 2" plastic foam, and some roofing nails with large, flat heads. Add a child-sized saw, drill, and screwdriver and screws.

Provide a lightweight toolbox so that the children can carry the tools with them to the place they are working. Talk about what they are pretending to build and repair.

If they are not already doing so, encourage girls to pretend to be carpenters, too. Watch carefully if nails or other sharp things are used for this play.

 outdoors 5–30 minutes 1–6 Fives

325

Fives can

- cooperate with friends in pretend play
- remember a short list

Going Shopping

Make a shopping activity box that includes some purses and wallets, pretend money, a pad and pencil, a set of car keys, and some string grocery bags. Put it in the Dramatic Play Center.

Sit in the kitchen and tell your Fives that you want to make a cake but you forgot to go to the grocery store. You are late for another appointment. Could they go to the store for you? Talk about what they will need to get at the store. Remind them to make a list so that they won't forget.

Don't be surprised at the ingredients they decide to buy for the cake! This is a good activity to do when there is a store set up in the classroom, in addition to the Dramatic Play Center.

 in or out 5–20 minutes 1–4 Fives

326

Fives can

■ cooperate with friends in pretend play

■ pretend about familiar experiences

Playing Doctors and Nurses

Put out an activity box of doctor and nurse things for your Fives to play with. Use only safe things, such as a toy or real stethoscope, a flashlight, pretend thermometer, short strips of gauze bandage material, plastic bandage strips or tape, and paper with pencils to keep records or write prescriptions. Do not put in bottles of candy pills. Encourage children to remember and talk about visiting the doctor.

You went to the doctor for a checkup, Monique.
Can you tell us what happened?

To help your Fives think of more play ideas, read books about going to the doctor with the children.

 in or out   10–20 minutes   1–6 Fives

327

Fives can

■ copy adult work

■ pretend about familiar experiences

Dressing Dolls and Caring for Doll Clothes

Buy or make simple doll clothes that are easy to put on. Ask interested Fives, parents, or volunteers to help with this. Have clothes that are loose or that fasten with buttons or snaps. Keep these in a dishpan on a low shelf for Fives to use. Encourage your Fives to dress the babies.

Add a toy ironing board with iron. Buy a pretend washer and dryer or make a set out of boxes. Talk about washing, drying, and folding clothes for babies. Then watch to see how children use these things in their play.

You put all the doll clothes into the laundry basket, Paul.
What are you planning to do?

 in or out   5–20 minutes   1–6 Fives

328

Fives can

- copy adult work
- pretend about familiar experiences

Dentist Play

Make a dentist activity box with some unbreakable hand mirrors, a book about going to the dentist, and pictures of toothbrushing. Talk with the children about what the dentist does. Let the children look at your teeth. Have them look at their own teeth in the mirrors. If the children have individual toothbrushes, have them brush their teeth and see if their teeth are clean after they brush. Have them look in the sink to see if anything brushed out of their teeth.

Encourage children to pretend to be dentists for dolls and toy animals. Help them figure out the things they need for play, such as how to make a dentist's chair or a waiting room. Supply rubber gloves, dentist's masks, and other props to use with the dolls. Read books about going to the dentist, too.

 indoors   5–20 minutes   1–6 Fives

329

Fives can

- copy adult work
- pretend about familiar experiences

Painters

Make a painter's activity box with painters' hats, big brushes, paint rollers with pans, buckets, paint scrapers, and plastic aprons or large shirts. Include pictures of people painting houses, furniture, or fences for children to look at. Arrange a field trip to a place where painters are working.

Talk with the children about the work painters do. Take the activity box outdoors and let the Fives use water for paint and pretend to be painters.

I see you have a hollow block to stand on so that you can reach up high to paint, Maria.
Do you remember what the painters stood on to paint?
That's right. It was called a scaffold.

 outdoors   5–30 minutes   1–8 Fives

330

Fives can

- copy adult work
- pretend about familiar experiences

Firefighters

Read a book about firefighters with your Fives. Take a field trip to a fire station, too. Then put out a firefighter activity box for your Fives to use as they play. Include short pieces of hose, firefighter hats, a blanket, a light toy plastic hammer to use as an ax, some firefighter badges made of aluminum foil over cardboard, and a bell. The children can use a wagon as the fire truck and put out pretend fires on the playground.

Talk about fire safety with your Fives. Remind them that real fires are dangerous. Ask local firefighters what you can teach your Fives to prepare them for fires. Help your Fives to practice these things in their play.

Stop, drop, and roll, Maggie.
Then the fire on your clothes will be out.

 outdoors   5–30 minutes   1–6 Fives

331

Fives can

- pretend about familiar experiences
- cooperate with friends

Post Office

Collect used envelopes, post cards, and lots of unopened junk mail. Put these into a post office activity box with bags to use as mail bags, boxes to sort mail, and stamps that come in junk mail. Talk with the children about the post office and what postal workers do. Visit the post office and read books about how mail is delivered. Let the children pretend with the things in the post office box. See if they will write letters, put stamps on envelopes, deliver mail to different people in the room, and open the letters they get. Use post office words, such as *address, deliver,* and *cancel.*

On a special day when cards are sent, such as Valentine's Day, have the children use the real post office to mail home a card that they have made in the Art Center.

 in or out   10–30 minutes   1–8 Fives

332

Fives can

- copy adult work
- pretend about familiar experiences

Playing Office

With your Fives, visit someone who works in an office. A short trip can be made to the office in your own building. Help the children see the kinds of equipment people use as they do office work, such as computers, copy machines, and pens and paper. Read books with your Fives about what office workers do. See what they know about this kind of work from their own experiences.

Put together an office activity box. Put envelopes and stationery, a small file box, a rubber stamp and stamp pad, a pad, and a pencil in the box. Make a pretend computer out of a cardboard box and add toy or real typewriters. Add a telephone book and address book to put near the telephones. Encourage your Fives to pretend about working in an office.

 indoors   10–30 minutes   1–8 Fives

333

Fives can:

- pretend about familiar experiences
- use realistic props in their pretend play

Mothers' and Fathers' Work Play

Talk with your Fives to find out what kinds of jobs their parents do. Be sure to include mothers and fathers working at home or outside the home.

Sammy, your father leaves for work before you get up in the morning. What does he do?
He drives a bread truck?
Tell us about what he does in his truck.

Make activity boxes for some of the jobs the children talk about. Ask parents for ideas that will help children pretend about jobs. They may have stationery, old uniforms, business cards, or other things to use as props. Be sure to ask parents for photographs that show them working at their jobs or have them come in to talk about their jobs if they can.

 in or out   5–30 minutes   1–8 Fives

334

Fives can

- copy adult work
- pretend about familiar experiences

Cleaning House

Put together a house-cleaning activity box with things you use to clean the house. Include dust rags, a spray bottle of water, an apron, rubber gloves, a small broom and a dustpan, a small mop, and a toy vacuum cleaner. Add clean, empty containers from household cleaners. Let interested Fives pretend about cleaning the Dramatic Play Center and other parts of the room.

Talk with children about the things people clean in their houses. Write down some of the things they say on a big piece of easel paper and read their ideas back to them.

What else do you help your mom and dad with when they are cleaning up, Desmond?

 in or out   10–30 minutes   1–8 Fives

335

Fives can

- copy adult work
- pretend about familiar experiences
- cooperate with friends

Library Play

Talk with your Fives about what librarians do. Talk about the children's visits to the library or bookmobile. Take a library field trip to help children see librarians at work. Set up a small place in the room where children can play library. Make a library activity box with library cards and envelopes, date stamps and ink pads, pencils, small used books, old magazines, and newspapers.

Let the children pretend with the things in the library activity box and give them books to put back on the shelves. Show your Fives how to put the books about the same topics together on the shelves. Use library words such as *check out, return,* and *due date.* Later, you may want to set up a classroom library with books the children can borrow.

 indoors   5–30 minutes   1–8 Fives

336

Fives can

- pretend about familiar experiences
- cooperate with friends

The Horse Show

Talk with your Fives about setting up a jumping course for a horse show. See if any of your Fives know about how a horse show works. Let children show how they would pretend being jumping and galloping horses. Then put out ten sturdy plastic crates, five 5'-long dowels, and posters numbered one to five. Add a box with 12" lengths of blue ribbons that each child can win. Allow children to arrange these things on the playground as a horse-jumping course that has five jumps.

Decide together where to put each jump on the course. Make sure your Fives can jump safely. Label each jump with a number poster. Your Fives can also set up bleachers for people to watch the show, sell tickets, or set up a food booth.

 outdoors   5–30 minutes   1–8 Fives

337

Fives can

- pretend about familiar experiences

Acting Out a Familiar Story

Read a familiar story to your Fives that has enough characters to act out. "Goldilocks and the Three Bears," "The Three Billy Goats Gruff," and "Little Red Riding Hood" are good choices.

Talk with your Fives about roles and costumes or props they will need for the parts of the story they want to act out. You may want to have a few rehearsals before the play is given.

Your Fives will retell the stories in their own words. Don't try to correct them, but be available to prompt them if they get stuck.

 in or out   5–20 minutes   1–20 Fives

338

Fives can

- copy adult work
- pretend about familiar experiences
- cooperate with friends

Rescue Squad Play

Put blankets, a first aid kit with bandage strips and gauze bandages, a flashlight, and a toy walkie-talkie in a rescue squad activity box. Read a book to your Fives about the job that rescue squad workers do. Visit your local rescue squad or see if an ambulance will visit your class. Explain how stretchers, blankets, or bandages are used. Talk with the children about what the rescuers do.

Why do the rescue workers need blankets, Brooke?
Yes, that's right. They want to keep people warm.
What do you think rescue workers do with a flashlight?

Encourage the children to pretend in their own way with the things in the rescue squad activity box. Add dolls and animals, wagons, and a doll-sized stretcher for your Fives.

 in or out   5–30 minutes   1–8 Fives

339

Fives can

- plan a pretend play activity
- cooperate with friends
- work on a long-term project

Putting on a Play

Act as a resource for interested Fives who want to put on a play. Some of the things you can help them do are

- decide what the play is about
- figure out the story and make up a beginning, middle, and end
- choose who plays which part
- make or choose props and costumes

Make sure you keep this activity fun for your Fives. Help more than one group do plays if there is lots of interest and not enough parts. Avoid taking over and turning the play into an adult production. Do not put pressure on the children for a perfect production.

 in or out   15–30 minutes   1–6 Fives

340

Fives can

- cooperate with friends
- work on a long-term project

Puppet Show

Make puppet activity boxes with puppets of characters in familiar stories. You can buy some puppets or you and the children can make some to use. Interested Fives can make puppets with ice cream sticks or tongue depressors, glue, paper, and watercolor markers or crayons. You and the children can make a puppet stage using a cardboard box or a table covered with a cloth. Make the stage wide enough so that two or three children can use it at one time.

Talk with your Fives about the voices their puppets will use. Help them practice with the puppets to tell a story. Show them how to hold puppets up so that their own hand is hidden from view. Make sure your Fives put the puppets back in the activity box when they are finished.

 indoors   5–15 minutes   1–6 Fives

341

Fives can

- copy adult work
- pretend about familiar experiences

Grocery Store

Make a little grocery store for your Fives to use in their pretend play. Put 10 to 15 empty, familiar food containers on a low shelf. Add other empty containers that children would see in the grocery store, such as dishwashing detergent bottles or dog food boxes. Be sure that all containers are safe, with no sharp edges. Add a toy shopping cart, a wagon, some small paper grocery bags, and plastic fruits and vegetables and plenty of play money. Put two toy cash registers on a little table for checking out. Let your Fives use these props in their pretend play.

Do you need a place to keep all your money to use in the store, Andrew?
Let's think. Is there anything you could use in this box of props?

 in or out   5–30 minutes   1–6 Fives

342

Fives can

- copy adult work
- pretend about familiar experiences

Pretend Bank

Talk with the children about what bank workers and customers do. See how much they can tell about their own visits to a bank. Set up a bank that has play money, including coins and bills. Also provide small boxes to use as cash drawers, a safe made out of a big cardboard box, and paper and pencils to keep records and use as checks.

Talk about the different coins and what they are worth. Help bankers sort the different coins and bills into different cash boxes. Have money for children who want to use the bank to deposit or withdraw money.

Virginia wants to deposit some money, Roy.
Be sure to give her a receipt.

 indoors   5–30 minutes   1–6 Fives

343

Fives can

- pretend about familiar experiences
- cooperate with friends

The Lemonade Stand

On warm days interested children might want to set up a lemonade stand. Help them plan what they will do. Have them use water and pretend it is any drink they wish, or make real lemonade. Help them set up a small table, a tablecloth, one or two chairs, a play cash register, play money, a large plastic pitcher, an ice bucket with ice, paper or plastic cups (a new cup for each buyer), napkins, and a trashbag.

Encourage your Fives to make signs for their lemonade stand. Decide together how much they want to charge for each cup and refills. Children can take turns making the lemonade, pouring it into cups, and selling it. Have a waiting list for this activity and continue the play until children lose interest. Make sure children clean up when they have finished.

 outdoors   5–30 minutes   1–5 Fives

344

Fives can

- copy adult activities
- pretend about familiar experiences
- cooperate with friends

Grown-Up Play Equipment

Add grown-up equipment to the Dramatic Play Center that children can use as they pretend. Include toy or real telephones of different kinds, cameras, radios, alarm clocks, and other safe small appliances that no longer work, and a typewriter. See if parents will help provide these items.

That's right, Jerry. That's an alarm clock.
Your mom brought it in for us to use.
Do you know how to set the alarm so that the bell rings?

Talk with your Fives to see how much they know about what these things are and how they are used. Let them play freely with these things used by grown-ups.

 indoors   5–30 minutes   1–6 Fives

345

Fives can

- know that people eat different things in different ways

Multicultural-Cooking Activity Box

Make a multicultural-cooking activity box that has food preparation and eating utensils used by various cultural groups. Include items such as bamboo steamers, chopsticks, clay pots, baskets, tortilla presses, and different kinds of dishes and pots or pans. Put out the activity box for children to use in their own creative pretend play. Add some of the utensils to the Dramatic Play Center for everyday use.

Ask your local librarian for picture books that show these things used in stories. Read the books to your Fives. Show them pictures of people using these cooking and eating utensils. Ask the children if they use these utensils at home. Have real cooking and eating activities that enable children to use the items. Some of your parents may want to help do this.

 indoors   5–30 minutes   1–6 Fives

346

Fives can

- copy adult activities
- pretend about familiar experiences
- cooperate with friends

Restaurant Play

Talk with the children about restaurant experiences they have had. See what they remember about fast-food and other types of restaurants. Ask questions about what happens in restaurants.

How do you get food in your favorite restaurant, Jimmy?
Do you go into the kitchen and take it out of the refrigerator?

Put out a restaurant activity box that has menus, trays, table place settings, aprons, a cash register, and play money. Talk about each item with your Fives. Encourage children to pretend about restaurants. Then let them play in their own way.

 indoors   5–30 minutes   1–6 Fives

347

Fives can

- copy adult activities
- notice different types of clothing

Dress-Ups From Many Cultures

Make a multicultural dress-up activity box with children's clothes from Asia, Africa, Central and South America, and Europe. Parents may be able to donate some of these things. Add picture books and pictures that show people wearing clothes like the ones in the box.

Talk with the children about the clothing. Tell them where the clothes come from. See if the clothes are familiar to any of the children. If the clothes have special names, use those words with your Fives. Encourage children to use the clothes as they play.

Yoshiko's mom gave us these tabis and this yukata.
Yoshiko, could you show us how to put these on?

 in or out   5–30 minutes   1–6 Fives

348

Fives can

- copy adult activities
- pretend about familiar experiences

Pretend to Swim

Make a swimming activity box with things people use at the beach, lake, or swimming pool. Include large towels, sunglasses, sun hats, and empty plastic suntan lotion bottles. Talk with the children about swimming experiences they have had and about water safety. Read picture books that tell about swimming in different places. Add an empty wading pool for children to use as they pretend.

Bring this activity box out in the winter and talk about summer memories. Let the children use the props in their own pretend play.

I'm glad you have sunglasses to protect your eyes.
Did you put on sunscreen to protect your skin?

 in or out   5–30 minutes   # 1–6 Fives

349

Fives can

- copy adult activities
- pretend about familiar experiences
- cooperate with friends

Sports Pretend Play

Collect sports outfits for a sports activity box. Include sports shirts, helmets, hats, shorts, pants, socks, jackets, and padding. Add some lightweight sports equipment, too. Ask parents to help you collect these things. Talk with the children about the sport that uses each thing in the box. Read books and show pictures of people playing the various sports. Be sure to include pictures of women as well as men.

Watch to be sure play does not become rough. Remind children that in pretend play, people never really hurt each other.

Julie, you have a tennis racket.
Are you going to serve to Brian?
Brian, see if you can return Julie's serve!

 in or out   5–30 minutes   # 1–8 Fives

350

Fives can

- notice different types of clothing
- cooperate with friends

Fancy Dress Play

Have frilly prom dresses, bridesmaid dresses, ballet outfits, sparkly cheerleader outfits, and fancy suits, cummerbunds, and bow ties for all children to use in dressing up. Add safe jewelry. See if parents will help you find these things in yard sales, attics, or thrift shops. Keep these in a fancy dress play activity box.

Encourage children to use these things in their own ways. Do not be surprised if boys want to try on these frilly things, too. Be ready for some very silly play.

You boys are certainly frilly today.
Who are you pretending to be?

 in or out   5–30 minutes   1–8 Fives

351

Fives can

- pretend about fantasy
- cooperate with friends

Super-Hero Play

Help your Fives do super-hero play without hurting one another. Have a super-hero activity box with masks, hats, costumes, and capes. Work with children to make other props, too. Talk with the children about super heroes. Watch a few super-hero shows yourself, so you will know what the children are talking about.

Talk about how super heroes are not real and their fighting is just pretend. Have children practice pretend fighting without really touching or hitting. Emphasize that is the way actors pretend. Supervise carefully and be ready to help children avoid becoming too rough in this play. Remind children that they have to turn back into their real selves when they take off their super-hero costumes.

 outdoors   5–30 minutes   1–6 Fives

Dramatic Play Center

Make the Dramatic Play Center easy for Fives to use.

- Don't put too much out at once, but have enough out so children do not fight over toys and props.

- Have open storage space to separate different kinds of things: dishes in one place, pots and pans on open shelves, dress-up clothes hung on hooks.

- Don't use a big box or toy chest for storage because children can't find things easily.

- Use picture labels for toys or other play things on shelves and storage places. These help children and adults know where things go at clean-up time.

- When play has been especially messy, help children clean up a little at a time. Name one thing at a time for them to find and put away in the proper place.

Make dress-ups fun and safe.

- Have dress-up clothes for girls and boys that are easy to put on and are not too long.

- Put loops on dress-up clothes so that children can hang them on low, safe hooks.

- Wash dress-ups often and use hard plastic hats that are easy to clean and sanitize.

- Have children wear socks with dress-up shoes and spray shoes often with disinfectant.

- Be sure that heels on dress-up shoes are not too high and that laces are tied or removed.

Have dramatic play outdoors as well as indoors.

- Put a play stove and sink outdoors where the children can use sand and water. Have house play equipment indoors too.

- Bring activity boxes outdoors to encourage many different types of pretend play. Be sure to have children collect and clean all the things they used outdoors before returning them to the activity box.

- Bathe baby dolls and wash doll clothes and dishes outdoors.

Bring in new ideas for dramatic play.

■ Read stories and then put out what children need to act out the stories.

■ Use pictures or take walking trips for new ideas.

■ Set up different pretend play places—kitchen, bedroom, store, garage, office, library.

■ Talk about different jobs children have seen adults do and give them what they need to act out those jobs.

■ Give children a chance to practice self-help skills as they play, such as pouring, washing tables, and sweeping.

Talk to children and get them to tell you about their play, but be sure not to interfere or take over.

■ Dramatic play lets you gives children a chance to use new words and new ideas. Introduce new words and ideas in a story before or after pretend play.

■ Talk about taking turns, sharing, and playing near and with others. Help children work out problems that come up when they play with each other.

■ Use words such as *make-believe* and *pretend* so that children start to understand the difference between real and make-believe.

■ Help children plan skits or puppet plays by helping them decide what to say, what part each child should play, and what props or costumes are needed.

■ If children need to continue their play at another time, make sure to put up a "Do not disturb" sign or find some other way to keep their play area and materials from being disrupted or cleaned up.

Materials and Notes

Music

electric keyboard

songbooks

charts with words to songs

drums of different kinds, musical instruments

tape player, earphones, music cassettes

- Plan music times in your daily schedule and add informal music to many other things you do with Fives.

- Encourage Fives to sing with the group, but don't force them to. Let a child watch or do a quiet activity while the rest of you sing if he or she does not want to join in.

- Sing, chant, or use records, tapes and compact discs often. Your Fives will love your singing even if you don't think your voice is good.

- Relax and enjoy the Fives' music even if it gets noisy. If the noise is too much inside, take the music outside. As your Fives get used to playing instruments, they will play both loud and soft.

- Put up the words to new songs where you can see them when you sing until you know all the words by heart. Be sure children can see the words, too, even though they will not be able to read most of them. Add pictures so that children can see what comes next.

- Teach new songs, but make time for Fives to sing the same songs over and over again.

- Share songs with parents. Ask parents to share their children's favorite songs with you. Ask the children to share their favorite songs.

- See Music Center Ideas and Songs and Rhymes at the end of this section.

Activity Checklist

Music

Music for Fives includes songs, chants, and rounds; moving to rhythms; making music with musical instruments; and listening to music made by others. Five-year-olds enjoy all kinds of music. They want to move to music in their own way and can make their own sounds by using everyday objects and simple musical instruments. They enjoy music by themselves and in a group. They remember words and melodies to many songs and can add their own words. You will hear Fives making up their own songs, too, and singing them as they play.

Check for each age group

	60–66 months	66–72 months
1. Adult sings with children daily, at both planned and informal times.	❐	❐
2. Children are encouraged to make up their own songs.	❐	❐
3. New songs are introduced regularly and repeated often so that children can learn them. Old favorites are sung often. Songs are contributed by parents and the children themselves.	❐	❐
4. Words to songs are displayed where children, teachers, and parents can see them. Children see how adults read the written words as they sing.	❐	❐
5. Children are encouraged but not forced to take part in group music activities.	❐	❐
6. Movement to music is included daily.	❐	❐
7. Dance props are available (scarves, wrist bells, ankle bells, pom-poms).	❐	❐
8. Music is on only when it is being used for children's activities or rest times, not as constant background noise.	❐	❐
9. Different types of music are used (special children's songs, classical, jazz, rock, and music enjoyed by different cultures and families of the children in the group).	❐	❐
10. Music Center is set up for daily free play with simple sound-making instruments and a simple tape player with headphones that children can use by themselves.	❐	❐
11. Adult helps children become aware of sounds and rhythms by planning activities with sounds and talking about them.	❐	❐

352

Fives can

- take things out and put them away
- care for materials

Music Center Tour

Set up a Music Center for your Fives. (You'll find Music Center Ideas on page 338.) Show children how to take out, use, and put away the things in the Center by acting out what to do. Talk about the things in the Center and how to use them carefully. Ask questions to see how much your Fives already know.

What do we do when we want to listen to music?
Yes, good! We put on the headphones and push this button to turn on the tape player.
What do we do when we're finished?
Right. We push this button and put the headphones in the dishpan.

 indoors   5–10 minutes   1–5 Fives

353

Fives can

- talk about familiar experiences

Music Pictures

In the Music Center hang <u>pictures</u> of people singing, dancing, or playing music. Make sure the pictures are down low where your Fives can see them. Look at the pictures with the children. Talk about them in many ways. Ask questions to see what the children can tell you about the pictures.

What are the people doing in the picture?
Yes, they are playing the drums. Do we have drums here?
Look, Jonathan sees them!
How are our drums different from the ones they are playing?

 indoors   1–5 minutes   1–4 Fives

Child-Created Songs

Make up little short songs about things the children do in the classroom. Sing them for children to hear.

Yolanda is building,
Building with the blocks.
Yolanda is building,
One block on top of another.

After your Fives see that you make up songs about familiar things, listen as children make up their own songs during everyday activities. You may also hear children chanting or singing songs without words as they play.

Fives can

■ make up their own simple songs

 in or out   1–5 minutes   1 Five at a time

Cozy Singing Time

Have a special, warm, cozy singing time with just one or two children. Sing a favorite song with them. See if they can sing along with you and then by themselves. Give them a little help if they need it, but allow them to do it all by themselves even if they do not know all the words. Try to do this with every child who is interested, fitting it in whenever you get a chance.

Come here, Ronnie. Sit with me for a little while.
Let's sing a song. Do you have a song you want to sing?

Encourage your Fives to bring their favorite songs from home. Don't be surprised if they make up new words to sing!

Fives can

■ remember and sing many songs

 in or out   3–5 minutes   1–2 Fives

356

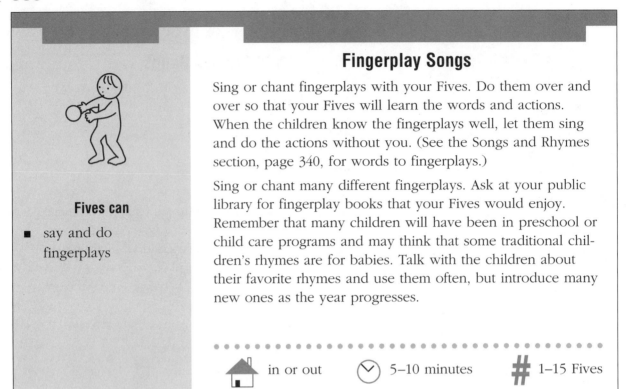

Fives can

- say and do fingerplays

Fingerplay Songs

Sing or chant fingerplays with your Fives. Do them over and over so that your Fives will learn the words and actions. When the children know the fingerplays well, let them sing and do the actions without you. (See the Songs and Rhymes section, page 340, for words to fingerplays.)

Sing or chant many different fingerplays. Ask at your public library for fingerplay books that your Fives would enjoy. Remember that many children will have been in preschool or child care programs and may think that some traditional children's rhymes are for babies. Talk with the children about their favorite rhymes and use them often, but introduce many new ones as the year progresses.

in or out   5–10 minutes   # 1–15 Fives

357

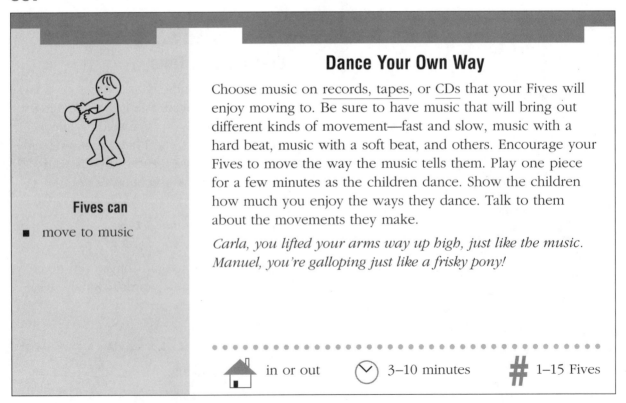

Fives can

- move to music

Dance Your Own Way

Choose music on records, tapes, or CDs that your Fives will enjoy moving to. Be sure to have music that will bring out different kinds of movement—fast and slow, music with a hard beat, music with a soft beat, and others. Encourage your Fives to move the way the music tells them. Play one piece for a few minutes as the children dance. Show the children how much you enjoy the ways they dance. Talk to them about the movements they make.

Carla, you lifted your arms way up high, just like the music. Manuel, you're galloping just like a frisky pony!

in or out   3–10 minutes   # 1–15 Fives

358

Fives can

- move to music
- recognize movements of familiar animals

Animal Music Games

Choose music on records, tapes, or CDs that reminds you of animals your Fives know about. Play the music for a few minutes while your Fives think about the animal they want to be. Ask them to tell you something about how the animal moves.

What animal did you choose, Annie?
You chose a cat?
How do you think a cat moves?
He walks lightly on the floor, and sometimes he slinks close to the ground.

Turn on the music again. Let the children move as they wish. Be sure they have plenty of room. After three or four minutes, turn off the music and ask the children to guess what animals they saw dancing.

 in or out   3–10 minutes   1–20 Fives

359

Fives can

- move to music

Dance with Props

Give your Fives props, such as long, colorful scarves, paper streamers, capes, or cheerleading pom-poms to dance with. Encourage them to experiment to find out how these move or swirl in different ways. Play music and let the children dance with the props. Try props on different parts of the children's bodies: streamers on wrists, waists, knees, and even as headbands. Try a long scarf around a child's waist and another around his wrist. As usual, watch carefully when you use long streamers or scarves that might trip or choke Fives.

Another time, let one child wearing props dance in the middle of the circle. Let the other Fives play drums to the rhythm the child is dancing.

 in or out   3–10 minutes   1–20 Fives

360

Fives can

- move to music
- imitate a familiar activity

The Popcorn Dance

Make <u>popcorn</u> with your Fives in a <u>popcorn popper</u> with a clear lid. Ask questions about how the popcorn moves when it begins to pop.

What is the popcorn doing, Alicia?
It's squiggling along the bottom of the pan.
What's the popcorn doing now, Sam?
It sure is! It's jumping up and popping open with a burst!

Put on some <u>popcorn-popping music</u>. Begin with a few children jumping up and popping. Continue until all your Fives are jumping up and down. At the end, turn off the music and encourage all your Fives to lie quietly on the floor.

 in or out   5–10 minutes   **#** 1–20 Fives

361

Fives can

- play simple musical instruments

Musical Instruments—Stop and Go

Give your Fives <u>musical instruments</u> to play as they listen to a <u>tape</u> that you can stop and start. Choose a variety of music so that children can play fast and slow, soft and loud. See if you can make a game of playing only when the music is on and stopping when it stops. It may be easier if you have the children put their instruments down when the music stops.

Let's practice how to put your instrument down on the floor when the music stops.
When the music starts, pick up your instrument and play to the music. Listen carefully.
Oh, oh! Did everyone stop when the music stopped?

Be patient with your Fives who are excited and want to keep playing. Most of all, enjoy the music.

 in or out   3–8 minutes   **#** 1–15 Fives

362

Fives can

■ remember and sing many songs

■ recognize some opposites

Fast/Slow Singing

Choose a familiar song your Fives enjoy. Try singing the song very slowly. Talk about how the song was sung. Then try singing the song fast. Talk about that, too. Be ready for lots of giggles when you sing fast.

Let's sing "I Know An Old Lady Who Swallowed a Fly."
Let's sing it as slowly as we can.
Listen. I'll show you how.
That was slow singing, wasn't it?
It made me sleepy to sing so slowly.
Can you sing it like that?

Play records, tapes, or CDs of fast and slow music. See if the children can clap along to the beat.

🏠 in or out   🕐 4–7 minutes   # 1–20 Fives

363

Fives can

■ count in rhythm

■ cooperate with friends

Clap and Chant

Have your Fives watch and listen as you chant and clap your hands in rhythm. Then see if they can clap and chant out the rhythm as you do.

Listen and watch. I'm going to clap and chant.
Miss Mary Mack, Mack, Mack. All dressed in black, black, black.
Can you clap and chant the way I'm doing?

Encourage children to take turns clapping and chanting for friends to copy.

Other familiar chants are "Teddy Bear, Teddy Bear" and "Who Stole the Cookie from the Cookie Jar?"

🏠 in or out   🕐 3–7 minutes   # 1–20 Fives

Fives can

- follow simple directions
- make music with a friend

Making Shakers

Collect juice cans or small plastic jars with lids for your Fives to fill to make their own shakers. Put out different things the children can choose to put into their cans, such as rice, dried beans, sand, stones, bells, or pebbles. Let the children take turns filling their cans in their own ways. Remind the children to leave lots of space so that the things inside can move to make noise. Secure all lids with strong tape and make sure children put their names on their shakers.

Use the cans at singing time. Help the children talk about how they made their shakers and what they put in them. Take turns listening to the different sounds the children's shakers make. When you have finished, put the shakers in a music activity box to use in the Music Center or on the playground.

 in or out   5–10 minutes   # 1–8 Fives

Fives can

- correctly use headphones and tape player when taught how

Choose and Play Tapes

Have a simple tape player and headphones set up for interested children to use. Add a variety of tapes, including tapes of favorite songs children have brought from home. Be sure the tapes are labeled so that children can tell what each one is. Remove and add tapes as children's interests change.

Teach the children which tape player buttons to push to make the music play, stop, and rewind. Be sure they know how to put the tape cassette in correctly. Explain what children must do to take good care of the tape cassettes. Once you are sure children can use these things carefully, encourage them to use them on their own.

 in or out   2–15 minutes   # 1–2 Fives

366

Fives can

■ remember and sing many songs

■ show interest in printed words

Seeing Words for Songs

Print clearly onto large sheets of easel paper the words to songs your Fives enjoy singing. Include pictures along with the words whenever possible. Hang them where everyone can see in the place where you and the children sing together. Point out the words and pictures when you sing these songs.

When you teach the children a new song, post the words where everyone can see. Read the words to the children and point them out as you sing the new tune. Explain that reading the printed words and seeing the pictures helps them learn the new song.

 indoors   2–15 minutes   1–20 Fives

367

Fives can

■ follow simple directions

■ relax to music

Relaxing to Music

Play quiet, relaxing music for your Fives. Ask them to lie down and get comfortable. Talk with them about relaxing their bodies to music.

Lie down on the floor. Close your eyes.
Feel your arms and hands get quiet and heavy.
Let your legs and feet rest on the floor.
Move your shoulders slowly up and down.
Can you feel your chest moving up and down and hear soft breathing?
It feels good to be quiet and get relaxed.
Listen to the music. Relax as you hear its softness.

 indoors   2–5 minutes   1–20 Fives

368

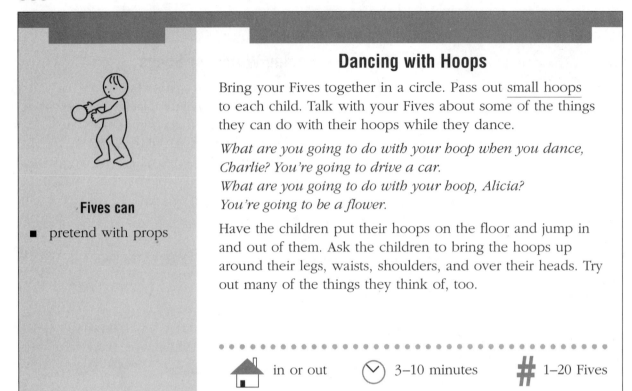

Fives can

- pretend with props

Dancing with Hoops

Bring your Fives together in a circle. Pass out small hoops to each child. Talk with your Fives about some of the things they can do with their hoops while they dance.

What are you going to do with your hoop when you dance, Charlie? You're going to drive a car.
What are you going to do with your hoop, Alicia? You're going to be a flower.

Have the children put their hoops on the floor and jump in and out of them. Ask the children to bring the hoops up around their legs, waists, shoulders, and over their heads. Try out many of the things they think of, too.

in or out   3–10 minutes   # 1–20 Fives

369

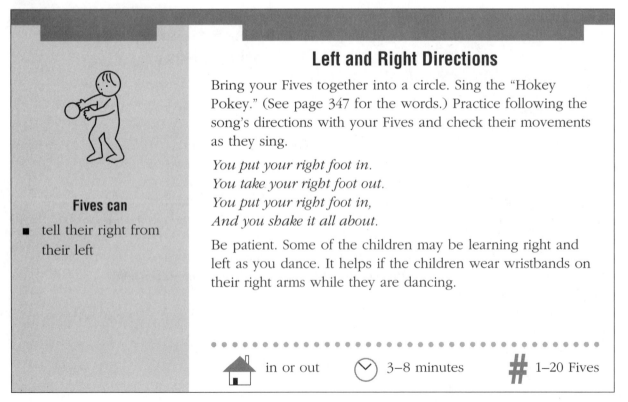

Fives can

- tell their right from their left

Left and Right Directions

Bring your Fives together into a circle. Sing the "Hokey Pokey." (See page 347 for the words.) Practice following the song's directions with your Fives and check their movements as they sing.

You put your right foot in.
You take your right foot out.
You put your right foot in,
And you shake it all about.

Be patient. Some of the children may be learning right and left as you dance. It helps if the children wear wristbands on their right arms while they are dancing.

in or out   3–8 minutes   # 1–20 Fives

370

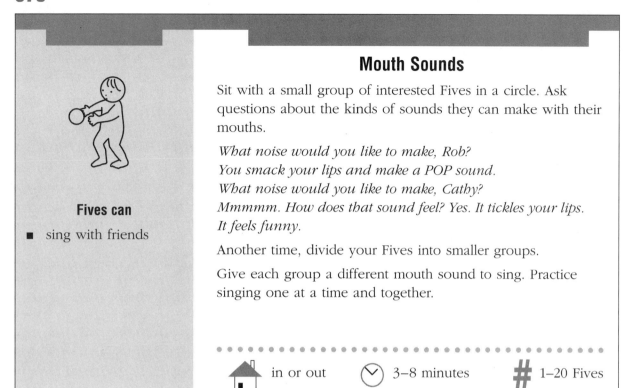

Fives can

■ sing with friends

Mouth Sounds

Sit with a small group of interested Fives in a circle. Ask questions about the kinds of sounds they can make with their mouths.

What noise would you like to make, Rob?
You smack your lips and make a POP sound.
What noise would you like to make, Cathy?
Mmmmm. How does that sound feel? Yes. It tickles your lips.
It feels funny.

Another time, divide your Fives into smaller groups.

Give each group a different mouth sound to sing. Practice singing one at a time and together.

in or out   3–8 minutes   # 1–20 Fives

371

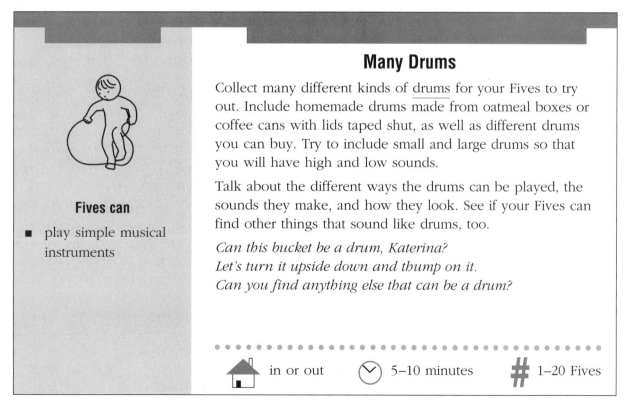

Fives can

■ play simple musical instruments

Many Drums

Collect many different kinds of drums for your Fives to try out. Include homemade drums made from oatmeal boxes or coffee cans with lids taped shut, as well as different drums you can buy. Try to include small and large drums so that you will have high and low sounds.

Talk about the different ways the drums can be played, the sounds they make, and how they look. See if your Fives can find other things that sound like drums, too.

Can this bucket be a drum, Katerina?
Let's turn it upside down and thump on it.
Can you find anything else that can be a drum?

in or out   5–10 minutes   # 1–20 Fives

372

Fives can

- move to music
- cooperate in a large-group activity for up to 20 minutes

March to Music

Show your Fives how to march around the room to music with a strong beat. Don't worry if your Fives do not make a straight line to march or if they don't move their feet in time to the music. Let them have fun marching in their own ways.

Do you hear the beat?
Lift your feet in time to the beat.
Can you clap and march at the same time?

Children could:

- March with drums, bells, or other instruments.
- Do an action while moving to the music, such as clapping or waving their arms.
- March around a chair or table.

 in or out　　 5–15 minutes　　 1–20 Fives

373

Fives can

- follow some directions
- play simple musical instruments

Play Your Kazoo

Make kazoos with a small group of Fives at a time. Cover one end of an empty paper towel roll with tissue paper. Secure with strong tape. Let the children color or put stickers on the rolls and choose the color of tissue paper they wish to use. Let children write their names on the kazoos they have made.

Show the children how to toot into their kazoos. See if they can play a song they know well on their new musical instruments.

Use a tape recorder to tape the music they play on their kazoos. Put the cassette tape in the Music Center so that they can listen to it later.

 in or out　　 2–20 minutes　　 1–5 Fives

374

Fives can

- cooperate in a large-group activity for up to 20 minutes

- make up simple songs

Orchestra Leaders

Talk about the job that an orchestra or band leader does. Talk about how he or she leads the players using arm movements to tell them whether to play fast or slow and when to start and stop. Help children learn some simple signals that tell them when to stop and start and how fast to play. Then let children take turns leading the orchestra as the other children play rhythm instruments.

Have a waiting list if lots of children want a turn leading. Do the activity on different days so that children do not become tired of the activity before everyone gets a chance to be leader.

Watch carefully. See if Carina wants you to play fast or slow.

 in or out   5–10 minutes   4–20 Fives

375

Fives can

- cooperate with friends

- move to music

Mirror Dance

Have a few Fives stand in front of a large, unbreakable mirror. Put on happy, lively music and encourage the children to dance or move the way the music makes them feel. Talk about the movements the children are making. Encourage the children to look at themselves and their friends while they dance.

Look at how Elena is moving her arms gently like a tree blowing in the wind.
Aaron, your dancing is fast and wild!

Encourage children to take turns trying new moves for others to copy by watching in the mirror.

 indoors   3–7 minutes   1–4 Fives

376

Fives can

- remember and sing many songs
- cooperate in a large-group activity for up to 20 minutes

What Song Am I Humming?

Choose some songs your Fives know very well. Try old favorites such as "Twinkle, Twinkle, Little Star" or "Row, Row, Row Your Boat." Hum one of them to the children. See if your Fives can guess the song and then sing the words with you.

Listen. I'm going to hum a song.
It's a song you know well. That's right, Raul.
It is "We Are The World."
Can you sing the words with me?

Encourage children to hum songs they know and have the other children try to guess the song.

 in or out   2–10 minutes   **#** 1–20 Fives

377

Fives can

- play simple musical instruments

Piano Playing

Have a toy piano, electric keyboard, or real piano that the children can play on their own. Be sure they know the rules for using the piano carefully, such as "play keys gently" and "use fingers, not fists to play."

Make or buy a simple color-coded songbook so that interested Fives can learn to play easy songs by matching the color to the piano key.

Use a waiting list to help encourage sharing if the piano is a favorite activity that many children want to do. Talk with children about the piano sounds they play.

You are playing all the high notes, Whitney.
Do you know where the low notes are?
Yes, I'd love to hear you play all the black keys.

 indoors   1–15 minutes   **#** 1–2 Fives

378

Fives can

- remember and sing many songs
- cooperate in a large-group activity for up to 20 minutes

Holiday Songs

At holiday times, teach the children a song or rhyme to go with the holiday. Make sure to learn songs for the different holidays celebrated by all children in the your group and for holidays of other cultures, as well. Ask parents, a music teacher, and your public librarian to help you find songs and music.

Collect songbooks, records, tapes, and CDs with holiday songs.

Don't be surprised if the children want to sing these songs all year, especially "Jingle Bells" or "Five Little Pumpkins."

 in or out   2–10 minutes   1–20 Fives

379

Fives can

- cooperate in a large-group activity for up to 20 minutes
- move to music

Copycat Dancing

Have children who are interested choose a partner to copy-cat dance with. Explain that one of each pair will create movements to the music while the other one copies. Have the pairs of children face one another, and then start some favorite music. See how children move and cooperate as they try to mirror each other's actions.

Stop the music after a minute or two so that the leaders can become the copiers. Encourage children to change partners, too.

 indoors   3–15 minutes   1–20 Fives

380

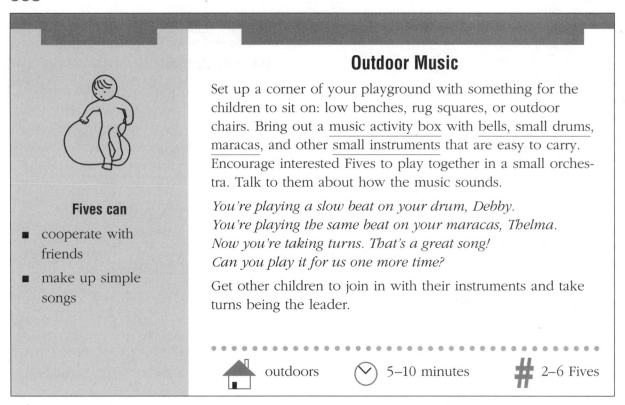

Fives can

- cooperate with friends
- make up simple songs

Outdoor Music

Set up a corner of your playground with something for the children to sit on: low benches, rug squares, or outdoor chairs. Bring out a music activity box with bells, small drums, maracas, and other small instruments that are easy to carry. Encourage interested Fives to play together in a small orchestra. Talk to them about how the music sounds.

You're playing a slow beat on your drum, Debby.
You're playing the same beat on your maracas, Thelma.
Now you're taking turns. That's a great song!
Can you play it for us one more time?

Get other children to join in with their instruments and take turns being the leader.

🏠 outdoors   🕐 5–10 minutes   # 2–6 Fives

381

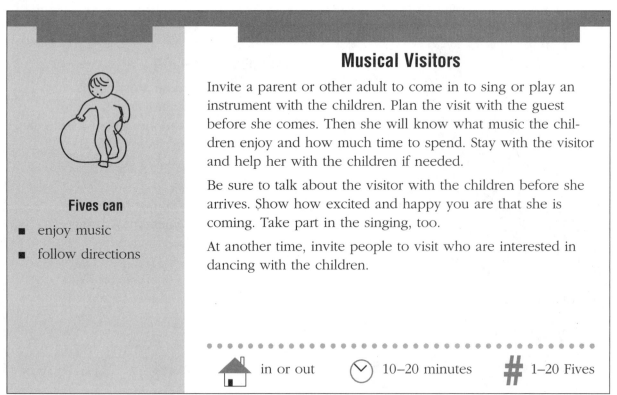

Fives can

- enjoy music
- follow directions

Musical Visitors

Invite a parent or other adult to come in to sing or play an instrument with the children. Plan the visit with the guest before she comes. Then she will know what music the children enjoy and how much time to spend. Stay with the visitor and help her with the children if needed.

Be sure to talk about the visitor with the children before she arrives. Show how excited and happy you are that she is coming. Take part in the singing, too.

At another time, invite people to visit who are interested in dancing with the children.

🏠 in or out   🕐 10–20 minutes   # 1–20 Fives

382

Fives can

- play simple musical instruments

Explore a New Instrument

Show the children a new <u>musical instrument</u>. Ask questions to help the children tell you as much as they can about the instrument. Show them how it sounds, and let each child try it out. If you have a <u>record</u> or <u>tape</u> that uses this instrument, play it for your Fives. Talk about the way to use and care for the instrument.

Did you ever see a musical instrument like this one?
That's right, Rasheed. It's called a kalimba, or thumb piano.
Can you show us how you play it?

If the instrument is very fragile, have the children listen only and keep it out of reach. Bring it out when you can watch carefully. Otherwise, let the children play the instrument once they know how it works. Add it to the Music Center.

 in or out　　 5–10 minutes　　 1–20 Fives

383

Fives can

- move to music
- cooperate in a large-group activity for up to 20 minutes

Dancing Like the Weather

Have children pretend to move like the wind, the rain, clouds, lightning, or snowflakes. This is fun to do on very windy, rainy, or snowy days. You can do this with or without music. Talk to children as they move.

Lizzie, you're moving just like a snowflake.
First you fall slowly to the ground.
Then you melt away.

On warm, sunny days, lie down on the grass with two or three of your Fives. Watch how the clouds move across the sky. When they get up, see if your Fives can move like the clouds.

 in or out　　 1–5 minutes　　 1–20 Fives

384

Fives can

■ make comparisons

■ copy sounds

What Does the Instrument Say?

Have one child play a rhythm instrument for his friends. When he is done, see if the friends can sing or chant to show how the music sounded. Have another child play the instrument, and have the children copy its sound again. Talk about whether it sounded the same as it did when the first child played.

Does the drum sound the same as it did when Charlie played it?

Yes, Denise. You played the drum loudly and Charlie played softly.

 in or out   4–10 minutes   # 2–5 Fives

385

Fives can

■ enjoy books

■ show interest in printed words

Song Books

Place some song books that have the words and music to songs children know in the Music Center. Look for music books with drawings or colorful pictures. As children look at the books, sing some of the songs with them. Point to the words they are singing. Explain that the printed notes on the pages tell you the tune to sing. Talk about how musicians read the music to find out what notes to play on their instruments.

You found the song about the dog, Bingo, Roger.
Look, here is Bingo's name. B-I-N-G-O.
Can you find Bingo's name somewhere else?
That's right! Let's sing the song.

 indoors   3–5 minutes   # 1–4 Fives

386

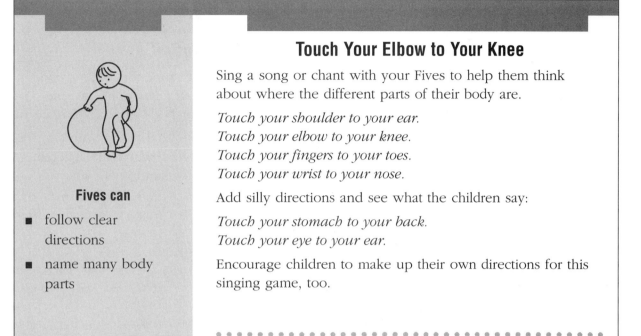

Touch Your Elbow to Your Knee

Sing a song or chant with your Fives to help them think about where the different parts of their body are.

Touch your shoulder to your ear.
Touch your elbow to your knee.
Touch your fingers to your toes.
Touch your wrist to your nose.

Add silly directions and see what the children say:

Touch your stomach to your back.
Touch your eye to your ear.

Encourage children to make up their own directions for this singing game, too.

Fives can

- follow clear directions
- name many body parts

in or out 2–5 minutes # 1–20 Fives

387

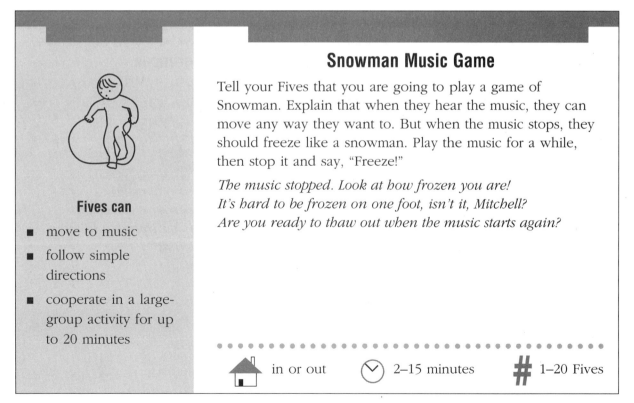

Snowman Music Game

Tell your Fives that you are going to play a game of Snowman. Explain that when they hear the music, they can move any way they want to. But when the music stops, they should freeze like a snowman. Play the music for a while, then stop it and say, "Freeze!"

The music stopped. Look at how frozen you are!
It's hard to be frozen on one foot, isn't it, Mitchell?
Are you ready to thaw out when the music starts again?

Fives can

- move to music
- follow simple directions
- cooperate in a large-group activity for up to 20 minutes

in or out 2–15 minutes # 1–20 Fives

Fives can

■ remember and sing many songs

Caring Songs

Be sure to include some songs about caring for others around the world in the songs your teach your Fives. Some favorite songs are "Reach Out and Touch Somebody's Hand," "We are the World," and "He's Got the Whole World in His Hands."

Write the words to these songs on a chart where the children, teachers, and parents can see. Use the chart to help you remember the words.

🏠 indoors　　🕐 3–10 minutes　　# 1–20 Fives

389

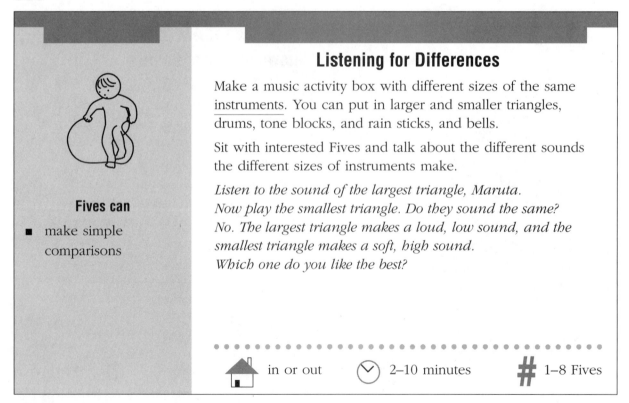

Fives can

■ make simple comparisons

Listening for Differences

Make a music activity box with different sizes of the same instruments. You can put in larger and smaller triangles, drums, tone blocks, and rain sticks, and bells.

Sit with interested Fives and talk about the different sounds the different sizes of instruments make.

Listen to the sound of the largest triangle, Maruta.
Now play the smallest triangle. Do they sound the same?
No. The largest triangle makes a loud, low sound, and the smallest triangle makes a soft, high sound.
Which one do you like the best?

🏠 in or out　　🕐 2–10 minutes　　# 1–8 Fives

390

Fives can

- move to music
- follow simple
  directions

Feel the Music Deep Inside You

When you play a piece of music for the first time, bring your Fives together in a circle. Tell them you are going to play something new. Ask them to listen to the music and show them the movements as you say the following words

When you feel the music deep inside you,
Tap it with your fingers. [Tap fingers on thighs.]
Bounce it in your knees. [Bounce up and down to the music.]
Feel it in your shoulders. [Move shoulders up and down.]
Now put it in your feet and let it take you all around the room.
[Walk or dance around the room in time to the music.]

indoors   2–10 minutes   # 1–20 Fives

391

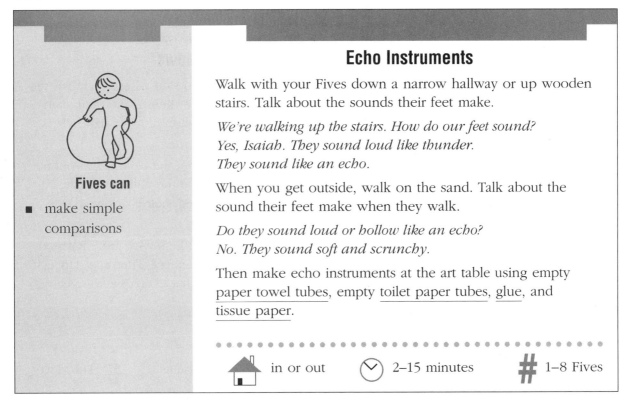

Fives can

- make simple
  comparisons

Echo Instruments

Walk with your Fives down a narrow hallway or up wooden stairs. Talk about the sounds their feet make.

We're walking up the stairs. How do our feet sound?
Yes, Isaiah. They sound loud like thunder.
They sound like an echo.

When you get outside, walk on the sand. Talk about the sound their feet make when they walk.

Do they sound loud or hollow like an echo?
No. They sound soft and scrunchy.

Then make echo instruments at the art table using empty paper towel tubes, empty toilet paper tubes, glue, and tissue paper.

in or out   2–15 minutes   # 1–8 Fives

Fives can

- imitate familiar
  sounds

Singing Familiar Sounds

Sit with a few of your interested Fives outdoors under a tree
or in a shady corner. Ask them to close their eyes and listen
to the sounds around them. See if they can sing to imitate the
sounds they hear.

Let's lie quietly and listen. What do you hear?
Maria, I hear that bird, too.
Can you sing a sound like the bird?
Tweeet, Tweeeeeeeet, Tweeet.
Jesse says he hears the sound of an airplane.
Can we sing like an airplane?

🏠 outdoors   🕐 3–8 minutes   # 1–8 Fives

Fives can

- move to music

Dancing Shadows

On a sunny day, take the children outside where they can see
the shadows their bodies make. Have them make their shadows dance to the music of simple instruments or hand clapping.

Another time, hang a white sheet from the ceiling and put a
bright light in back of the sheet. Have the children move
between the light and the sheet to see their shadows dance
on the sheet.

While one to three children dance, others who are interested
can watch from the other side of the sheet. Then the dancers
and watchers can change places so that everyone will get
a turn shadow dancing.

🏠 in or out   🕐 5–15 minutes   # 1–10 Fives

394

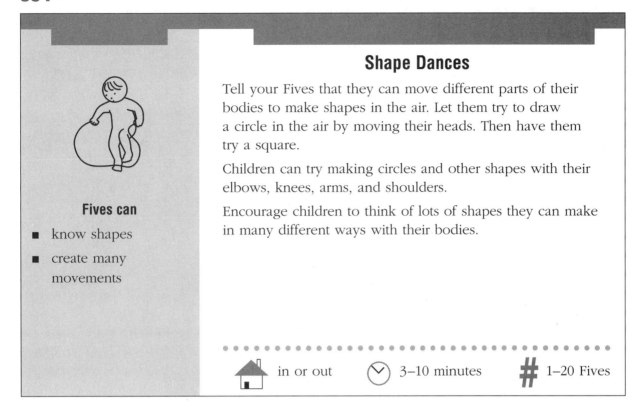

Fives can

- know shapes
- create many movements

Shape Dances

Tell your Fives that they can move different parts of their bodies to make shapes in the air. Let them try to draw a circle in the air by moving their heads. Then have them try a square.

Children can try making circles and other shapes with their elbows, knees, arms, and shoulders.

Encourage children to think of lots of shapes they can make in many different ways with their bodies.

in or out   3–10 minutes   # 1–20 Fives

395

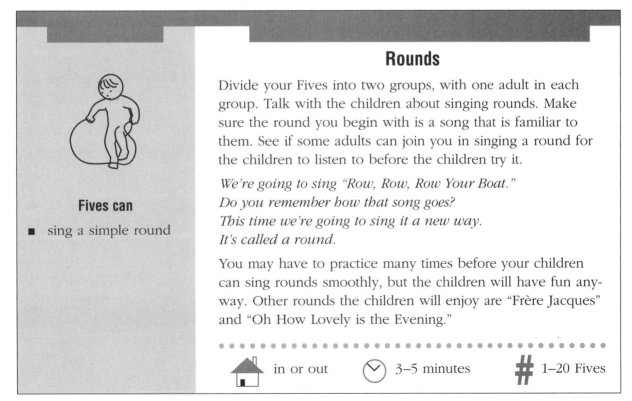

Fives can

- sing a simple round

Rounds

Divide your Fives into two groups, with one adult in each group. Talk with the children about singing rounds. Make sure the round you begin with is a song that is familiar to them. See if some adults can join you in singing a round for the children to listen to before the children try it.

We're going to sing "Row, Row, Row Your Boat."
Do you remember how that song goes?
This time we're going to sing it a new way.
It's called a round.

You may have to practice many times before your children can sing rounds smoothly, but the children will have fun anyway. Other rounds the children will enjoy are "Frère Jacques" and "Oh How Lovely is the Evening."

in or out   3–5 minutes   # 1–20 Fives

Music Center

■ Choose a small, quiet corner out of traffic for a Music Center. Use low shelves or other sturdy furniture to keep music noises in and other noises out. A carpet on the floor and big soft pillows will cut down on noise, too.

■ Put sturdy musical instruments and toys neatly on shelves. Use picture and word labels to help Fives remember where things are to be put away. Keep smaller musical instruments in a labeled box or dishpan. If your Music Center must share space with other toys, keep the instruments in an activity box and bring them out often for children to use.

■ Have two or more of the instruments children enjoy the most. This will cut down on fights.

■ Include a simple tape player with headphones and cassette tapes for children to use.

■ Put out only a few musical instruments to begin with. Show children how to use them. Add new things often. Always show and tell your Fives about all of the things you add.

■ Buy or make musical instruments and toys such as the following:
wrist bells, melody bells, cowbells, bells on sticks
many kinds of shakers
sturdy toy piano
xylophone with mallet
cymbals (large and finger-size)
clackers, clave tone blocks, castanets
rhythm sticks
kalimba (thumb piano)
scraping instruments with sticks, such as guiros
tambourines
sandpaper blocks

■ If you use harmonicas, whistles, horns, recorders, kazoos, or other mouth instruments, make sure to wash them with bleach solution and air dry after each use. Keep them in a separate box and bring them out only when you can supervise. Also be sure that instruments have no loose or broken parts that could cut or choke a child.

- Change toys and instruments in the Music Center often.

- Keep children from being crowded in the Music Center. Give them plenty of choices for other interesting things to do if they can't fit in right away. Use a sign-up sheet or other system to make sure children do get a turn after a short wait. Or have music for a larger group outside of the area if there is lots of interest.

- Have movement in a large enough area so that Fives will not bump into one another. Give them a chance to calm down with a quiet song after they dance.

- Help Fives keep the Music Center neat and organized. Make sure the area is cleaned up after each day's use.

- Try music outdoors. This will give you lots of space for movement or dance. Set up a small music corner for small-group musical instrument play. If you can't have music outdoors, move furniture and other equipment aside to make a bigger space.

- Add dance props for movement and dance. Try musical instruments, dress-ups, plastic hoops, masks, long streamers, and scarves. Watch carefully to be sure the children do not trip or hurt themselves when they do movement activities with these dance props.

Songs and Rhymes

A Hunting We Will Go

A hunting we will go, a hunting we will go.
Hi-ho the merrio, a hunting we will go.

Bear Hunt

We're going on a bear hunt.	*[slap hands on thighs to make*
Here we go!	*walking sounds]*
Let's go look for a bear.	
Here's a hill—	*[make hill with hands]*
We can't go under it.	*[make hand go down]*
We can't go around it.	*[make hands go around)*
We'll have to climb it.	
Let's climb!	*[climb with arms]*
Climb, climb, climb, climb.	
Wow! That was hard work.	*[wipe brow]*
Let's walk on.	*[slap thighs to make walking*
We're going on a bear hunt.	*sounds]*

Continue with:	
Here's a lake . . . row	*[do movement for all of these,*
Here's a swamp . . . squish	*making walking sounds*
Here's a jungle with vines	*between each]*
. . . swing	
Here's a field of very tall	
grass . . . swish	
Here's a pond . . . swim	
Oh, here's a cave.	*[point to cave]*
Let's go inside.	
Ooooh! It's dark in here!	*[close eyes]*
And the walls are cold and	*[stretch out hands to feet]*
slippery!	
Aah! Here's something warm,	
and big, and fuzzy.	
EEK! It's a bear!!	
Run, Run, Run!	*[slap thighs fast]*

[Do all verses and actions quickly in reverse.
After pretending to run down the hill, say,]

Look! There's our house!
Quick, run inside! Lock the door!
Whew! We're safe!
Let's go on a bear hunt again sometime.

Creative Activities

Did You Ever See a Lassie (or Laddie)

Did you ever see a lassie, a lassie, a lassie?
Did you ever see a lassie go this way and that?
Go this way and that way, go this way and that way.
Did you ever see a lassie go this way and that?

The Farmer in the Dell

The farmer in the dell, the farmer in the dell,
Hi Ho the Derry O, the farmer in the dell.
The farmer takes a wife . . .
The wife takes a child . . .
The child takes a nurse . . .
The nurse takes a dog . . .
The dog takes a cat . . .
The cat takes a mouse . . .
The mouse takes the cheese . . .
The cheese stands alone . . .

Five Little Monkeys

Five little monkeys	*[Hold up five fingers.]*
Jumping on the bed,	*[Hump fingers on palm of other hand.]*
One fell off	*[hold up one finger.]*
And bumped his head.	*[rub head.]*
They ran for the doctor	*[run fingers across other hand.]*
And the doctor said,	
"No more monkeys jumping	
on the bed!"	*[Point and shake finger.]*
[Continue with four, three, two, and one monkey.]	

Head and Shoulders, Knees and Toes

Head and shoulders, knees and toes, knees and toes.
Head and shoulders, knees and toes, knees and toes.
Eyes and ears and mouth and nose.
Head and shoulders, knees and toes, knees and toes.

Here We Go 'Round the Mulberry Bush

Here we go 'round the mulberry bush, the mulberry bush, the mulberry bush.
Here we go 'round the mulberry bush, so early in the morning.

Hush Little Baby

Hush, little baby, don't say a word, Momma's gonna buy you
*   a mocking bird.*
If that mocking bird won't sing, Momma's gonna buy you
*   a diamond ring.*
If that diamond ring turns brass, Momma's gonna buy you
*   a looking glass.*
If that looking glass gets broke, Momma's gonna buy you
*   a billy goat.*
If that billy goat won't pull, Momma's gonna buy you a cart
*   and bull.*
If that cart and bull turn over, Momma's gonna buy you a dog
*   named Rover.*
If that dog named Rover won't bark, Momma's gonna buy you a
*   horse and cart.*
If that horse and cart fall down, you'll still be the sweetest little baby
*   in town.*

If You're Happy and You Know It

If you're happy and you know it, clap your hands. (clap, clap)
If you're happy and you know it, clap your hands. (clap, clap)
If you're happy and you know it, then your face will surely show it.
If you're happy and you know it, clap your hands. (clap, clap)
Additional verses: (2) Stamp your feet; (3) Nod your head; (4) Pat
*   your knees; (5) Wave good-bye*

I'm a Little Teapot

I'm a little teapot short and stout.
Here is my handle, here is my spout.
When I get all steamed up, hear me shout,
"Just tip me over and pour me out."

It's Raining, It's Pouring

It's raining, it's pouring,
The old man is snoring.
He went to bed
And bumped his head,
And didn't wake up till morning.

Jack and Jill

Jack and Jill went up the hill to fetch a pail of water.
Jack fell down and broke his crown and Jill came tumbling after.

Creative Activities

Jack Be Nimble

Jack be nimble.
Jack be quick.
Jack jump over the candlestick.

Lazy Mary

Lazy Mary will you get up, will you get up, will you get up?
Lazy Mary will you get up, will you get up this morning?

Little Duckie Duddle

Little Duckie Duddle
Went wading in a puddle,
Went wading in a puddle quite small.
Said he, "It doesn't matter
How much I splash and splatter,
I'm only a duckie, after all. Quack, Quack."

Little Green Frog

Ah—ump went the little green frog one day.
Ah—ump went the little green frog.
Ah—ump went the little green frog one day.
And his eyes went blink, blink, blink.

Little Jack Horner

Little Jack Horner sat in a corner,
Eating his Christmas pie.
He stuck in his thumb and pulled out a plum,
And said, "What a good boy am I."

Little Miss Muffet

Little Miss Muffet
Sat on a tuffet
Eating her curds and whey.
Along came a spider
And sat down beside her
And frightened Miss Muffet away.

Little Turtle

There was a little turtle
He lived in a box.
He swam in a puddle,
And he climbed on the rocks.
He snapped at a mosquito,
He snapped at a flea,
He snapped at a minnow
And he snapped at me.
He caught the mosquito.
He caught the flea.
He caught the minnow.
But he didn't catch me.

London Bridge

London bridge is falling down, falling down, falling down,
London bridge is falling down, my fair lady.

Miss Lucy Had a Baby

Miss Lucy had a baby,
She named him Tiny Tim,
She put him in the bathtub
To see if he could swim.

He drank up all the water,
He ate up all the soap,
He tried to eat the bathtub,
But it wouldn't go down his throat.

Miss Lucy called the Doctor,
Miss Lucy called the Nurse,
Miss Lucy called the lady
With the alligator purse.

"Mumps," said the Doctor,
"Measles," said the Nurse.
"Nothing," said the lady
With the alligator purse.

Out went the Doctor,
Out went the Nurse,
Out went the lady
With the alligator purse.

"Little Turtle" reprinted with permission of Macmillan Publishing Company from *Collected Poems* by Vachel Lindsay. Copyright © 1920 by Macmillan Publishing Company, renewed 1948 by Elizabeth C. Lindsay.

Creative Activities

Miss Mary Mack

Miss Mary Mack, Mack, Mack,
All dressed in black, black, black,
With silver buttons, buttons, buttons
All down her back, back, back.

She asked her mother, mother, mother,
For fifteen cents, cents, cents,
To see the elephant, elephant, elephant
Jump over the fence, fence, fence.

He jumped so high, high, high,
He touched the sky, sky, sky,
And didn't come back, back, back
Until the Fourth of July, ly, ly.

Miss Polly Had a Dolly

Miss Polly had a dolly that was sick, sick, sick,
So she telephoned the doctor to come quick, quick, quick.
The doctor came with her bag and her cap.
And she knocked on the door with a rat-a-tat-tat.
She looked at the dolly and she shook her head,
"Miss Polly, put that dolly straight to bed, bed, bed."
She wrote on the paper for the pill, pill, pill,
"I'll be back tomorrow with the bill, bill, bill!"

Muffin Man

Do you know the muffin man, the muffin man, the muffin man?
Do you know the muffin man who lives on Drury Lane?

Oats, Peas, Beans

Oats, peas, beans and barley grow;
Oats, peas, beans and barley grow;
Do you or I or anyone know
How oats, peas, beans and barley grow?

Old MacDonald

Old MacDonald had a farm, E-I - E-I - O
And on his farm he had a cow, E-I - E-I - O
With a moo moo here
And a moo moo there
Here a moo, there a moo
Everywhere a moo moo
Old MacDonald had a farm, E-I - E-I - O
[Additional verses with other animals]

On Top of Spaghetti

On top of spaghetti, all covered with cheese,
I lost my poor meatball, when somebody sneezed.
It rolled off the table, and onto the floor,
And then my poor meatball rolled out of the door.
It rolled in the garden and under a bush.
And then my poor meatball was nothing but mush.
But the mush was as tasty, as tasty could be,
And early next summer, it grew into a tree.
The tree was all covered with beautiful moss.
It grew lovely meatballs and tomato sauce.
So if you eat spaghetti, all covered with cheese,
Hold onto your meatball and don't ever sneeze!

Open, Shut Them

Open, shut them, open, shut them, give a little clap.
Open, shut them, open, shut them, lay them in your lap.
Creep them, creep them, creep them, creep them right up to your
  chin.
Open wide your little mouth, but do not let them in.

Pop Goes the Weasel

All around the cobbler's bench the monkey chased the weasel.
The monkey thought 'twas all in fun.
Pop goes the weasel.

Pease Porridge Hot

Pease porridge hot, pease porridge cold,
Pease porridge in the pot, nine days old.
Some like it hot, some like it cold,
Some like it in the pot nine days old.

Put Your Right Hand In (Hokey Pokey)

Put your right hand in.
Put your right hand out.
Put your right hand in
And you shake it all about.
You do the Hokey Pokey and you turn yourself around;
That's what it's all about.
[Continue with left hand, right foot, left foot, whole self.]

Ring Around the Rosy

Ring around the rosy,
A pocket full of posies.
Ashes, ashes,
We all fall down.

Rock-A-Bye Baby

Rock-a-bye baby, in the tree top,
When the wind blows, the cradle will rock,
When the bough breaks, the cradle will fall.
And down will come baby, cradle and all.

Rub-a-Dub-Dub

Rub-a-dub-dub, three men in a tub,
And who do you think they be?
The butcher, the baker, the candlestick maker.
Turn them out, knaves all three.

See Saw, Margery Daw

See saw, Margery Daw, Johnny shall have a new master;
He shall have but a penny a day because he can't work any faster.

Sing A Song of Sixpence

Sing a song of sixpence, a pocket full of rye.
Four and twenty blackbirds baked in a pie.
When the pie was opened the birds began to sing,
Wasn't that a dainty dish to set before the king?

Swing Our Hands

Swing our hands, swing our hands, swing our hands together.
Swing our hands, swing our hands, in our circle now.
Tap our toes, tap our toes, tap our toes together
Tap our toes, tap our toes, in our circle now.
Additional verses: (2) Shake our heads; (3) Move our hips;
(4) Bend our legs; and others

Take Me Riding in Your Airplane

Take me riding in your airplane.
Take me riding in your airplane.
Take me riding in your airplane.
I want to go riding in your airplane.
[Add motions to the song.] Additional verses: (2) Bumpety bus;
(3) Motorcycle; (4) Bicycle; (5) Rowboat; (6) Rocket ship; and others

Teddy Bear

Teddy bear, teddy bear, turn around,
Teddy bear, teddy bear, touch the ground.
Teddy bear, teddy bear, show your shoe,
Teddy bear, teddy bear, that will do!

There Was a Duke of York

There was a Duke of York.
He had ten thousand men.
He marched them up the hill.
And then he marched them down again.
When you're up, you're up.
And when you're down, you're down.
And when you're only halfway up
You're neither up nor down.

This is the Way We Wash Our Clothes

This is the way we wash our clothes, wash our clothes, wash our
*   clothes.*
This is the way we wash our clothes, so early in the morning.
Additional verses: (2) Hang up our clothes; (3) Iron our clothes;
(4) Fold our clothes; (5) Put on our clothes

Twinkle, Twinkle, Little Star

Twinkle, twinkle, little star, how I wonder what you are.
Up above the world so high, like a diamond in the sky,
Twinkle, twinkle, little star, how I wonder what you are.

Wheels on the Bus

The wheels on the bus go round and round, round and round,
*   round and round.*
The wheels on the bus go round and round all through the town.
Additional verses: (2) Baby goes wah wah wah; (3) Lights go blink
blink blink; (4) Driver says move on back; (5) Money goes clink
clink clink; (6) People go up and down; (7) Wipers go swish,
swish, swish

Where is Thumbkin?

Where is thumbkin? Where is thumbkin?

Here I am, here I am. (Hold up thumbs.)
How are you today, sir?
Very well, I thank you.
Run away, run away. (Put hands behind back.)
[Continue with pointer, tall man, ring man, and pinky.]

Where Oh Where Is Pretty Little Susie?

Where, oh where is pretty little Susie?
Where, oh where is pretty little Susie?
Where, oh where is pretty little Susie?
Way down yonder in the pawpaw patch.

Who Stole the Cookie from the Cookie Jar?

Who stole the cookie from the *cookie jar?*	*[Children look around.]*
[Name] stole the cookie from the *cookie jar.*	*[Point to a child.]*
Who, me? *Yes, you!* *Couldn't be!* *Then who?*	*[Child points to self and shakes head.]*
(Name) stole the cookie from the *cookie jar.*	*[Point to another child.]*
	[Continue until all children have been named. The last child says:]
Yes, I stole the cookie from the *cookie jar and I ate it all up!*	*[Rubs tummy and smiles.]*

Yankee Doodle

Oh, Yankee Doodle went to town a riding on a pony,
He stuck a feather in his cap and called it macaroni.
Yankee Doodle keep it up; Yankee Doodle Dandy,
Mind the music and the step and with the girls be handy.

Frère Jacques (Round)

Frère Jacques, Frère Jacques.
Dormez-vous? Dormez-vous?
**Sonnez les matines. Sonnez*
  les matines.
Din, don, din.
Din, don, din.
*[*Second group starts singing from the beginning.]*

Are you sleeping?
Are you sleeping?
Brother John? Brother John?
**Morning bells are ringing,*
Morning bells are ringing.
Ding, dong, ding.
Ding, dong, ding.
*[*Second group starts singing from the beginning.]*

Oh, How Lovely is the Evening (Round)

Oh how lovely is the evening.
Is the evening.
**When the bells are sweetly ringing,*
Sweetly ringing.
Ding dong. Ding Dong.
*[*Second group starts singing from the beginning.]*

Row, Row, Row, Your Boat (Round)

Row, row, row your boat
**Gently down the stream.*
Merrily, merrily, merrily, merrily
Life is but a dream.
*[*Second group starts singing from the beginning.]*

Activities for Learning from the World Around Them

Index

of Activities for Learning from the World Around Them

Here's Why

Like most young children, Fives are curious and fascinated by the world around them. You can enjoy this with them in many ways. They can tell you about why they think things happen and even carry out simple experiments and come to their own conclusions. Fives depend on their senses—hearing, sight, smell, taste and touch—as they come to understand the world. They have not yet learned to deal with abstract concepts, so some of their conclusions may be a bit puzzling to you.

Real things in nature are fun for Fives to observe and learn about. Many of the science and nature topics that Fives enjoy the most are about animals, insects, gardens, plants, the weather, snakes, rocks, rivers, and other bodies of water. These topics can be used to encourage children to think, and move toward reading, writing, and math as they record their discoveries. However, it is most important for Fives to have lots of time outdoors to roll in grass or snow, feel the wind, let sand fall between their fingers, and experience nature in many ways.

If your Fives have already taken part in lots of fun activities to help them learn about numbers, shapes, and sizes, they will now know many words about these ideas. Fives are beginning to really understand that numbers mean "how many." They can count and will often count things all by themselves. They understand sizes and are able to compare sizes quite well. By the end of the kindergarten year, they should be ready to begin very simple adding.

There are many activities in this section to help the children continue learning without feeling pressured or bored. In the real-life activities, such as cooking and measuring, children can learn how numbers are important in our lives. Fives will also enjoy playing number, shape, and size games with real objects that they can move around. All these early experiences about the world help children get ready for much of the learning that will come later in school.

Materials and Notes

Science and Nature

natural things, magnifying glass

sand, measuring cups and spoons

simple microscope

nature and science books

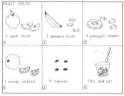

labels and instructions

small animal

- Since many science and nature activities in this section are open-ended and have no single correct answer, most can be done with either younger or older Fives.

- Fives learn best about science and nature through their senses. Allow Fives to have many chances to explore nature in their own way. Give children words for what they experience and listen to their thoughts. Remember that your most important job is to join in, share discoveries, and help children see new things.

- Set up a Science and Nature Center. Fill it with interesting natural things for the children to explore and games for them to play. Add pictures and books that give more information about things the children explore. Change items in the center often. Encourage children and parents to add to the center, too.

- Make sure to keep things safe. Avoid glass containers. Be sure that plants are not poisonous and that animals and insects will not harm children. If in doubt, be cautious and check things out.

- Fives will ask many questions about science and nature. Try to answer them as simply as you can. Help children use their senses and thinking skills to find answers. Don't be afraid to admit that you do not know an answer. Show Fives how to look in books or ask others to find information.

- Ask parents to help with science and nature activities. They can help on field trips, bring in new and interesting natural things, and find the information you need. At home, they can continue the science and nature activities you have begun with their child.

Activity Checklist

Science and Nature

Science and Nature for Fives includes exploring natural things both indoors and out, learning words about natural things, and beginning what can be a lifelong interest in our environment. Learning about what plants and animals need to live, how to protect the environment, different kinds of weather, and dinosaurs are only a few of the science and nature activities Fives enjoy. Fives who are interested can record their discoveries in many ways.

Check for each age group

	60–66 months	66–72 months
1. Children have a daily outdoor time, weather permitting.	❏	❏
2. Adult and children share natural things they notice, such as life cycles of plants and animals, the weather, erosion.	❏	❏
3. Adult shows appreciation and respect for nature when with the children; shows curiosity and interest rather than disgust about insects, snakes, and so on; has a positive attitude about going outdoors in many kinds of weather.	❏	❏
4. Adult encourages children to explore nature in safe ways.	❏	❏
5. Adult asks interested children questions about their science and nature experiences to encourage talking and thinking things through.	❏	❏
6. Sand and water play with a variety of toys is available daily, both indoors and outdoors. The sandbox is protected from animal droppings and children wash their hands before using the water table.	❏	❏
7. A Science and Nature Center is set up for children to use daily, with natural things to explore, books and pictures that add information, and science and nature games. Things in the center are changed often, with the nature and science interests of the children considered.	❏	❏
8. Safe science and nature experiment materials are provided, such as magnifying glasses, magnets, and sink-or-float games.	❏	❏
9. Children are encouraged to record discoveries according to their own abilities (drawing, dictating stories, writing, tape recording, and so on).	❏	❏
10. Cooking activities in which the children take a meaningful part are provided regularly.	❏	❏

Activities for Learning from the World Around Them

396

Fives can

- show curiosity and delight about natural things
- talk about things that interest them

Ever-Changing Science and Nature Center

Set up a Science and Nature Center where there are things for the children to explore and experiment with. If possible, place the area near a window. Have a table where children can do activities and a shelf to hold games, books, and natural things. Change things in the area often. Add new games and pictures. Be sure to add things that the children bring in and find interesting. Tell the children about the new things and join them when they show interest.

Do you have new rocks for our collection, Nicky? Tell me about them. I'll write what you say. Then we can leave your story with the rocks so that everyone will know how you found them.

See page 388 for more Science and Nature Center ideas.

 indoors   1–30 minutes   1–4 Fives

397

Fives can

- do simple cooking
- follow sequences

Cook with Fives

Read Ideas for Cooking with Fives on page 402. Then choose a simple recipe Fives can follow. Print the recipe on a big chart or show the recipe with pictures and words. Talk about what the printed words or pictures tell them to do. Encourage the children to talk about the foods they are using. Let children taste and smell the foods as they work, but make sure to keep germs from spreading by following sanitation rules: wash hands, use clean spoons to stir, and so on. Encourage children to eat what they have cooked. Help them remember the cooking sequence when finished.

Do you remember how we made the corn muffins? What did we do first? Right! We always wash hands before we cook. What did we do next?

 indoors   10–20 minutes   1–8 Fives

398

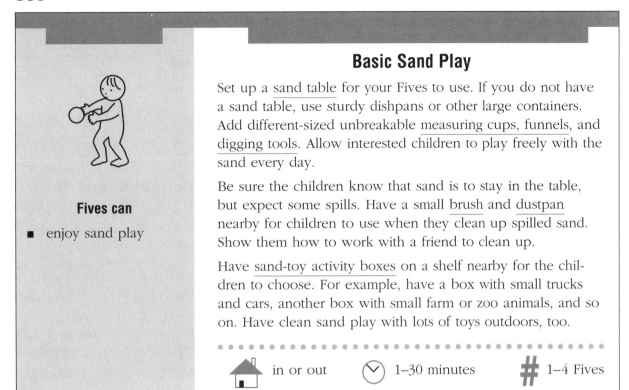

Fives can

■ enjoy sand play

Basic Sand Play

Set up a sand table for your Fives to use. If you do not have a sand table, use sturdy dishpans or other large containers. Add different-sized unbreakable measuring cups, funnels, and digging tools. Allow interested children to play freely with the sand every day.

Be sure the children know that sand is to stay in the table, but expect some spills. Have a small brush and dustpan nearby for children to use when they clean up spilled sand. Show them how to work with a friend to clean up.

Have sand-toy activity boxes on a shelf nearby for the children to choose. For example, have a box with small trucks and cars, another box with small farm or zoo animals, and so on. Have clean sand play with lots of toys outdoors, too.

🏠 in or out   🕐 1–30 minutes   # 1–4 Fives

399

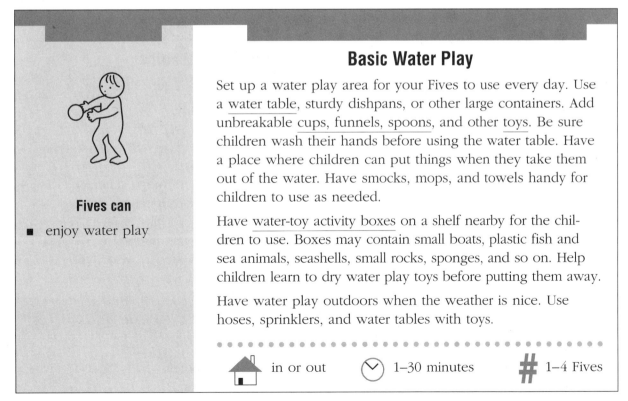

Fives can

■ enjoy water play

Basic Water Play

Set up a water play area for your Fives to use every day. Use a water table, sturdy dishpans, or other large containers. Add unbreakable cups, funnels, spoons, and other toys. Be sure children wash their hands before using the water table. Have a place where children can put things when they take them out of the water. Have smocks, mops, and towels handy for children to use as needed.

Have water-toy activity boxes on a shelf nearby for the children to use. Boxes may contain small boats, plastic fish and sea animals, seashells, small rocks, sponges, and so on. Help children learn to dry water play toys before putting them away.

Have water play outdoors when the weather is nice. Use hoses, sprinklers, and water tables with toys.

🏠 in or out   🕐 1–30 minutes   # 1–4 Fives

400

Fives can

- experiment as they play

- enjoy sand and water play

Water and Sand

Give your Fives a fun change by mixing sand and water together for play. Do this in two dishpans if you don't want to get lots of sand wet. Have one pan for sand and the other for water, and let the children mix up the two with spoons, cups, and other unbreakable sand and water toys.

You can also add water to the outdoor sand area if you wish.

Talk with the children about how the texture and firmness of the sand changes as water is added. Show them how to mold the damp sand and see if dry sand molds as well.

Press the damp sand into the bucket, Dana. Now turn it over and see if it has the bucket shape. Now try to make a mold with this dry sand. What happens?

 in or out   2–30 minutes   1–4 Fives

401

Fives can

- talk about things that interest them

Tuning in to the Weather

Each day, take a little time to talk with your Fives about what the weather is like. Have them close their eyes and try to remember what it was like when they arrived in the morning. Then let them check by looking out the window or going outdoors to see.

Help the children tune into the signs of the weather, such as the clouds, wind, sun, rain or other precipitation, dryness, or humidity. Talk about how the weather looks or feels. Talk about what children wear and do in the different types of weather. Encourage them to draw pictures of what the weather looks like.

How did the weather feel when you left your house this morning, Jack? It was cold, wasn't it? What did you do to keep warm?

 in or out   1–5 minutes   1–15 Fives

Activities for Learning from the World Around Them

402

Fives can

- talk about things that interest them

- know that what they say can be written and read

Weather Flannelboard

Buy or make flannelboard pictures that relate to the weather, including a bright sun, raindrops, snow, clouds (both gray and white). You may also want to have figures of a boy and girl, with the clothes they need for different weather, such as coats, boots, umbrellas, shorts, etc.

After talking about the weather, let children play with the flannelboard and the cutouts. Encourage them to make a picture of what the weather looks like today, but also let them play freely with the weather pieces. Talk with your Fives about the pictures they make.

If they wish, you can write down what they say about the weather pictures they make and read their stories back to them, as well as to other children.

 in or out   1–5 minutes   1–2 Fives

403

Fives can

- enjoy sand and water play

Digging in the Dirt

Set aside an out-of-the-way place on the playground where children can dig in the dirt with safe digging tools. Add sturdy toy trucks and bulldozers. Let children add twigs, stones, rocks, and other props that they find on their own.

As the weather changes, talk with the children about how the dirt changes.

It is so hot and sunny. The dirt is really dusty and hard. How is your digging going, Juan?
What are you making with the bulldozer, Sally?

If you wish, add a trickle of water from a hose or allow children to add water. Then they can see what happens as dirt becomes wet. Allow extra time for cleanup. Children may also need a change of clothes.

 outdoors   4–30 minutes   1–10 Fives

Activities for Learning from the World Around Them

404

Fives can

- be responsible with lots of guidance
- follow simple routines

Taking Care of Classroom Pets

Teach your Fives how to care for any pets in the classroom. Talk about how pets need many of the same things people do—a clean place to live, healthful food, water, exercise, and rest. Make picture/word instructions to guide children as they care for pets. (See page 389 for sample instructions.)

I'm glad you looked at our guinea pig's cage, Deanna. Does Squeeky need anything today? Is his cage dirty? Would you like to help me clean it?

Be sure that classroom pets are not disturbed too much, handled roughly, or overfed. Have children wash hands after handling pets or caring for them.

 in or out   3–15 minutes   **#** 1–4 Fives

405

Fives can

- think about the sounds they hear
- do simple matching

Sound-Picture Matching Game

Put one small thing into each of five margarine tubs with lids. Use things that will sound different when shaken in the tub. For example, use a bell, block, crayon, cotton ball, and a scoop of sand. Make a little picture card of each thing in the tub.

Show your Fives how to shake the tubs, listen carefully, look at each picture, and then try to guess which pictured thing is in each tub. Show them how to put each sound tub with its matching picture card. Then the children can open the tubs to see if they guessed correctly.

Leave the set of tubs and picture cards in a box on a shelf in the Science and Nature Center for children to use on their own once you have shown them how.

 indoors   4–15 minutes   **#** 1–3 Fives

406

Fives can

- experiment as they play
- draw simple conclusions and talk about what they think

Recording Experiment Results

Do simple experiments with your Fives, such as finding out what kinds of things sink and float or what magnets are attracted to. Encourage the children to talk about the things they discover, and to draw their own conclusions. For example, if the children find that magnets do not stick to wooden pencils, doors, bookcases, and trees, then help them see that all those things are made of wood. They can then conclude that magnets are not attracted to wood.

Write down what children say about their discoveries and read their ideas back to them. Encourage them to experiment and think, whatever their conclusions are. You can also use experiment record sheets for children to fill in. Sample sheets can be found at the end of this section.

 in or out   5–20 minutes   # 1–6 Fives

407

Fives can

- experiment as they play
- use clues to draw simple conclusions

Magnet Experiments

Have a magnets activity box with several magnets for the children to use to see what magnets do and do not attract. Talk with your Fives about what they discover. Encourage them to record their findings by drawing pictures or by dictating ideas to an adult.

Was the magnet attracted to the window, Jinsy?
No? What should I write on your picture of the window?

Children can also fill in an experiment record sheet like the one on page 396. Be sure that all the items shown on the record sheet are in the activity box for your Fives to try.

Note: Be sure that children do not use magnets near computer disks or video or cassette tapes.

 in or out   2–25 minutes   # 1–4 Fives

408

Fives can

■ experiment as they play

■ use clues to draw simple conclusions

Sink-or-Float Game

Put some things that sink and some that float next to your water table or in a dishpan filled with water. Let your Fives experiment to find out what each thing does in the water. Talk about sinking and floating with the children.

Some children may be interested in recording what they found out. Encourage any children who are interested to draw pictures of what they discovered about which things sink and which float. Or if children wish, you can help them mark a record sheet such as the one on page 395 to show what they discovered.

What do you think the wooden block will do, Jason? Will it sink or float? Yes, it floats! Are you going to mark the picture of the block on your record sheet?

 in or out   5–15 minutes   1–4 Fives

409

Fives can

■ experiment as they play

■ talk about their discoveries

Spice Packets Matching Game

Shake spices or extracts onto cotton balls. Put each cotton ball into its own empty film container. Punch holes in the top so that children can smell the different fragrances. Make two of each. Label the containers on the bottom. Store the containers in a sturdy box in the Science and Nature Center. As children sniff the containers, encourage them to talk about the different smells. See if they can match the ones that are the same, and then check the labels to see if they were right. (It does not matter if children peek at the labels—they will be learning either way they play!)

You put the two mint containers together, Kim. See, here's the name. M-I-N-T, mint. Have you ever eaten anything made with mint?

 in or out   2–20 minutes   1–6 Fives

410

Fives can

- tell heavy from lightweight objects
- do matching and some sorting

Heavy-Light Cans

Collect nine empty frozen-juice cans with metal lids. Fill three to the top with sand or pebbles. Fill three one-quarter full. Leave the last three empty. Tightly seal the lids onto all the cans with strong tape. Have your Fives pick each of the cans and talk about which ones feel heavy, medium, and light. Then help the children sort the cans onto mats that you have labeled with the names (and pictures) of the three weight groups.

Which ones are you finding first, Noah?

Leave the set of cans in the Science and Nature Center for the children to use on their own once you have shown them how to do the activity. Add another set of cans that are half full to add more challenge.

 in or out   5–15 minutes   1–3 Fives

411

Fives can

- experiment as they play
- use clues to draw simple conclusions

Outdoor Streams and Rivers

On a warm day let a hose run on a dirt area of the playground. Allow children to play in the little streams and rivers the water makes as it flows. Let children dig little roads for the water with sturdy trowels and sticks. Talk about how the water flows downhill.

You're digging a little pool for the water, Sally. How can you get the water to fill up your pool?

Add some narrow plastic plumber's pipes or plastic gutters for the children to use as stream beds. They can arrange them over and over to see how the water flows.

Later, see if some children who played in water want to tell you about the things they discovered. Write what they say on a chart and read their words back to them.

 outdoors   3–30 minutes   1–15 Fives

Activities for Learning from the World Around Them

412

Fives can

- sort things in different ways, usually by color

Nature Picture Sorting Game

Look at How to Make Picture Card Sorting Games on page 392. Then mix up two sets of nature picture cards. For example, mix the fish cards with the flower cards. Encourage children to look at all the pictures and sort them in their own way. See if your Fives sort them into the fish and flower categories or if they sort them by some other aspect, such as color. Ask children to explain why they put the pictures into the groups.

I see you put all the fish into this pile, Evie. And there are flowers in this pile. Why did you put these cards together? Oh! They are your favorite pictures!

Add more challenge by putting similar sets of cards together, such as flowers and trees or animals and birds.

 in or out   2–15 minutes   1–4 Fives

413

Fives can

- show curiosity and delight about natural things
- talk about things that interest them

Nature Walks

Take short nature walks with your Fives often. You will find many nature walk ideas in Tips for Nature Walks and Field Trips on page 390. Encourage children to look at how natural things change with time and season. Show delight as children share their discoveries.

Ezra sees geese flying overhead. Listen to them! Where do you think they are going?

Look carefully at the twigs on this tree. Do you see anything different?

Encourage any children who are interested to draw or tell a story about the things they observe on their walks, but do not force children to participate.

 outdoors   10–30 minutes   1–15 Fives

414

Fives can

- show curiosity and delight about natural things

- talk about things that interest them

Bird Feeders

Have your Fives help make bird feeders to put up in the play yard or near a window where the children will be able to see them. Ideas for making simple bird feeders are on page 393. You can turn these ideas into picture/word instructions to guide your Fives. As birds visit the feeders, help the children notice them. Talk about how the birds are like other living things and how they are different. Notice the parts of the birds with the children—talk about eyes, beaks, feet, wings, and feathers. Compare these parts on the different birds you see.

Britt says that the cardinal has a short, fat beak.
Can you think of a bird that has a longer beak?

Encourage children to take responsibility for making sure the feeders are kept full.

 in or out   1–12 minutes   # 1–20 Fives

415

Fives can

- show curiosity and delight about natural things

- begin to understand graphs

"Birds We See" Chart

Hang up pictures of the birds in your Science and Nature Center. Also have picture books of familiar birds for children to use. Talk about the birds and have children take part as you look up birds whose names you do not know.

Make a big chart to document the birds children spot. You will find a sample chart on page 394. As children spot a type of bird, show them how to make a mark next to the bird's picture on the chart. Talk about which type of bird is seen most often and which birds are seen more rarely. Add new birds to the chart as the children spot them.

Wow! It's easy to see the bird we see most frequently!
That's right, Tamara. The sparrow has lots of marks!
Which bird did we see only once?

 indoors   1–10 minutes   1–20 Fives

416

Fives can

- play matching games
- sort by color, then by other aspects, such as size

Leaf-Matching Game

Collect four or more very different <u>leaves</u>. Find other leaves that closely match the ones you already have in color, size, and shape. Your Fives can help you to collect the leaves. Put all the leaves out for the children to see. See if they can match the leaves that look alike.

This is a maple leaf, Sonya.
Can you find another maple leaf that looks the same?

See if children can sort leaves by color, size, shape, or in other ways, too.

How are you sorting the leaves, Dennis?
Oh, yes, I see. These are the crunchy ones and these are the soft ones.

 in or out   3–15 minutes   1–4 Fives

417

Fives can

- play simple games, but have trouble with following rules and losing
- do simple matching

Animal Lotto Game

Buy or make an <u>animal-matching or lotto game</u> that has game boards with pictures of animals and picture cards to match to the pictures on the boards. Give one board to each child who wants to play. Then you can hold up one picture at a time for all players to see. Ask who has that same picture on his board. Give the picture card to the child who has the same picture on his board and let him use it to cover that picture. Continue playing until all pictures are used.

Help children understand that the point of the game is to get all pictures covered, not for one person to cover all his pictures first.

Make or buy other matching games with pictures of flowers, fish, trees, birds, or other natural things.

 in or out   8–20 minutes   2–8 Fives

418

Fives can

- show curiosity and delight about natural things
- talk about things that interest them

Bug Search

Search for insects with your Fives. Remind them that bugs are delicate and should not be hurt. Encourage them to just look and not touch so that the bug can go about its interesting business. Be sure to protect children from insects that bite or sting.

Use posters, pictures, and picture books about insects with your Fives to find out more about the insects you and the children discover. Talk about insect body parts, how they live, and how they are the same or different from other animals. You can work with the children to make a bug book for the Book Center that has Fives' drawings and stories about insects.

Here's what Paul said about the cockroach he saw.
The roach was big and brown. It ran under the dumpster.

 in or out   2–15 minutes   1–10 Fives

419

Fives can

- enjoy simple experiments
- talk about their discoveries
- use clues to draw simple conclusions

How Things Swing

Have some of your Fives watch children who are swinging. Talk about what people do to swing higher and to stop. Then set up a swinging experiment. Hang a 4' string from a hook. Help children tie objects of different weights to the string, such as a feather, a piece of cloth, a doll, and a small block. See if your Fives can figure out which things make the swing go best, the heavy things or the light ones.

Children can help you make a chart that shows what they found out, with their drawings of things that swing well on one side and those that do not on the other. Add their words to the chart, too.

Try the experiment with longer and shorter strings, too.

 in or out   5–15 minutes   1–20 Fives

420

Fives can

- recognize familiar sounds and voices

Sounds of Real Things

Use a tape recorder to record sounds of real things the children know. Play the sounds one at a time as your Fives listen. See if the children can figure out what is making each sound. Try some of these sounds on your tape:

- child laughing
- toilet flushing
- telephone ringing
- car horn honking

- water running
- dog barking
- hammer pounding
- cat meowing

You can make a picture game to go with the tape by collecting or drawing pictures that go with the sounds. Put the pictures with the tape for the children to use. Also make recordings of the different children's voices in your group. Children can match names or pictures to the voices.

 indoors   5–15 minutes   1–20 Fives

421

Fives can

- show curiosity and delight about natural things

- take some responsibility when reminded

Caring for Plants

Make safe plants a regular part of your classroom. Give each interested child a small potted plant to nurture as his or her own for the year. Teach children how to help care for the plants. They can water, fertilize, trim, repot, and be sure their plants get enough light. Keep a small watering can and mister handy to use. Put up a checklist so that children can check off that they have cared for their plant every week.

Know the names of the plants in the room and use them as you talk about the plants with the children. Talk about the plant parts, too. Some children will be interested enough to follow through, and others will be more interested in alternative activities. Be ready to find helpers who will care for plants that are ignored.

 in or out   2–15 minutes   1–5 Fives

Activities for Learning from the World Around Them

422

Fives can

- show curiosity and delight about natural things
- sort things in different ways, usually by color

Rock Collections

Show interest in the pebbles and rocks that your Fives find. Make a special place where they can be collected or displayed in the Science and Nature Center. Have picture books and posters about rocks nearby that can be used to find out what types of rocks the children find. Talk about the rocks with the children—discussing texture, color, size, and shape.

Encourage children to sort the rocks in many ways.

How did you sort the rocks, Nathan?
Oh! These are all the rocks you found, and these are the rocks other children found.
How can you tell them apart?

 in or out   1–12 minutes   # 1–8 Fives

423

Fives can

- show curiosity and delight about natural things
- sort things in different ways, usually by color

Exploring Seeds

Go on seed hunts with your Fives at different times of the year. You can search for seeds in the grass during outdoor times or take walks in the neighborhood to hunt for them. Talk about the colors, sizes, and shapes of the seeds as well as how they are part of a plant's growing cycle. Have children sort the seeds by color, size, shape, which plants they came from, and in many other ways.

Children can tape seeds they found onto blank sheets of paper to make a seeds book. They can tell you where they found the seeds, and you can add their words to the pages. Also encourage children to write their own words if they wish.

 in or out   8–20 minutes   # 1–15 Fives

424

Fives can

- show curiosity and delight about natural things

- talk about many things that interest them

Magnifying Glass Mysteries

Set up magnifying glass mysteries in the Science and Nature Center. Ask children to find out about tiny things, such as the tiny parts of flowers, banana seeds, or mites on plants. Provide safe plastic or glass magnifiers with thick wooden or plastic frames. Encourage your Fives to talk about the new things they can see when things are enlarged.

There are some tiny surprises living on these leaves, Emma. You can use the magnifying glass to see them better. Can you draw a picture of what you see? How do those mites look?

What other parts of the flower can you see, Josh? Use the magnifying glass to find out.

 in or out   1–7 minutes   1–4 Fives

425

Fives can

- show curiosity and delight about natural things

Bubbles of All Sizes

Use liquid dishwashing detergent to make a bubble solution to use with your Fives. Add a little water to thin the detergent, but be sure to try it out before using it. Talk about the rainbow of colors in the bubbles and how the wind carries bubbles away. Let your Fives try these bubble ideas:

- Blow into a cup of bubble solution with a straw to make lots of small bubbles.
- Dip a straw into bubble solution, take it out, and blow softly.
- Use a plastic bubble wand from a jar of bubble liquid.

You can make huge bubbles for your Fives to chase by dipping a stretched-out wire hanger into bubble liquid and then waving it in the air.

 in or out   3–20 minutes   1–20 Fives

426

Fives can

- show curiosity and delight about natural things
- ask and answer questions

Pet Visits

Encourage parents to bring family pets in to visit once in a while. Be sure that the times of these visits are planned ahead so that no pet fights can happen. Be sure that all pets are safe and ask parents how to best make sure things go well. Allow a few children to get close to the pet at a time so that the pet will not be frightened and become excited. Be sure children wash hands after handling pets.

Encourage the child whose pet is visiting to tell the other children all about the pet—what it eats, where it sleeps, and anything else the others are curious about. You can write down the children's answers. After several pets have visited, read about each one and see if the children remember whose pet is being described.

 in or out 3–15 minutes 1–10 Fives

427

Fives can

- ask and answer questions
- begin to understand measurement

Freezing/Melting

On a warm day, have some of your Fives pour water into ice cube trays and also into a small bowl. Then have them help you put the trays and bowl into the freezer. Check on how the water is freezing several times with your Fives. Use a thermometer to measure the water's temperature each time. Talk about the changes the children see. Let them feel the water as it turns to ice. Later, put the ice cubes into dishpans for outdoor play. Be sure children do not put ice cubes into their mouths. Have crushed ice for eating.

On another day, have children help you freeze juice to make juice bars. Talk about how the juice freezes and melts. If you have ice outdoors in winter, have the children bring some indoors and put it in a bowl to observe and discuss.

 in or out 5–15 minutes 1–20 Fives

428

Fives can

- experiment as they play
- talk about their discoveries

The Warmth of the Sun

Help your Fives notice how the sun warms things on the earth. Try these ideas:

- Feel warm sunny spots that come through windows in the classroom. Compare shady and sunny spots outdoors.
- Have water play outdoors in the sun and in the shade. Talk about how the water temperature differs.
- Melt ice in the shade and in the sun. See which melts faster.
- Drink a cup of water that has been in the sun and a cold cup of water. Talk about which is warmer.

Ask parents for permission to use sunscreen when children go outdoors on hot sunny days. Talk about why sunscreen is needed.

 in or out   1–12 minutes # 1–20 Fives

429

Fives can

- recognize familiar things by touch

Nature Feelie Bag

Make four or five feelie bags by putting plastic margarine tubs into big, clean socks. Put one natural thing into each bag— a shell, an acorn, a feather, a rock, and a pine cone. Make a picture/word card showing each natural thing.

Have children look at the picture cards and talk about what the natural things are and how they might feel. Then let a child reach into one of the bags and guess which of the pictured things he is feeling.

How does the thing feel, Carlos? Smooth and soft?
What do you think it is? Look at the pictures.

Allow children to play this game on their own or with a friend. Change the natural things and the pictures often.

 in or out   3–15 minutes # 1–4 Fives

430

Fives can

- show curiosity and delight about natural things

- ask and answer questions

Growing Herbs

Have children help you plant <u>herbs</u> in <u>rich potting soil</u> in <u>small pots</u> and place them in a bright sunny place. Use seeds or small plants of basil, chives, oregano, mint, tarragon, and other easy-to-grow herbs. Have your Fives help care for the plants. Encourage children to talk about how these plants smell and how they are used in cooking. Encourage children to gently rub the leaves of the plants and then sniff each smell. Compare how the plants are different.

That's oregano, Maurice. We use oregano in pizza and spaghetti sauce. Which herb do you like to smell the most?

When the plants are big, you and the children can taste some of the leaves or use them in cooking.

 in or out   2–6 minutes   1–10 Fives

431

Fives can

- show curiosity and delight about natural things

- ask and answer questions

Exploring Trees

Help your Fives make comparisons about <u>trees</u>. Inspect the bark, leaves, flowers, seeds, shape, and height through the seasons.

Have many <u>books and posters</u> for your Fives to use to find out more about trees. Also, encourage children to make their own books about the different trees they see. They can draw pictures and you can write down their words. Encourage interested children to write by copying words you write for them or by using their own invented spelling. (See page 99 for more information on invented spelling.)

If there are no trees in your area, then help your Fives notice all they can about other plants they see.

 outdoors   3–20 minutes   1–10 Fives

432

Fives can

- do simple experiments
- show curiosity and delight about natural things

Pressed Flowers

When your Fives notice an abundance of small flowers, have them find out if it is OK to pick a few to press. Make sure they are a common type and that no permission is needed from owners. Show Fives how to place a flower between two sheets of wax paper and then put it under a heavy weight so that it will dry flat. Have the children find something to use as the heavy weight. Have interested children check the flower every day and talk about how it has changed.

Labels with the flower names can be placed between the wax paper sheets with the flower. The see-through sheets holding the dried flowers can be displayed in sunny windows, or the wax paper sheets can be opened so that children can see what happened to the flower.

 in or out   3–15 minutes   1–4 Fives

433

Fives can

- do simple experiments
- use clues to draw simple conclusions

What Will Ants Eat?

On a day when you and the children notice ants in the outdoor area, do a little experiment to see what the ants like to eat. Have children choose some foods to put on little plates outdoors, near the ants (but away from the building!). Have children check the plates periodically to see if the ants have discovered the foods. When ants are interested in eating some of the foods, talk with the children about what the ants do and do not like. Talk about the tastes of the different foods. See if children can come to conclusions about the kinds of foods their ants like best.

That's right, Latarsha. The cookie and the peach are sweet. The ants are not interested in the celery. How does the lettuce taste? What flavors do these ants like best?

 outdoors   3–20 minutes   1–8 Fives

434

Fives can

- experiment as they play
- talk about their discoveries

Mixing-Color Experiments

Put out clear plastic test tubes or other small clear plastic containers. Fill several larger containers with water your Fives have colored with food coloring. Add plastic eye droppers. Show children how they can use the eye droppers to mix different colors in the test tubes by adding a few drops of the colored water.

You made green water in your test tube, Chris. What colors did you use to get that new color?

Allow your Fives to experiment freely with the colored water. Provide aprons or smocks to keep clothes clean.

Have children write about their results.

 in or out　　 2–20 minutes　　 1–8 Fives

435

Fives can

- experiment as they play
- talk about their discoveries

Experimenting with Flashlights

Allow your Fives to experiment with sturdy flashlights in many areas of the room—to flash them on the ceiling, on the floor, in dark corners, and in bright spaces (but not in other people's faces). Help children talk about how the light changes as the flashlight is used in different places and at different angles and distances. Add colored plastic wrap with rubber bands so that children can cover the lights to see what happens.

Your light is green, Yolanda. How did you make that color?

Explain that flashlights use batteries for energy to make light. Help the children change batteries or bulbs when needed. Remind children always to turn off the flashlight when they are through using it.

 indoors　　 2–20 minutes　　 1 Five per flashlight

436

Fives can

- be responsible with lots of guidance
- follow simple routines

Save Energy and Resources

Practice saving energy and resources with your Fives. Talk about why we do all these things to help save the earth:

- Turn off lights and water when they are not needed.
- Close doors and windows to conserve heat and air conditioning.
- Recycle plastic milk bottles, aluminum cans, and paper.
- Reuse safe, clean junk materials for artwork.
- Take good care of toys and equipment.

Pay special attention to children who help save resources.

Thanks for turning off the lights, Daniel. You are right. We won't need them while we're outdoors.

 in or out   1–10 minutes   1–20 Fives

437

Fives can

- be responsible with lots of guidance
- talk about their discoveries

Gardens

Look at Gardening with Fives on page 399. Decide whether you will have small gardens for each child or one large garden for the whole group. Collect all the materials you will need and talk to the children about how they will be gardening. As you do each part of gardening with your Fives, talk about what plants need to grow, how we care for gardens, and how the plants change.

Encourage children to show what they know about gardening in their own creative artwork. Add gardening props to the Dramatic Play Center so that children can act out what they have learned in their own way. Write down the stories they tell you about gardening and read their words back to them, or have children write their own stories, using invented spelling.

 outdoors   3–30 minutes   1–8 Fives

438

Fives can

- begin to understand measurement
- make comparisons

Plant Growth Charts

Have your Fives plant some seeds that grow into tall plants (try scarlet runner bean seeds) in pots. Label each pot with a different color of construction paper. Cut 11" strips of each color construction paper. As the plants grow, have children use the strips of construction paper to measure them each day. They can hold the strip next to the plant, mark the plant's height, and then cut the strip at the mark. Be sure they use the right color for each plant.

Show children how to glue the paper strips onto a big chart that compares the growth of each plant. (See page 401 for a sample chart.) Look at the chart with your Fives. Talk about which plant is growing the fastest or slowest, and whether any plants are growing at the same rate.

 outdoors   3–30 minutes   1–8 Fives

439

Fives can

- experiment as they play
- talk about their discoveries

Reflections

Have safe mirrors of many sizes for children to look into. Encourage them to experiment with the mirrors in many ways. Talk with the children about how much they can see in smaller or larger mirrors and how they can move mirrors to see different things or people.

Challenge your Fives to find reflections in other things around them. See if they find reflections in:

- windows
- puddles of water
- a shiny slide
- a metal spoon
- bright pots and pans

On chart paper, list all the reflections the children found.

 in or out   1–10 minutes   1–20 Fives

440

Fives can

- show curiosity and delight about natural things
- ask and answer questions

Things in the Sky

Talk about the sky when you are outside with your Fives. Lie down on your back with the children and look up. Help them notice the movements of the sun and clouds. Talk about the different colors of the sky on different days and at different times. If children are with you when it is dark, share the moon and stars with them, too. See if children can talk about what the cloud shapes remind them of.

I see a big white fluffy cloud that looks like a dog.
See? There's its head and mouth, and the long part is its tail.
You think it looks like a cat running, Lois?
Oh, yes, I see what you mean.

Put out picture books and posters about things in the sky, too.

 outdoors 2–12 minutes 1–20 Fives

441

Fives can

- play with flannelboards
- read a few words

Nature Flannelboards

Look at Directions for Making a Flannelboard on page 398. Put out one or more flannelboards for the children to use. Have different sets of nature cutouts made from felt that the children can choose to use with the board. Store each in its own container. Add words that show the names for the things, too. See if children attach the words to the pictures.

- sky things (stars, moon, clouds, sun)
- fish things (water plants, brightly colored fish, water birds)
- farm things (barn, fence, animals)
- jungle animals
- dinosaurs
- leaves and trees
- flowers

 indoors 2–15 minutes 1–2 Fives

442

Fives can

- sort by color, then by other aspects, such as size

Seashells

Have a collection of seashells in the Science and Nature Center for your Fives to inspect. Have several of each kind of shell. Encourage children to sort them into different groups—color, size, shape, or other aspect that they find interesting. Have books and pictures that show different shells nearby so that you and your Fives can find out more about each kind of shell. Talk about the names of the shells as the children play with them.

You sorted all the scallop shells into one pile, Trina. Do you know what kind of shells these are? I think you're right. How can you tell?

Children can trace or draw the shells to make shell pictures or wash them to see how the colors change when they get wet.

 in or out   1–20 minutes   # 1–10 Fives

443

Fives can

- begin to understand measurement

What Thermometers Tell Us

Set up an experiment with sturdy thermometers that children can put into bowls of ice water and warm water. Add a sign that says, "What happens to the red line when the thermometer is in cold or warm water?" Allow children to find out the answer. Help them see the red thermometer indicator as it moves. Some children may want to use a recording sheet like the one on page 397 and a red crayon or marker to show what they found. Others may want to draw their own pictures or dictate their results for you to write down.

Place big thermometers with easy-to-see numbers indoors and outdoors where your Fives can discover how the indicator moves as the weather is hotter or colder. Look at the thermometer often with the children and talk about what it tells us.

 in or out   1–3 minutes   # 1–8 Fives

444

Fives can

- show some interest in maps
- talk about things that interest them

Where We Live on the Earth

Place a globe of the world where children can see and touch it. Tell them that the globe is a model of the earth and that we live on the earth. Point out the land and the oceans, but do not name all the countries or expect children to be interested in the details. Talk about things that are familiar to the children. Show them

- where they live
- where they are going if they take a long trip
- where mountains or beaches are that they have visited
- where children in the class are from

Yoshiko is from Japan. This is Japan on our globe.
Yoskiko had to cross a big ocean to get here.
How did you come from Japan, Yoshiko?

 indoors   2–8 minutes   1–4 Fives

445

Fives can

- learn lots about dinosaurs
- ask and answer questions

All About Dinosaurs

Have a collection of toy dinosaurs for the children to use. You may want to have small and large sets. Be sure to have several of the most popular types to avoid fights over toys.

Place picture books and posters about dinosaurs out in the classroom. Use these with interested children to answer questions and find out more. Help interested children learn the correct name for each dinosaur, what it ate, and how it lived. Explain that dinosaurs lived long ago, but are not alive now. Encourage interested children to make drawings and books about dinosaurs to use in the Science and Nature Center.

Charlie, you wrote this book about dinosaurs.
Do you want to read it to us?
I see that you and Dianna both did illustrations for the book.

 in or out   2–30 minutes   1–8 Fives

446

Fives can

- talk about their discoveries
- begin to understand measurement

How Much Did It Rain or Snow?

Place a container with a flat bottom and straight sides outdoors to catch any rain, sleet, or snow that falls. Check the container each day with your Fives to see how much precipitation there was. Use a ruler and help children measure. Then let them empty the container. They can mark the amount of precipitation on a graph each day and compare to see when there was more or less.

Have children guess whether there will be anything in the container before they actually look. Talk about the signs in the sky that help us know when we will have precipitation.

Marika says that the container will be empty, but Jason remembers that it rained last night. What do you think, Simon?

 outdoors   3–10 minutes   1–5 Fives

447

Fives can

- begin to understand measurement
- do simple experiments
- talk about their discoveries

What a Compass Tells Us

Show your children how a compass works. Let them experiment by holding the compass in many places to see where north is. Explain about directions by looking at the globe and also by seeing where familiar things are that are near their building. Draw a simple, big map with interested children that shows where the playground and other landmarks are in relation to the building. Help your Fives experiment to see where the sun rises and sets. Draw these on the map, too.

Have several safe, sturdy compasses for your Fives to use on their own, both indoors or out.

Where is the needle pointing, Josh?
Now try moving over here.
Is the needle still pointing north?

 in or out   1–7 minutes   1–10 Fives

448

Fives can

- show curiosity and delight about natural things
- talk about their discoveries

The Power of the Wind

Hang a wind sock or a bunch of plastic streamers outdoors where your Fives can easily see it. Help the children notice how the wind makes the sock move in different ways and in different directions. Use a compass to find out the direction in which the wind is blowing. Talk about how you cannot see the wind, but you can see and feel how it moves. Help children notice the wind in these ways, too:

- Show children how to lick one finger and hold it up outdoors—the wind will make it feel cold.
- Use pinwheels of different types.
- Watch trees, grass, and bushes move in the wind.
- Make paper fans to make your own wind.

Have children create their own stories about the wind.

 in or out   1–7 minutes   1–20 Fives

449

Fives can

- begin to understand measurement
- talk about their discoveries

Weather Reporter Book

As children keep track of the weather each day, suggest that they make a weather reporter book. Each day the weather reporter can collect information about weather conditions—temperature, wind, precipitation, clouds, sun, and so on—and create a page for the book by drawing or writing. These pages can be added to a loose-leaf binder that is kept in the Science and Nature Center. The weather reporter can later explain to others about what he or she found out.

As pages accumulate in the book, look back at all the different types of weather the children have experienced. Help them see how conditions change with the seasons.

Wow! I remember the day when it was so snowy. Here's Audrey's weather report for that day.

 in or out   1–7 minutes   1–20 Fives

450

Fives can

- experiment as they play
- talk about their discoveries

Microscopes

Have a simple, sturdy microscope for children to look through to see familiar things up close. Use the instructions that come with the microscope to make slides. You might show a strand of hair, a small piece of a leaf, a little soil, and a piece of yarn. Focus the microscope so what the children see is clear.

Talk with the children about how things look different when they are magnified. Compare what they see when using a microscope and a magnifying glass.

How does the leaf look through the microscope, Danny? It doesn't look like a leaf at all? What do you see?

 in or out   1–7 minutes   1–2 Fives

451

Fives can

- sort by color, then by other aspects, such as size

What Is It Made Of?

Put into a box at least two things made of each of these materials: metal, wood, rubber, plastic, clay, wool, cotton, and glass. Add labeled construction paper sheets (laminated or covered with clear contact paper if you wish) that children can sort the items onto. Have your Fives look at each thing and talk about how it feels, looks, or sounds. Encourage children to figure out what each thing is made of. Help them sort the things onto the correct sheet of construction paper.

What do you think the key is made of, Tracy? How does it look and feel? That's right. Do you know where the metal things go?

Help your Fives notice what everyday things are made of.

Can you tell what these two tables are made of?

 in or out   2–15 minutes   1–20 Fives

452

Fives can

- show curiosity and delight about natural things

- experiment as they play

Prisms

Bring in a collection of prisms that make rainbows when sun-light passes through them. Hang crystal prisms in sunny windows and use clear plastic prisms that the children can hold and move to catch the light. Point out the rainbows, inspect the colors, and encourage children to experiment to make a rainbow.

That's right, Chio. I see the rainbow on the wall, too.
Let's see how many colors it has.

Provide art materials in the rainbow colors. Then see if the children begin to include rainbows in their artwork.

Look for rainbows during rainstorms. If you are lucky enough to find one, celebrate the event with your Fives.

 in or out　　 1–7 minutes　　 1–15 Fives

453

Fives can

- show curiosity and delight about natural things

- draw some recognizable figures

Look and Draw Natural Things

Bring art materials outdoors for your Fives to use. Encourage interested children to concentrate on natural things, such as flowers, grass, trees, or animals, and to draw what they see. Give children clipboards or something else to use as a portable, sturdy surface for drawing. Then they can move around and get up close to what they want to draw.

Talk about the pictures children have created. Write down their words if they wish. Have plenty of natural things indoors for children to draw if they are interested.

Are you finished with your drawing, Phillip? Would you like to tell me something about it? Yes, I see the brown ants you drew. What were they doing?

 in or out　　 1–7 minutes　　 1–20 Fives

454

Fives can

- do simple experiments
- talk about their discoveries

Which Things Melt?

On a hot sunny day, have your Fives help you put a variety of objects out in the sun in individual margarine tubs. For example, you might try a crayon, a candle, a piece of chocolate, a piece of hard candy, a wooden block, a metal key, and a stone. Talk about the warmth of the sun. Ask the children if they know what will happen when the things are left in the sun. Wait several hours and then look again. Talk about which things melted and which did not. See if they can tell how things that melted are the same or different.

Bring the things into a cooler place. Check them with the children after they solidify. Use the words *liquid* and *solid*. Later, cook grilled cheese sandwiches with the children. Talk about how the cheese changes when it gets hot.

 in or out   1–7 minutes   1–20 Fives

455

Fives can

- experiment as they play
- talk about their discoveries

Which Things Dissolve?

Set up clear plastic containers, water, spoons, and a variety of things for children to put into the water, such as paint powder, flour, sand, dirt, and sugar. Put up a sign that says, "Which things dissolve in water?" Show children how to add a spoonful of one thing to a container of water, stir it, and then see what happens. Talk about which things dissolve in water. Allow children to experiment freely. Talk to them about their discoveries. See if they notice that if they add more of some things to the water, the thing no longer dissolves as well, or that things tend to dissolve better in warm water than in cold.

What happened when you put the first spoon of sugar into the cup, Antoine? What happened when you added more sugar?

 in or out   1–7 minutes   1–20 Fives

- Have a table where many interesting natural things can be put for children to inspect.

- Have a sand or water table nearby.

- Make sure there is plenty of light.

- Have a place to put pictures about science and nature. Put up pictures that show natural things children are interested in. Change the pictures often.

- Have a place to put books that give more information about the science and nature things your Fives enjoy.

- Have lots of unbreakable jars, boxes, or containers ready to put natural treasures in. Some will need lids with holes punched in them for air.

- If living things are part of the Science and Nature Center, be sure they are well-cared-for—cages cleaned, food and water provided daily, no rough handling.

- If wild living things are brought in or discovered, encourage your Fives to respect the creature's life, even if the living thing is only a small insect or worm.

- Be sure that nothing in the area is poisonous or dangerous to a child.

- Pay lots of attention to the Science and Nature Center. Show your own curiosity and interest as you share discoveries with the children.

- Change or add to the area often. Help the children notice the changes.

- If a child cares about something he or she has brought in, be sure it is protected and sent home again.

- Add natural things to other areas of the room. Have plants, pets, pictures, or mobiles wherever they can safely fit in.

- Keep pets such as gerbils or mice out of children's reach. These pets are fun to watch but can bite small fingers, even when children are supervised. And children can easily harm the pets. A sturdy aquarium cage with a wire mesh top is the best home for these animals.

- Make sure any animals that children come into contact with are healthy and will not pass on any illness. If any child is scratched or bitten, disinfect the injury and let the parent know what happened.

Sample Picture/ Word Instructions for Caring for Pets

Caring for Our Hamsters

1. Lift the top off the cage.

2. Take out the wheel.

3. Take out the food dish and water bottle.

4. Put dirty cedar chips into the trash.

5. Put in 1" of new cedar chips. Use a ruler to measure.

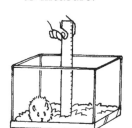

6. Replace top so hamster doesn't get out.

7. Clean the water bottle and food dish.

8. Dry the water bottle and food dish.

9. Fill the water bottle.

10 Fill the dish with food.

11. Put the water bottle, food dish, and wheel in cage.

12. Replace the top.

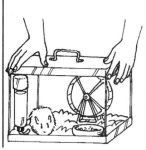

13. Wash and dry your hands.

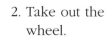

Activities for Learning from the World Around Them

389

Tips for Nature Walks and Field Trips

- Many of the trips you take with Fives should be short. Most trips can be walks of no more than 20 to 30 minutes. Very special trips can last a morning, an afternoon, or even a full day, but be sure to keep the children's regular schedule for meals and snacks, toileting, and rest.

- Be sure there are enough adults along and that their full attention is on the children at all times. The longer the trip, the more adults you will need. If a trip lasts a full day, then it is best to have one parent or teacher for every three or four children.

- If a child is difficult to handle, then have one adult supervise that child and another easy child.

- Take the same walks over and over again, but look for different things each time.

- If you drive in private vehicles, make sure each child is seat-belted safely with his or her own safety restraint. Seat belts should never be shared. Be sure to follow all safety rules if school buses are used.

- Have each child wear a name tag.

- Get permission slips from parents. For walks around the block or to a nearby park, one blanket permission for all outings should be enough. But always make sure all parents know where you will be going and when you will be back.

- Let parents know before you take any trip so they can dress children properly. Send notes home to parents if parents do not visit your classroom every day. A note on the parents' message board works well for parents who pick up their children. Remind children to tell their parents about upcoming trips, too. But do not depend on children to be the only messenger.

- Have extra clothing available so that no child ever has to be too cold or too hot.

- Make sure to be back on time. If you will be late, contact someone who can tell the parents.

- If your trip will be longer than usual, take along a snack and anything else you might need for the children.

- If you are going farther than just around the block, always bring children's emergency information and a small first-aid kit.

- Some Fives may want to be independent and wander away from the group. If this is a problem with a child you are supervising, always hold that child's hand and watch carefully. Be serious with the children and explain how important it is for their safety to stay with the adults.

- Whenever possible, encourage children to enjoy plant and animal life in its natural place. For example, instead of picking wildflowers, help children learn to enjoy them, but leave them for others, too. Instead of catching bugs, encourage children to watch the bugs do the things they do without being disturbed.

- Some ideas for nature walks and trips with Fives are

  the children's playground

  a walk around the block

  children's backyards that are nearby

  a pet store

  a zoo

  a big grassy field

  a children's science museum

  a farm

  a forest or woods

  a park with trees and flowers

  an aquarium

  a greenhouse filled with plants

  a pumpkin patch

  a Christmas tree farm

  an orchard (when in flower and when in fruit)

  a pond, river, or stream (but only with extra supervision)

  a beach (but only with extra supervision)

  a duck pond to feed the ducks (but only with extra supervision)

How to Make Picture Card Sorting Games

- Have a set of 10–20 picture cards that children can sort into various piles by an attribute they choose, such as color or size.

- Have different sets of cards representing different aspects of nature, such as flower picture cards, animal cards, fish cards, and so on. Sets can be combined so that children can sort by type, such as sorting the fish cards into one pile and the land animals into another.

- Pictures of the same thing shown differently may be also be used. For example, you may have one picture of a whole apple to match to a picture of an apple cut into slices, or a picture of a bunch of tulips that matches a picture of a single tulip.

1. Collect or draw pictures for the cards. You can find pictures in catalogs, magazines, newspaper ads, or children's activity books.

2. Glue each picture onto a sturdy piece of cardboard or onto an index card.

3. Cover the cards and board with clear contact paper or laminate to protect the pictures.

4. Store each set of cards in its own individual container.

Activities for Learning from the World Around Them

Ideas for Making Bird Feeders

1. Mix peanut butter with cornmeal until you can roll the mixture into a doughy, not-too-sticky ball. Your Fives can help knead the mixture with their hands. Add birdseed, if you wish. Make sure there is enough cornmeal in the mixture so that the birds don't choke on the peanut butter.

2. Put a big ball of the mixture into a mesh onion bag. Hang the bag outside.

OR

Cut clean, empty 6-oz cardboard frozen juice containers so that they are 1" in height. Punch a hole through the cardboard at the open end. Tie a loop of string through the hole as a hanger. Have your Fives help you press the mixture into the cans. Hang outside.

Peanut Butter and Birdseed on Toast

1. Toast bread lightly. Stale bread collected from children's parents is fine for the birds. Your Fives may want to taste this before birdseed is added. Use fresh toasted bread for children to eat.

2. Have your Fives use dull plastic knives to spread peanut butter on toast.

3. Use a dull darning needle to thread a loop of yarn through one corner of the toast.

4. Have children sprinkle birdseed onto the sticky peanut butter.

5. Hang the toast outside for the birds.

Sample "Birds We See" Chart

Make a mark when you spot the bird.

Sparrow

Cardinal

Mockingbird

Pigeon

Chickadee

Activities for Learning from the World Around Them

Sink-or-Float
Sorting Game
Record Sheet

Mark the things that float.

Crayon	Wooden Bead
Nail	Wooden Block
Pencil	Magnet
Rock	Small Ball
Leaf	Key

Record Sheet for What Sticks to Magnets

Mark the things that stick to the magnet.

Crayon	Wooden Bead
Nail	Wooden Block
Paper Clip	Plastic Spoon
Rock	Metal Spoon
Leaf	Key

Activities for Learning from the World Around Them

What Do Thermometers Tell Us?

Mark how high the red line goes when you put the thermometer in the two bowls of water.

Cold Water   *Warm Water*

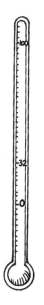 

Directions for Making a Flannelboard

1. Cover a board with a large, wide piece of felt or flannel cloth. For the board, use wood, very sturdy cardboard, or an old bulletin board. A rectangle of 2' × 2½' works well, but you can make a larger or smaller board if you wish. You can even make individual flannelboards, 11" × 14".

fold edges to back

Front

2. Fold the cloth over the back of the board, making sure the front is pulled smooth. Sew the ends together, or staple and cover securely with heavy tape.

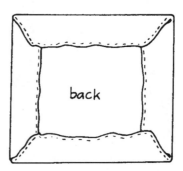

back

3. When you use the board, lean it at an angle against a wall or bookcase. Then the flannel pictures will stay on better. When your Fives use the board, have them place it flat on a table or floor so that the pictures will not fall off.

4. To make pictures, cut out ones you want to use. Cover the front with clear contact paper and glue felt material or sandpaper on the back. Or use pens to draw on felt material. You can buy pictures for use with flannelboards. Check school supply catalogs for prices and ideas.

Gardening with Fives

Group Garden

Fives will enjoy growing a garden, but their interest will come and go, depending on what is happening. For example, some children will be interested in planting seeds, others will like watering, and others will want to pick flowers or harvest the foods you grow. Many of your children will be interested in bits and pieces rather than the long-term picture that you enjoy so much. This is normal and appropriate for young children.

■ Plant a small garden in a sunny, protected place where children can see it.

■ Plant quick-to-grow vegetables (lettuce, radishes) and flowers (zinnias, marigolds). If your program is open through the summer, plant other things that take longer to grow (tomatoes, green beans, pumpkins, summer squash) but that the children will find interesting to watch.

■ Tend the garden well, keeping it weeded, watered, and harvested. Encourage children to help in every step, but do not expect that they will always be interested.

■ If you do not have a good place for a garden outdoors, plant small vegetables such as radishes, lettuce, or small tomato plants in containers. Dishpans or large flowerpots filled with rich potting soil can be used if kept in a sunny place and watered regularly.

Individual Gardens

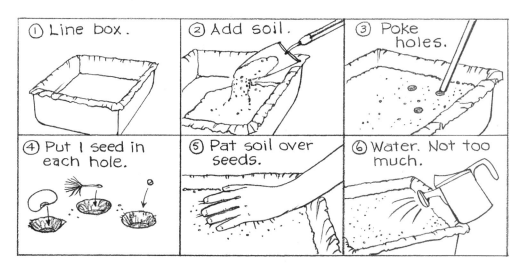

① Line box.

② Add soil.

③ Poke holes.

④ Put 1 seed in each hole.

⑤ Pat soil over seeds.

⑥ Water. Not too much.

Gardening Instructions

■ Copy the garden recipe onto a large chart or onto individual cards.

■ Talk about the pictures with small groups of children before they plant.

- While children make gardens, have them look at the pictures to see what they need to do.

- Help children talk about what they are doing.

- Optional:

    a. If children use plastic dishpans, do not have them line the box (step 1).

    b. Children can use a measuring stick to poke holes. Make a measuring stick by marking a straw, stick, or coffee stirrer 1/4" from one end. Tell children to make holes as deep as the mark.

    c. Place large-holed chicken wire on top of soil. Have the children plant only one seed in each wire space. This avoids overcrowding plants.

    d. Allow children to choose their own seeds. Set up seeds so that children can see how many of each type to take. Provide a picture of what the seed will grow into.

Tip: Give children a piece of masking tape to stick seeds onto until they're ready to plant. They're easy to remove, and small seeds won't blow away or get lost.

- Encourage the children to observe and care for their own gardens.

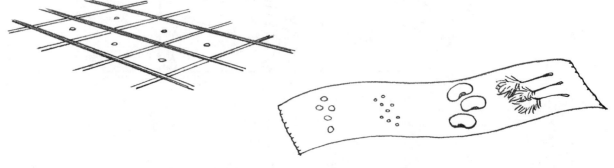

Sample Plant
Growth Chart

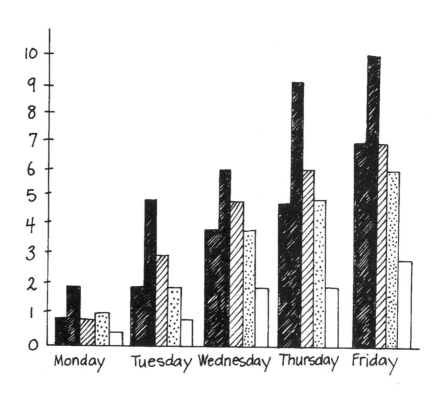

Ideas for Cooking with Fives

1. Copy these recipes on larger pieces of cardboard to make recipe cards.

2. Put each card in a row on a low table or counter from left to right.

3. Put each ingredient and utensils in front of their cards.

4. Have each child start on the left and follow the steps to complete the recipe.

Cornmeal Muffins

Flour Mixture
$\frac{2}{3}$ cup sifted flour
2 T. sugar
$1\frac{1}{2}$ tsp. baking powder
$\frac{1}{8}$ tsp. salt

1. Sift.

2.

3. Stir.

4.

5.

6.

7. Stir just to moisten dry ingredients.

8. Pour into 2 small lined muffin tins. Bake 13 minutes at 400°.

Activities for Learning from the World Around Them

Framed Egg

1 slice bread

1. Cut out circle.

2. Butter both sides.

3. Brown 1 side. Turn.

4. Crack egg into cup.

5. Slip egg into frame.

low heat

6. Cover till white is set.

7. Uncover. Cook till egg is firm.

These recipes are from *Cook and Learn* by Beverly Veitch and Thelma Harms. Menlo Park, CA: Addison-Wesley Publishing Company, 1981. See also the recipes on pages 199 and 200 of this book.

For more ideas on cooking with children, try:

Cook and Learn by Beverly Veitch and Thelma Harms
Addison-Wesley Publishing Company
Jacob Way
Reading, Massachusetts 01867

Creative Food Experiences for Children by Mary Goodwin and Gerry Pollen
Center for Science in the Public Interest
1755 S. Street N.W.
Washington, DC 20009

Cool Cooking for Kids by Pat McClenahan and Ida Jaqua
Fearon-Pitman
6 Davis Drive
Belmont, CA 94002

More than Graham Crackers by Nancy Wannamaker, Kristen Hearn and Sherrill Richarz
NAEYC
1834 Connecticut Avenue, N.W.
Washington, DC 20009

Materials and Notes

Number, Shape, and Size (Math)

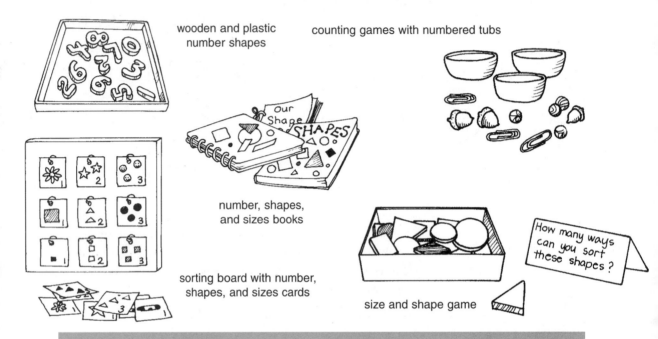

wooden and plastic
number shapes

counting games with numbered tubs

Our
Shape

SHAPES

number, shapes,
and sizes books

sorting board with number,
shapes, and sizes cards

How many ways
can you sort
these shapes?

size and shape game

- Count real things with your Fives often. Talk about numbers of things as you go through the day with the children so that they see how numbers are used and why they are useful.

- Keep number, shape, and size activities fun and interesting for Fives. Do not push children to memorize numbers or turn math into a boring task that children do not enjoy.

- Some children in your group will be able to understand numbers very well, while others will not yet be interested. Challenge each child at his or her own level. Add a little number talk to everything each child is interested in.

- A Math Center should be set up in a quiet area of the room where Fives can use a variety of number, shape, and size materials and games.

- Tell parents about some of the number, shape, and size games you play with children. Encourage parents to talk about these things with their children at home.

- Many of the activity ideas for younger and older Fives can be used with either age group because they are open-ended and can be challenging to children with a wide range of abilities.

Activity Checklist

Number, Shape, and Size (Math)

Number, Shape, and Size (Math) activities for Fives help children think about and compare how many, how much, and what size or shape as they play games and solve real-life number-related problems. Many math activities include reading or writing some of the numbers or drawing shapes, but not all children will be interested in this type of activity. Number, shape, and size activities focus on using ideas and words in the preschool setting so that when children are older, doing mathematics in school will come more easily.

Check for each age group

	60–66 months	66–72 months
1. Children take part in routines where counting is used, such as counting how many children brought their lunch to school or being sure there are the right number of chairs for children who want to work together.	❐	❐
2. Adult asks questions to help children think about number, shape, and size but does not quiz children on these things.	❐	❐
3. Number, shape, and size are part of many different activities, not just those in the Math Center. For example, counting is used to keep score for basketball or to see how many blankets are needed for the dolls.	❐	❐
4. Teaching about number, shape, and size is developmentally appropriate. Hands-on activities are used instead of memorization and worksheets. Interest is encouraged but not forced.	❐	❐
5. Math Center with number books, age-appropriate games, and lots of small things to count is set up for children to use freely.	❐	❐
6. Adult often plays number games with children and helps when needed.	❐	❐
7. Adult encourages Fives to estimate numbers of things and then count to check.	❐	❐
8. Interested children are helped and encouraged to read and write simple numbers, but emphasis is still on hands-on math activities.	❐	❐
9. Older Fives are encouraged to combine small numbers of real things to see how simple addition works.		❐

456

Fives can

■ show interest in
numbers, shapes, and
sizes

■ play simple games

Math Center

Set up a Math Center in a quiet part of the room where you
and your Fives can do fun number, shape, and size activities.
Have lots of games for counting, matching, sorting and
comparing; number, shape, and size books and pictures or
posters; pencils, watercolor markers, and paper. You will find
many ideas for activities in this section of the book.

Place books and materials for activities on a low shelf for
children to use freely. Show children how to do each new
activity and give help as children play. Change activities and
books every week.

 indoors   5–30 minutes   **#** 1–6 Fives

457

Fives can

■ read some written
numbers

■ count 10 or more
objects

Number Books

Have lots of picture-number books in the Book Center and
in the Math Center for your Fives to use. Look at these books
with the children. Encourage them to count the pictures on
the pages. Talk about the written numbers. See if the children
can tell you the number names.

This number is 9, James.
And look, the word nine *is printed under the number.*
N-I-N-E. That's how you spell nine.
Can you guess what this word on the next page is?

 in or out   2–20 minutes   **#** 1–5 Fives

Activities for Learning from the World Around Them

458

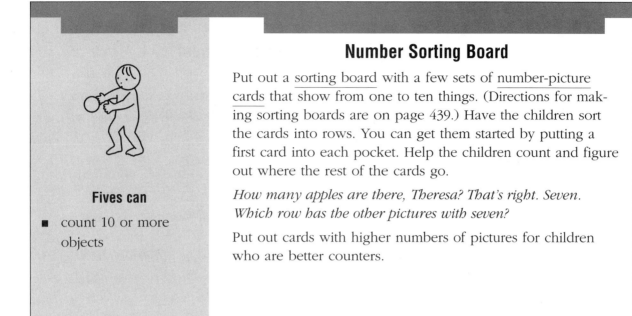

Fives can

- count 10 or more objects

Number Sorting Board

Put out a sorting board with a few sets of number-picture cards that show from one to ten things. (Directions for making sorting boards are on page 439.) Have the children sort the cards into rows. You can get them started by putting a first card into each pocket. Help the children count and figure out where the rest of the cards go.

How many apples are there, Theresa? That's right. Seven. Which row has the other pictures with seven?

Put out cards with higher numbers of pictures for children who are better counters.

🏠 in or out   🕐 5–20 minutes   # 1–2 Fives

459

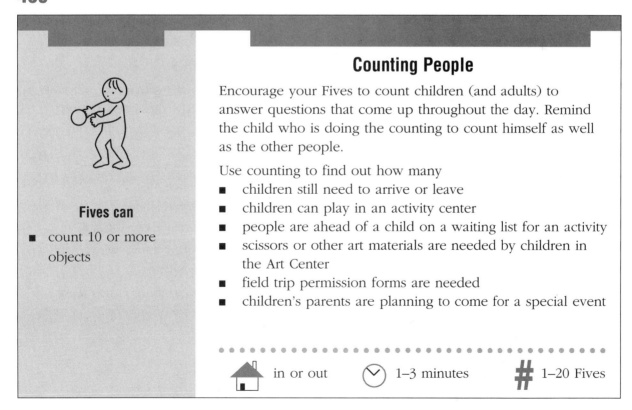

Fives can

- count 10 or more objects

Counting People

Encourage your Fives to count children (and adults) to answer questions that come up throughout the day. Remind the child who is doing the counting to count himself as well as the other people.

Use counting to find out how many
- children still need to arrive or leave
- children can play in an activity center
- people are ahead of a child on a waiting list for an activity
- scissors or other art materials are needed by children in the Art Center
- field trip permission forms are needed
- children's parents are planning to come for a special event

🏠 in or out   🕐 1–3 minutes   # 1–20 Fives

460

Fives can

- write numbers 1 to 5 but not perfectly

Writing Numbers

Give your Fives many chances to practice writing numbers but only when they are really interested. Have paper, pencils and markers for them to use. Be sure there are examples of clearly written numbers for them to look at and copy in the Math Center.

Help children write numbers whenever they want to in their play in other areas, too.

You can get a marker and some paper to make some money for your store, Shameeka.
You want to help too, Tony? That must be a four-dollar bill. I see you made a four.

 in or out   1–15 minutes   1–6 Fives

461

Fives can

- sort by many features—each thing in group shares one characteristic

Sorting Buttons

Make a collection of many colorful buttons that are different sizes, shapes, textures, and colors. Place these in a button-sorting activity box. Encourage your Fives to sort the buttons in many ways:

- Make a pile of buttons that are the same color.
- Find all the buttons that are the same size.
- Find all the buttons that are the same shape.
- Make a line of buttons from the smallest to biggest.

Encourage children to sort in their own creative ways. Ask them to explain how they sorted the buttons.

You made two groups of buttons, Kenya. What makes these buttons the same? And how is this group of buttons different?

 indoors   1–20 minutes   1–4 Fives

462

Fives can

- sort by many features—each thing in group shares one characteristic

Sorting Feelie Shapes

Cut out five circles, squares, triangles, and rectangles from sturdy cardboard. Use glue to cover one of each shape with sandpaper, fuzzy cloth, satin cloth, bumpy cloth, or vinyl. Trim the edges evenly. Put out four or more shallow boxes. Encourage the children to sort the shapes into the boxes in as many different ways as they can think of. Help them get started if needed by suggesting one feature to sort by.

Let's sort all the shapes that have corners into one box.
We can sort the ones with rounded edges into another.

To add new challenge to this sorting game, add other shapes, such as hearts, stars, ovals, or octagons. Or add different-sized shapes, too.

 in or out   2–20 minutes   1–4 Fives

463

Fives can

- count 10 or more objects

- name written numbers 1 to 5

- begin to learn names of numbers 6 to 10

Number-Sorting Tubs

Use ten clean margarine tubs. Use a permanent marker to write the number 1 in the bottom of the first tub. Make one dot in the bottom of that tub, too. Continue marking each tub until you have tubs that show 1 through 10.

Put out the tubs, along with lots of colorful ½" beads. Show your Fives how to put one bead into the tub that says 1, two into the tub that says 2, and so on. Then see how the children play the game on their own. Talk about putting in only one bead into the tub for each dot.

Javier, how many beads did you put into this tub?
Let's count them and see. That number is eight.
Did you put eight beads into the tub?
You did!

 indoors   3–12 minutes   1–2 Fives

464

Many Small Things to Count

Keep many small things in the Math Center for children to count and sort. They can count things into number-sorting tubs, boxes, paper bags, or other containers you have numbered. Here are ideas for small things children can count. You, the children, and their parents will have lots of other ideas.

- small plastic farm or zoo animals
- small plastic dinosaurs
- acorns
- rocks and pebbles
- seashells
- colorful pegs
- clothespins
- small toy cars or trucks

Fives can

- count 10 or more objects
- name written numbers 1 to 5
- begin to learn names of numbers 6 to 10

 in or out   2–12 minutes   1–20 Fives

465

"Which Number Is It?" Riddles

Play easy number riddle games with your Fives often. Give clues about a number you want them to guess and see if they can figure out what the number is. When they have guessed correctly, hold up a card that shows that number.

I'm thinking of a very small number.
We have this many tables in our room.

Allow a child to choose a card and then give clues so that everyone can guess the number.

Randy, can you give us a clue about the number on the card you drew?

Fives can

- count 10 or more objects

 in or out   2–12 minutes   **#** 1–20 Fives

466

Fives can

- know what calendars are used for

- understand time words (*week, morning, afternoon*)

Exploring the Calendar

Hang a colorful calendar where your Fives can easily see and touch it. Talk with the children to see what they know about calendars—the days, months, and year. Show children what day it is today. Let each child help you mark her birthday. Show children when other special days are, too. Talk about the numbers and dates. Count up how many days it is until a special day.

Are you trying to find your birthday, Emma?
Here is the September page. Do you see your name?
That's right, it's there on the 9!

The calendar can be used briefly each day with a large group of Fives. Talk about what day it is and any special events that are coming up. Keep the large-group discussion very short.

 indoors   1–5 minutes   1–20 Fives

467

Fives can

- understand the day's schedule

- understand time words, such as *day* and *week*

Time Talk

Use time words with your Fives often. See if they know what happens in the morning, afternoon, and night, as well as early or late. Use time words and time numbers, too. Have a big clock with clear numbers to show children the time on the clock when they are interested.

You got here really early today, Kathleen. See the clock? It's only 7:15 in the morning.

The clock says it is ten minutes to eleven. Do you remember what that means? That's right. It's time to clean up. We have ten minutes until morning outdoor time.

 in or out   1–2 minutes   1–20 Fives

468

Fives can

- understand how numbers are used

- learn to solve simple problems

Talking Through Real "How Many" Problems

Help the children see how numbers work by talking through real "how many" problems throughout the day. For example, talk through how you figure out if there are enough chairs for the number of people who can work in a center or how to share play dough fairly.

Is there enough play dough for everyone at the table? How many people are there? That's right, Jimmy. There are four people. How can we divide the play dough so that each person will have a fair share?

 in or out 1–4 minutes 1–8 Fives

469

Fives can

- understand the words *one* and *many, less* and *more*

- begin to understand measurement

Balance Scales

Set up one or two balance scales for your Fives to use in the Math Center. Explain to all children how the scales work—the side that is heavier goes down while the side that is lighter goes up. Help them understand that the scales must be used gently. Put out some familiar small things, such as plastic and wooden blocks or small toys the children can weigh to find out which weigh more and which weigh less. Encourage children to feel the weights of each thing and then try them on the scale.

Here are a plastic block and a wooden block, Jason. Hold them. Which is heavier? You can see if you are right. How can you find out? Which one went down on the scale? Right! The one that went down is heavier than the other.

 in or out 2–15 minutes 1–3 Fives per scale

Activities for Learning from the World Around Them

470

Fives can

- become familiar with written numbers
- name written numbers 1–5

Numbers in the Neighborhood

Take a walk around the neighborhood and see how many written numbers you and your Fives can spot. Look for numbers on speed limit signs, on houses, on the pumps at gas stations, in advertisements on store windows, and wherever else they appear. See if the children can name the numbers they find. If not, say the numbers for them.

Talk about what the numbers tell people.

Martin found a number! See, it's on the speed limit sign. Do you know what that number tells us? Do you know the name of the number? Right, there is a three. This number is a five. Both numbers together say thirty-five.

 outdoors   10–20 minutes   **#** 1–10 Fives

471

Fives can

- become familiar with written numbers
- do simple matching and sorting

Sorting Written Numbers

Make sets of cards with numbers from 1 to 10 written clearly in different colors and sizes on each card. Write only one number on each card. Look at the cards with your Fives and talk about the sizes and colors of the numbers, as well as the names.

See if the children can sort the same numbers in many different ways.

We put all the same colors into piles.
Now let's see if we can find all the cards with the same numbers.
This is a five. Can you find another five, James?
Great, you found lots of them!
Which number do you want to do next?

 in or out   5–20 minutes   **#** 1–4 Fives

472

Fives can

- know names of familiar coins
- learn how many cents are in a penny, nickel, and dime

Money Matching and Sorting Games

Use plastic play money coins or real coins to make money-matching or sorting games. You will find three fun Money Matching and Sorting Games to make on pages 436–438.

Place the games on the shelf for children to choose when they go to the Math Center. Show your Fives how to play. Use the names of the coins, talk about the numbers the children see, and encourage the children to count easy numbers in many ways.

You put the right number of pennies on the card, Sarah. Can you count them?

Show children how to put the games away after playing.

 indoors   1–15 minutes   1–2 Fives

473

Fives can

- write some numbers
- understand a little about how money is used

Making Money

Let children inspect some real one-, five-, ten-, and twenty-dollar bills. Talk with them about how the numbers printed on the money tell us how much the bill is worth. Talk about which bills are worth the most. Help the children notice the words and pictures that are on the bills.

Cut out rectangles of plain paper that are the same size as real dollar bills. Set up a money-making activity in which children use watercolor markers, pencils, and crayons to make their own bills. Talk about the numbers the children write on their own money. Children can use the money they make in their pretend play or keep it for themselves. Keep the money-making things in an activity box in the Math, Art or Writing Center.

 in or out   5–10 minutes   1–5 Fives

474

Fives can

■ begin to understand fractions

Fraction Words

Give your Fives the chance to learn a little about fractions. Use the words *equal, half, third,* and *quarter* in real situations. For example, when helping children to share play dough, talk about dividing it into equal parts. Or at snack, serve foods such as sandwiches, apples, or bananas that are cut into equal pieces.

We're having fresh tomatoes and crackers for snack.
I'll cut the tomatoes so we can each have a half.
How many pieces did I cut this tomato into?
Right, I cut the tomato into two pieces—two halves.
Each half is the same size. They are equal.

 in or out   1–3 minutes   1–20 Fives

475

Fives can

■ arrange things in order, from little to big

Sequencing from Little to Big

Make sets of five or six different things ranging from tiny to large, such as candles, socks, spoons, or bolts. Have parents help you collect the things. Ask your Fives if they can arrange each set in a line from smallest to biggest.

Anita, you found the big and little socks.
Here are some more socks. Where do you think they should go?

 in or out   2–20 minutes   1–3 Fives

476

Fives can

- name triangle, circle, and square
- tell some shapes by touch

Shapes Feelie Bag

Make a feelie bag by putting a plastic container into a big, clean sock. Put a flat plastic circle, square, and triangle into the feelie bag. Ask the child to pull out a shape you name. Show a picture of the shape if you need to and talk about how it feels.

The square has four corners and straight sides.
Can you feel the square, Jason?

Try these ideas to add new challenges:

- When a child can tell one shape from another, add a rectangle.
- Ask the child to reach into the bag, feel one of the shapes, and then try to guess what it is.

 in or out   2–15 minutes # 1–4 Fives

477

Fives can

- sort by many features—each thing in group shares one characteristic
- name triangle, circle, and square

Shape-Sorting Board

Put out a sorting board with shape cards to sort. Begin with shape cards that are the same size and color. (Directions for making several sorting boards are on pages 439–440.) Help the child get started by talking about how you sort shapes as you do the first few cards. Then see how much the child can do by herself.

You know this shape, Martine.
That's right, it's a square.
Can you put it in the row with the other square?

 in or out   3–20 minutes # 1–2 Fives

478

Fives can

- know some written numbers

- hop about 5 yards on either foot

Hopping Number Squares

Use chalk to draw a hopscotch pattern on a sidewalk or use masking tape to make one on the floor indoors. Number the squares from one to ten.

Show children how to hop from the first square to the last. They can hop or jump, and it's fine if they step on lines. See if they can count as they hop. Talk about how many squares they hopped in and the name of each number.

Here you go, Jana!
One, two, three, four.
Are you going to stop or hop to the five?
Oh! You are hopping back to the one!

 in or out   1–12 minutes   1–4 Fives

479

Fives can

- begin to understand measurement

- know fraction words, such as *half, quarter*

Lots of Measuring

Provide many measuring experiences for children as they play and help. Have a box of measuring cups and spoons that children can choose as they play with sand or water. Encourage children to measure as they help you prepare art materials such as paint or play dough. Have cooking activities for the children where they measure foods. Use measurement words often as the children measure in many ways.

I'm glad you are helping me fill the water table, Patrick.
Let's use these empty gallon milk containers.
How many gallons do you think we will need?
Maybe twenty? Let's count and see. The table is about half full now. How many gallons have we put in so far?

 in or out   1–20 minutes   1–8 Fives

480

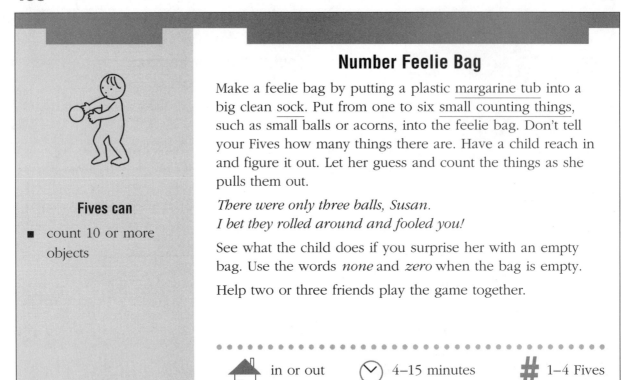

Fives can

- count 10 or more objects

Number Feelie Bag

Make a feelie bag by putting a plastic margarine tub into a big clean sock. Put from one to six small counting things, such as small balls or acorns, into the feelie bag. Don't tell your Fives how many things there are. Have a child reach in and figure it out. Let her guess and count the things as she pulls them out.

There were only three balls, Susan.
I bet they rolled around and fooled you!

See what the child does if you surprise her with an empty bag. Use the words *none* and *zero* when the bag is empty.

Help two or three friends play the game together.

in or out   4–15 minutes   # 1–4 Fives

481

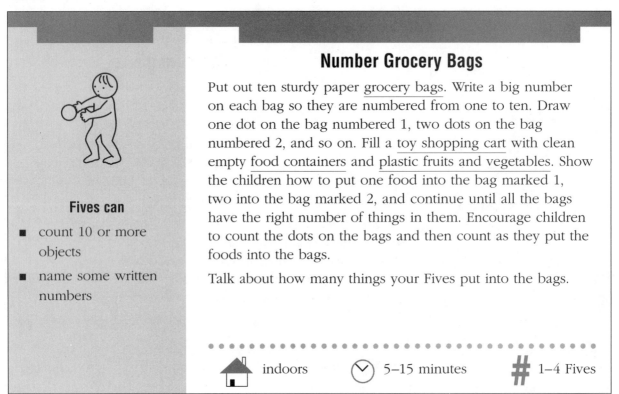

Fives can

- count 10 or more objects

- name some written numbers

Number Grocery Bags

Put out ten sturdy paper grocery bags. Write a big number on each bag so they are numbered from one to ten. Draw one dot on the bag numbered 1, two dots on the bag numbered 2, and so on. Fill a toy shopping cart with clean empty food containers and plastic fruits and vegetables. Show the children how to put one food into the bag marked 1, two into the bag marked 2, and continue until all the bags have the right number of things in them. Encourage children to count the dots on the bags and then count as they put the foods into the bags.

Talk about how many things your Fives put into the bags.

indoors   5–15 minutes   # 1–4 Fives

482

Fives can

- match some written numbers
- name some written numbers

Number Matching Game with Cards

Have several colorful decks of playing cards in the Math Center for children to use. Show them how they can match all the cards with the same numbers. Use just half of the deck with the lowest numbers for beginners, and add more cards as children want more challenge.

This is a three, Elana. Can you find the other cards that have three on them?

You can also show children how to spread out the cards face down and turn them over one at a time to play an easy version of "Concentration." Allow your Fives to play with the cards in their own creative ways.

 in or out 3–15 minutes 1–3 Fives per deck

483

Fives can

- name some written numbers

What Number Are You Feeling?

Make a feelie bag by putting a plastic container into a big, clean sock. Put three different wooden number shapes into the feelie bag. Ask the child to find the number shape you name. Show pictures of the numbers if you need to and talk about how each would feel.

Try these ideas to add new challenges:

- Ask the child to reach into the bag, feel one of the numbers, try to guess what it is, and then pull it out to see.
- Put one number into each of nine feelie bags. See if children can feel the hidden number and then match a number card to each.

 in or out 3–15 minutes 1–3 Fives

484

Fives can

- begin to understand measurement

Rulers and Tape Measures

Use rulers and tape measures with your Fives to find out how long or high things are. Have them help as you measure. Encourage them to help count inches, centimeters, or whatever measurement you are using. Point out the printed numbers as you measure. Some things you can measure with your Fives are

- distance from door to wall
- how tall the children are
- how far children can jump

See if your Fives can think of lots of other things to measure.

Amanda wants to find out how tall Mr. Bunny is.
How can we measure our rabbit?

 in or out　　 1–15 minutes　　 1–10 Fives

485

Fives can

- compare sizes
- begin to understand measurement

Comparing Block Sizes

Put out four wooden unit blocks that are different lengths and a bucket of inch cubes. Line up cubes along the length of a unit block, counting out each one. Count with the children as they put cubes on the other blocks. After they have finished, talk about which blocks held more cubes and which held fewer. Compare the sizes of the blocks.

How many cubes did you put on your block, Karen?
Which block is the longest?
Which block is the shortest?

Put out a foot-long ruler so that children can measure their unit blocks in another way.

 inside　　 5–10 minutes　　 1–5 Fives

486

Fives can

- begin to understand measurement
- count up to 20 objects
- write some numbers

Measuring: What Smaller Measures Equal a Larger One?

Set up a measuring experiment with teaspoons, tablespoons, and sets of graduated measuring cups. Have a dishpan of sand for children to measure. Put up a sign that asks, "How much sand does it take to make a cup?" Talk about the names of the different measures with the children. Look at the numbers on them. Show children how they can fill a smaller measure, level off the sand with a plastic knife, and then pour it into the one-cup measure, repeating until the cup is full. Encourage children to count the number of measures it takes to fill the cup.

Show interested Fives how to fill out a recording sheet about what they found. (See the sample on page 441.)

 in or out   5–20 minutes   1–4 Fives

487

Fives can

- begin to understand measurement
- count up to 20 objects
- write some numbers

Measuring: Is Sand the Same as Potting Soil?

Set up a measuring experiment with tablespoons and sets of graduated measuring cups. Have a dishpan of sand and another of potting soil. Put up a sign that asks, "How much does it take to fill a cup?" Let children fill a smaller measure with either sand or potting soil, level it off with a plastic knife, and then pour it into the one-cup measure, repeating until the cup is full. Have your Fives keep track of the number of measures it takes to fill the cup with sand or with potting soil. They can use a recording sheet, like the sample on page 442. Try this experiment using other things to measure, too.

It take 16 tablespoons of sand to fill a cup.
How many tablespoons of potting soil does it take, Karl?
That's right! It takes 16. It takes the same amount.

 indoors   2–8 minutes   1–4 Fives

488

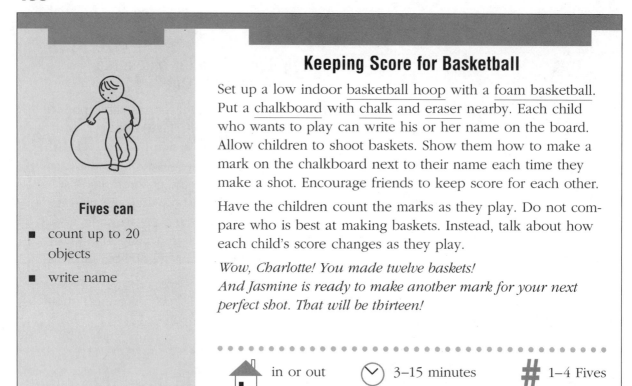

Fives can

- count up to 20 objects
- write name

Keeping Score for Basketball

Set up a low indoor basketball hoop with a foam basketball. Put a chalkboard with chalk and eraser nearby. Each child who wants to play can write his or her name on the board. Allow children to shoot baskets. Show them how to make a mark on the chalkboard next to their name each time they make a shot. Encourage friends to keep score for each other.

Have the children count the marks as they play. Do not compare who is best at making baskets. Instead, talk about how each child's score changes as they play.

Wow, Charlotte! You made twelve baskets!
And Jasmine is ready to make another mark for your next perfect shot. That will be thirteen!

in or out   3–15 minutes   # 1–4 Fives

489

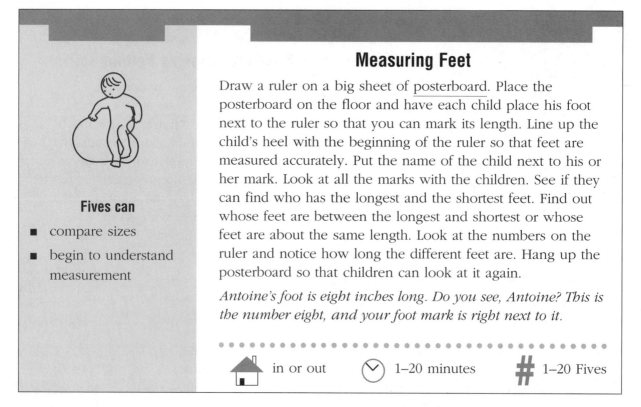

Fives can

- compare sizes
- begin to understand measurement

Measuring Feet

Draw a ruler on a big sheet of posterboard. Place the posterboard on the floor and have each child place his foot next to the ruler so that you can mark its length. Line up the child's heel with the beginning of the ruler so that feet are measured accurately. Put the name of the child next to his or her mark. Look at all the marks with the children. See if they can find who has the longest and the shortest feet. Find out whose feet are between the longest and shortest or whose feet are about the same length. Look at the numbers on the ruler and notice how long the different feet are. Hang up the posterboard so that children can look at it again.

Antoine's foot is eight inches long. Do you see, Antoine? This is the number eight, and your foot mark is right next to it.

in or out   1–20 minutes   # 1–20 Fives

490

Fives can

- play group games
- count up to 20 objects

"May I?" Game

Stand on one side of the playground and have all interested children line up along a wall or fence on the other side of the playground, facing you. Then give them an instruction that tells them how many steps they should move toward you. After you give the instruction, the children must ask, "May I?" If you say, "Yes you may," then they can all move according to the instruction. If you say, "No you may not," then they must wait for the next instruction. Give instructions for funny kinds of steps, such as the following:

- 7 twirling steps
- 20 tiny baby steps
- 12 scissor steps
- 10 squatting steps

- 4 backward hops
- 9 tiptoe steps
- 12 shaky steps
- 6 rub-your-tummy steps

 in or out   3–10 minutes   1–4 Fives

491

Fives can

- count up to 20 objects
- some name written numbers

Hopping on the Number Line

Buy or make a big number line that can be used on the floor. Make it out of a material that will stand up to children hopping on it, such as sturdy canvas. Number the line from 1 to 20 with 9" to 12" between each number. Then play a hopping game with a small group of Fives in which children take turns as you give them directions for how many spaces they should hop. Give both hopping ahead and hopping back directions.

Kerry, you can hop ahead three spaces.
What number did you land on?

Help children figure out how to share a space if needed. Have everyone follow directions until they reach the end of the line. Let children give directions, too.

 in or out   5–15 minutes   1–3 Fives

492

Fives can

- count up to 20 or higher

- understand the words *higher* and *lower*

- read and write some numbers

Higher, Lower Number Guessing Game

Show your Fives a number line that is numbered from 1 to 10. Point to a number on the line and talk about the numbers that are higher and lower than that number. Then write down a number between one and ten. Do not let the children see what you wrote. Say, "I am thinking of a number between one and ten. Can you guess what it is?" Have them guess one number at a time, saying if the number they guessed is higher or lower than the one you chose. Show them what the choices are by showing them the number line. Play until they guess the number. Later, children can take turns writing down a number and giving the clues. For more challenge, see if children can do the problem in their heads or use numbers between 1 and 20.

 in or out   2–15 minutes   # 1–20 Fives

493

Fives can

- sort by many features—each thing in group shares one characteristic

Sorting Shoes

Have a group of children who want to play sit with you in a circle. Have everyone take off their shoes and put them into the middle of the circle. Then sort all the shoes into different piles, in many ways—by color, type of shoe, the way the shoe fastens, and so on. Encourage the children to decide which pile the shoes should be in.

Kendra says to put all the shoes with laces into this pile.
How does this shoe fasten? That's right. It has a buckle.
Does it go with the shoes that have shoelaces?
Let's make a new pile for shoes with buckles.

Try sorting other types of clothing, such as jackets or mittens and gloves.

 indoors   5–20 minutes   # 1–20 Fives

494

Fives can

- begin to understand that adding and subtracting changes numbers

Talking About Real-Life Addition and Subtraction

As you do simple addition and subtraction to figure out real problems, talk about what you are doing and thinking with interested Fives. See if they can help you figure out easy answers when they can see the real things that are being added or subtracted. Use the words *adding* and *subtracting* as you talk.

Let's put the balls into the box so that we can bring them in.
I already put two in. Jana is adding one more.
How many will we have in the box?

There are four potatoes in the bowl.
Zac's going to subtract one by putting it on his plate.
How many will be left in the bowl?

 in or out   2–4 minutes   # 1–20 Fives

495

Fives can

- match some written numbers

Delivering Mail to Houses

Make twenty colorful construction paper houses. Use a marker or crayon to draw windows, doors, and other house parts. Clearly write a number from 1 to 20 on the house doors. Cover the houses with clear contact paper or laminate them to make them sturdy. Number 40 envelopes from 1 to 20 so that you have two envelopes with each number. Mix the envelopes and put them into a tote bag.

Show your Fives how to pretend to be mail carriers. Spread the houses out on the floor or on a table. The children can deliver the mail by placing each envelope on the house with the same number. Use fewer houses to make the game easier. Add people and street names to the addresses, or use higher numbers to make the game more challenging.

 indoors   5–20 minutes   # 1–3 Fives

496

Fives can

- sort by many features—each thing in group shares one characteristic

More Challenging Shape Sorting

Buy a set of shapes that differ by color, size, and thickness. As children become good sorters, have them decide how to sort the shapes in different ways—by shape, color, size, or thickness.

You are right, Jordan. It's green. It's a green circle. Can you put it with all the other circles?

See if children can sort the shapes first by one feature, and then into smaller groups based on another feature. For example, help interested children find all the circles first and then sort them by size into groups of big, medium, and small circles.

 in or out   5–20 minutes   1–4 Fives

497

Fives can

- understand the words *big* and *little*, *tall* and *short*

- begin to understand measurement

Graphing Everyone's Height

Make a line graph that shows how tall everyone in your group is. (There is a picture of a line graph in Graph Ideas on page 443.) If there are lots of children, use the wall in a hallway or outdoors. Have each child take a turn standing along the wall and mark the height of each one. Mark the height of the adults in the group, too. Put each person's name near their mark.

Talk about the big graph with your Fives. Measure and write down the heights with interested children. Compare same and different heights. Add marks for other heights, too, such as a classroom pet or children's family members.

Can you find the tallest mark on the graph, Marcia? That's right. It's Tonya's daddy.

 in or out   3–20 minutes   1–20 Fives

498

Fives can

- understand the words *one* and *many, more* and *less*

- begin to understand graphing

Using Bar Graphs to Compare

Make bar graphs with your Fives to compare numbers of things that they are interested in. You will find directions for making bar graphs in Graph Ideas on page 443. Help children compare the different categories shown on the graphs. Talk about *more, less, equal* (or the *same*) and help your Fives count to find out how many.

You're looking at the new graph we made, Kendra.
This bar shows how many boys we have, and this shows how many girls. Can you find your name? Are there more boys or girls? I think so, too!
Let's see how many we have of each.
Can you help me count?

 indoors   3–20 minutes   1–15 Fives

499

Fives can

- sort by many features—each thing in group shares one characteristic

Sorting Children

Tell the children that you are going to play a "children-sorting" game. Ask children who want to play to sit in a big circle. Sort the children in various ways and help them decide which group to go into. Some aspects to sort by are

- color of shirt
- type of shoes
- color of hair
- favorite food
- who likes dogs
- who has sisters or brothers

Compare the sizes of the different groups. Give children lots of chances to use their own sorting ideas, too.

Wow! Which is bigger—the group of children that likes broccoli or the group that does not?

 in or out   5–20 minutes   1–20 Fives

500

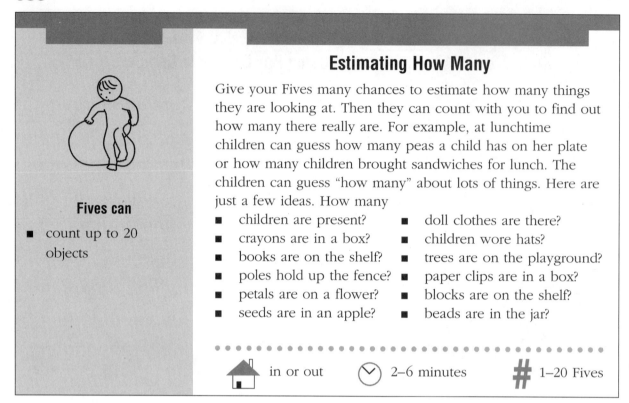

Fives can

- count up to 20 objects

Estimating How Many

Give your Fives many chances to estimate how many things they are looking at. Then they can count with you to find out how many there really are. For example, at lunchtime children can guess how many peas a child has on her plate or how many children brought sandwiches for lunch. The children can guess "how many" about lots of things. Here are just a few ideas. How many

- children are present?
- crayons are in a box?
- books are on the shelf?
- poles hold up the fence?
- petals are on a flower?
- seeds are in an apple?

- doll clothes are there?
- children wore hats?
- trees are on the playground?
- paper clips are in a box?
- blocks are on the shelf?
- beads are in the jar?

🏠 in or out   🕐 2–6 minutes   # 1–20 Fives

501

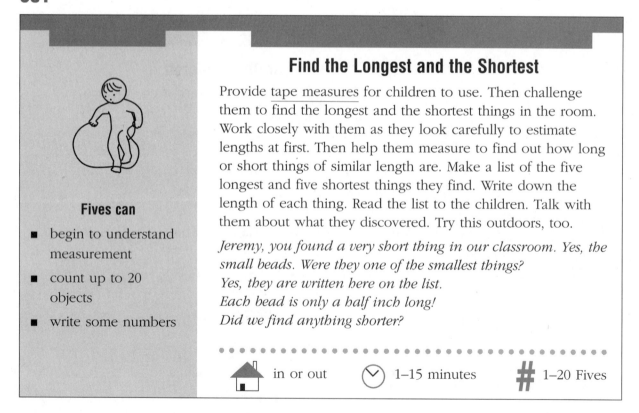

Fives can

- begin to understand measurement
- count up to 20 objects
- write some numbers

Find the Longest and the Shortest

Provide tape measures for children to use. Then challenge them to find the longest and the shortest things in the room. Work closely with them as they look carefully to estimate lengths at first. Then help them measure to find out how long or short things of similar length are. Make a list of the five longest and five shortest things they find. Write down the length of each thing. Read the list to the children. Talk with them about what they discovered. Try this outdoors, too.

Jeremy, you found a very short thing in our classroom. Yes, the small beads. Were they one of the smallest things?
Yes, they are written here on the list.
Each bead is only a half inch long!
Did we find anything shorter?

🏠 in or out   🕐 1–15 minutes   # 1–20 Fives

502

Fives can

- play simple board games

- sometimes have trouble following rules or losing

Counting to Play Simple Board Games

Put out several simple board games that require counting how many moves to make by throwing a number cube or turning a number spinner. Use games such as "Trouble" or some that you draw yourself on posterboard. Children can use buttons as markers for the homemade games.

Explain to the children how each game is played. Show them how to count while moving their marker one space for each number they say until they reach the number that came up on the dice or spinner. A child can play a game on her own if she wishes, or a few friends can play together if competition does not cause upsets.

Move the marker one hop for each number you say, Hillary. Be careful. Try not to skip over any spaces.

 in or out   8–20 minutes   1–4 Fives

503

Fives can

- count up to 20 objects

- follow complex directions with some help

Taking Surveys

Help your Fives learn to take simple surveys about questions that interest them. Have a clipboard with pencil attached for the survey taker and a survey recording sheet. (Sample survey recording sheets are on pages 445–446.) Look at the survey sheet with the child and talk about what the question says. Then during activity time, help the survey taker ask all children in the class the question. Show him how to mark in the correct place on the sheet to show how each child answered. Give the child a list with the names of all people in the class to check off as he questions each child.

When everyone has been asked, show the child how to tally the scores. Talk about which answers had the most responses. The survey taker can later report what he found out.

 in or out   8–20 minutes   1–2 Fives

504

Fives can

- begin to learn to tell time on the hour and half hour

Beginning to Tell Time

Explain to your Fives about what the hands on a big clock mean. Help them notice when the hands are in different positions, such as an exact hour or half past an hour. Call their attention to the small minute marks. Show them how they can count how far the big hand has moved to see how many minutes it is past the hour the small hand is pointing to. Keep things simple and brief so that children do not get bored.

Wow! Look at the clock! Can you tell what time it is?
See the small hand? What number is it pointing to?
And the big hand is pointing to the twelve, so that means it is three o'clock. We need to get ready to go home, don't we?

 indoors   1–3 minutes   1–20 Fives

505

Fives can

- do simple adding with 1, 2, 3, and 4
- count up to 20 objects
- write some numbers

How Many Ways Can You Make a Number?

Use permanent markers to draw on posterboard or sturdy cloth to make counting mats like those shown on page 447. Make several for each number up to 10. Have a variety of small counting things that children can use. Take out one mat and show interested Fives how you can combine sets of different numbers and get a larger number in several ways. For example, show them that you can put 1 thing in a set and 3 in another to get 4 or you can put 2 things in one set and 2 in the other and also get 4.

Encourage children to experiment by moving counting things around to see how many ways they can make a larger number out of smaller numbers. Children can show what they discovered on recording sheets (sample shown on page 448).

 in or out   5–20 minutes   1–4 Fives

506

Fives can

- show interest in written words
- write some numbers
- count up to 20 objects

Balance Scale Problems

Set up some balance scale problems your Fives can solve. Put out a balance scale, the things they will need to weigh, and a Balance Scale Problems recording sheet for them to use to show what they find out. (A sample recording sheet is on page 449.)

Read the problems to the children. Encourage them to experiment until they find out the answers. Remember that recording answers is optional and should only be done by children who are really interested.

What did you find out, Theodore?
Which weighs more, three square blocks or your shoe?
Your shoe? How did you figure that out?
Do you think that is true for Maria's shoe, too?

 in or out   2–12 minutes   1–2 Fives per scale

Counting Songs and Rhymes

Baa, Baa, Black Sheep

Baa, baa, black sheep,
Have you any wool?
Yes sir, yes sir,
Three bags full.   (hold up three fingers)
One for the master,   (hold up one finger)
One for the dame,   (hole up two fingers)
And one for the little child   (hold up three fingers)
Who lives down the lane.

The Bee Hive

Here is the bee hive,   (put hands together)
Where are the bees?   (make a fist)
Hiding out
Where nobody sees.   (put hand behind back)
They are coming out now.
They are all alive—   (bring hand out)
One, two, three, four, five.   (put up one finger at a time)

Five in the Bed

There were five in the bed
And the little one said,
"Roll over, roll over!"   (roll one hand over the other)
So they all rolled over
And one fell out.
There were four in the bed
And the little one said, etc.

Five Little Monkeys

Five little monkeys   (hold up five fingers)
Jumping on the bed,   (jump fingers on palm of other hand)

One fell off   (hold up one finger)
And bumped his head.   (rub head)
They ran for the doctor   (run fingers across other
And the doctor said,   hand)
"No more monkeys jumping
   on the bed!"   (point and shake finger)
(Continue with four, three, two, and one monkey.)

Five Little Pumpkins

Five little pumpkins	*(hold up five fingers)*
Sitting on a gate.	
The first one said,	*(hold up one finger)*
"Oh my, it's getting late!"	
The second one said,	*(hold up two fingers)*
"There are witches in the air!"	
The third one said,	*(hold up three fingers)*
"But we don't care!"	
The fourth one said,	*(hold up four fingers)*
"Let's have some fun!"	
The fifth one said,	*(hold up five fingers)*
"Let's run, run, run!"	
Whoooo went the wind,	
And out went the light,	
And the five little pumpkins	
Rolled out of sight.	*(roll one hand over the other)*

Johnny Works with One Hammer

Johnny works with one hammer	*(pretend to hammer with one fist)*
One hammer, one hammer, one hammer	
Johnny works with one hammer	
Now he works with two.	*(pretend to hammer with two fists)*
Continue with:	
two hammers	*(use both fists)*
three hammers	*(use two fists, one foot)*
four hammers	*(use two fists, two feet)*
five hammers	*(use two fists, two feet, nod head)*
Then he goes to sleep.	*(close eyes, put head on folded hands)*

One Little, Two Little, Three Little Children

One little, two little, three little children
Four little, five little, six little children
Seven little, eight little, nine little children
Ten little children right here.
(Sing this, using fingers instead of children.)

One, Two, Buckle My Shoe

One, two, buckle my shoe;
Three, four, open the door;
Five, six, pick up sticks;
Seven, eight, lay them straight;
Nine, ten, a big fat hen!

Six Little Ducks

Six little ducks that I once knew	*(hold up six fingers)*
Fat ones, skinny ones, tall ones too.	
But the first little duck with the	*(wiggle one finger)*
feather on his back,	*(wiggle one finger)*
He led the others with a quack,	*(open and close fingers*
quack, quack.	*to thumb)*

Down to the river they did go	
Wibble wobble, wibble wobble,	*(with palms together, move*
to and fro.	*hands back and forth)*
But the first little duck with the	
feather on his back,	
He led the others with a quack,	*(open and close fingers*
quack, quack.	*to thumb)*

This Old Man

This old man, he played one, he played nick-nack on my thumb,
With a nick-nack paddy-whack, give a dog a bone,
This old man came rolling home.
Additional verses: (2) shoe; (3) knee; (4) door; (5) hive; (6) sticks;
(7) up in heaven; (8) gate; (9) spine; (10) once again

Three Little Kittens

The three little kittens
They lost their mittens
And they began to cry,
"Oh, mother dear,
We sadly fear
Our mittens we have lost."
"What, lost your mittens?
You naughty kittens!
Then you shall have no pie."
"Meow, Meow, Meow, Meow, we shall have no pie.
Meow, Meow, Meow, Meow, we shall have no pie."

Activities for Learning from the World Around Them

The three little kittens
They found their mittens
And they called out with joy,
"Oh, mother dear,
See here, see here,
Our mittens we have found."
"What, found your mittens?
You good little kittens!
Then you shall have some pie."
"Meow, Meow, Meow, Meow, we shall have some pie.
Meow, Meow, Meow, Meow, we shall have some pie."

Two Little Blackbirds

Two little blackbirds sitting on a hill.
One named Jack and one named Jill.
Fly away Jack, fly away Jill.
Come back Jack, come back Jill.
Two little blackbirds sitting on a hill.
One named Jack and one named Jill.

Two Fat Sausages

Two fat sausages	*(hold thumbs up in front)*
Sizzling in the pan.	*(move thumbs up and down)*
One went POP!	*(put finger in mouth and pop)*
The other went BAM!	*(slap open hands together)*

Money Matching and Sorting Games

Most five-year-olds know that money is a desirable thing to keep. You may notice that they put the money from money games into their pockets or cubbies. Money from these games will also wander to the Dramatic Play Center as children use it in their imaginary play. Avoid making an issue about this. Talk with the children about how important it is to keep the game pieces together. Have extra pennies and play money on hand to replace the pennies that become lost. If money becomes a big problem, have sheets of money pictures the children can cut out for their play. You can also make homemade money by laminating the sheets and then cutting out the money you need for the games.

Real Pennies Matching Game

1. Cut out 10 posterboard cards that are about 5" × 7".

2. Glue one penny to the first card, two pennies to the second, three to the next, and so on until you have cards with up to ten pennies glued onto them. Print the number that shows how many pennies are on each card.

3. Cover the cards with clear contact paper.

4. Place at least 55 pennies in a container. It is best to use a container with a lid.

5. Show your Fives how to put one penny on top of each penny on the cards.

6. Talk about the numbers of pennies on each card.

This game is easier when you glue the pennies in rows, but to make the game more challenging, glue the pennies so that they are not in any special pattern.

Activities for Learning from the World Around Them

How Many Pennies Equal a Nickel, Dime, and Quarter?

1. Cut out three posterboard cards that are about 5" × 7".

2. Glue a nickel to the first card, a dime to the second, and a quarter to the next.

3. Trace around five pennies to make penny outlines on the card that has the nickel. Make ten penny outlines for the dime and twenty-five for the quarter. Print a clear 5 on the nickel card, a 10 on the dime card, and a 25 on the quarter card.

4. Cover with clear contact paper.

5. Place at least 40 pennies into a container. It is best to use a container with a lid.

6. Show your Fives how to put one penny onto each penny outline on the cards. Talk about which coin is worth the most pennies.

Coin and Bill Matching Game

1. Use paper play money with one-, five-, and ten-dollar bills as well as plastic coins of 1, 5, 10, and 25 cents.

2. Glue one piece of each type of money to its own 5" × 7" card. Cover with clear contact paper.

3. Place several of each coin and bill into a container with the cards.

4. Show children how to spread out the cards and look carefully at the coins and bills. Help the children notice the differences in coin sizes and colors and the different numbers they see.

5. Then show the children how to take one piece of money from the container, look at it carefully, and place it on the card with the matching coin or bill.

6. Make the game easier by using only coins or bills, using only two coins, or having the children sort all the money into piles of coins and bills.

(Note: Have extra play money on hand to replace pieces that become lost.)

Activities for Learning from the World Around Them

How to Make Sorting Boards and Boxes

Sorting Board 1: Wooden with Cup Hooks

1. Get a rectangular board about 36" wide × 30" long. Make sure it is smooth, with no rough edges.
2. Draw four lines to divide the board into fifths.
3. Screw in six cup hooks of three different sizes in each section. You'll need 30 hooks in all.
4. Provide enough washers of three different sizes to match the hooks.
5. Hang up one washer on a matching hook. Let the child hang the rest.

Sorting Board 2: Cloth with Cloth Pockets

1. Cut out 25 cloth 2½" × 5" rectangles. Hem ¼" on all sides of each.
2. Sew the rectangles onto a sturdy piece of 36" × 40" cloth in five rows to make pockets. Be sure to leave the tops (a 5" side) of each pocket open. Sew only the two sides and the bottom.
3. Hang this sorting board on a wall, the back of a bookcase, or a closet door.
4. Make sets of cards to fit into the pockets. Be sure that when the card is in the pocket, most of the picture can still be seen.

A shoe bag also works well as a cloth sorting board for bigger pictures.

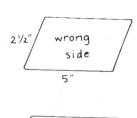

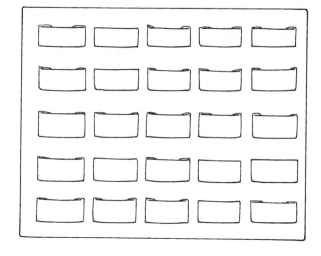

Sorting Board 3: Cardboard with Pockets

(This board is not as sturdy as Boards 1 and 2.)

1. Use 25 sturdy brown envelopes, library card pockets, or envelopes with the flaps turned in and glued down to make them sturdier.
2. Glue the envelopes onto a large posterboard, making five evenly spaced pockets in five lines.
3. Put the sorting board on a low table or floor for children to use. Or try hanging it down low where children can reach it.

Sorting Box

1. Use a grocery box with dividers, such as a box for large soda bottles.
2. Cover the box with colored contact paper, if you want.
3. Use strong tape to make the dividers sturdy.
4. Turn the box on its side so that the dividers become shelves.
5. Put a picture in each space to show children what they will be sorting. Help them get started.

Sample Measuring Recording Sheets

How many make a cup?

Tablespoon

_____

Quarter Cup

_____

Third Cup

_____

Half Cup

_____

Compare—How many of each make a cup?

Which takes more to fill a cup—sand or potting soil?

Draw a picture or write the number to show how many.

Sand

Potting Soil

Tablespoon

_____

Tablespoon

_____

Quarter Cup

_____

Quarter Cup

_____

Third Cup

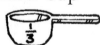

_____

Third Cup

_____

Half Cup

_____

Half Cup

_____

Activities for Learning from the World Around Them

Graph Ideas

Line Graphs

Line graphs are good for comparing children's heights, but bar graphs are better for making other comparisons that Fives will understand.

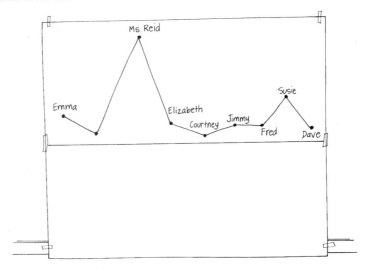

Bar Graphs

Make bar graphs with your Fives so that they can compare numbers of things that interest them.

Children can take part in making these graphs by putting their name cards onto the graph to show their choice for certain categories. Then you can help them compare the numbers of names that were put under each to see which had more and which had fewer names.

The easiest graphs for children to help make and understand are graphs that have only two bars. Here are some examples:

■ How many children are boys and how many are girls?
■ Who likes and who dislikes a certain food?
■ How many children wore a coat and how many did not today?
■ How many children wore long pants, and how many wore shorts?
■ How many children do or do not have sisters or brothers?

Harder graphs with more bars can be used when children understand simple bar graphs. Here are some ideas:

■ How many children have different kinds of pets?
■ How many children enjoy different games?
■ How many children like certain foods?
■ How many children did different activities over the weekend?
■ How many children wore different types of clothes to school?
■ How many children have sisters or brothers?
■ How many children like which colors the best?

Making Different Types of Bar Graphs

1. Set up a large graph with bars that can have categories listed at the bottom or side.

Floor Graph

Use a large sheet of plastic that is divided into eight bars. Make lines with masking tape or permanent marker. Mark off a large space for the different categories, such as different types of pets, at the bottom of the bars.

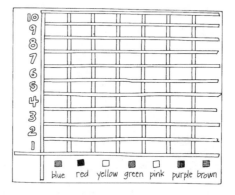

Wall Graph

Use a large sheet of paper that is divided into as many bars as there are categories. Make a large space for the category names, such as the names of different types of pets, at the bottom of the bars.

2. Give each child a card made of paper or cardboard with his or her name on it. Be sure each card is of equal size.
3. Help children place their cards onto the bars they choose. Look at the categories with the children and help them decide where their names should go. Help children place their cards in straight rows, close together in each bar. Place the first child's card at the bottom of the bar and add cards so that the bar becomes higher as children add their name cards.
4. Talk about which category has more names, which has fewer, and whether any categories have the same number.

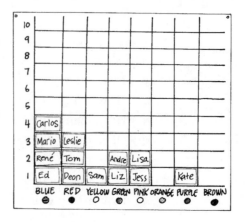

Activities for Learning from the World Around Them

Sample Survey
Recording Sheets

(You may help the child color in the boxes next to the color words.)

Name _____

How many children like each color?
Mark how many.

Red ☐ _____

Orange ☐ _____

Yellow ☐ _____

Green ☐ _____

Blue ☐ _____

Purple ☐ _____

Black ☐ _____

Brown ☐ _____

Pink ☐ _____

White ☐ _____

Activities for Learning from the World Around Them

How many people wore warm
clothes today? Mark how many.

Hat

_____

Jacket or Coat

_____

Scarf

_____

Mittens or Gloves

_____

Earmuffs

_____

Boots

_____

No Warm Clothes (Brrr!)

_____

Activities for Learning from the World Around Them

Illustration for
"How Many Ways
Can You Make a
Number?"

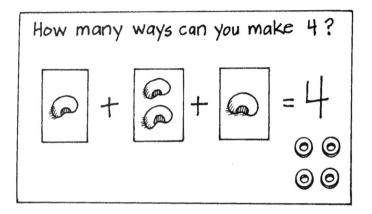

Name _____

How many ways can you make a 5?

+		= 5
+		= 5
+	+	= 5
+	+	= 5

Activities for Learning from the World Around Them

Sample Balance Scale Problems Recording Sheet

Name _____

Write or draw what you find out.

How many cars equal the weight of a block?

Which weighs more—10 bears or your shoe?

How many paper clips equal the weight of an acorn?

Which weighs more—a pencil or a marker?